AF564729

Software Engineering

SOFTWARE ENGINEERING

Nishit Mathur

CENTRUM PRESS
NEW DELHI-110002 (INDIA)

CENTRUM PRESS
H.O.: 4360/4, Ansari Road, Daryaganj,
New Delhi-110002 (India)
Tel: 23278000, 23261597, 23255577, 23286875
B.O.: No. 1015, Ist Main Road, BSK IIIrd Stage,
IIIrd Phase, IIIrd Block, Bangalore-560085 (INDIA)
Tel: 080-41723429
Email: centrumpress@gmail.com
Visit us at: www.centrumpress.com

Software Engineering

First Edition, 2011

PRINTED IN INDIA

Printed at Tarun Offset Printers, Delhi-110053

Contents

Preface

Software engineering is a profession dedicated to designing, implementing, and modifying software so that it is of higher quality, more affordable, maintainable, and faster to build. It is a "systematic approach to the analysis, design, assessment, implementation, test, maintenance and reengineering of software, that is, the application of engineering to software."

It first appeared in the 1968 NATO Software Engineering Conference, and was meant to provoke thought regarding the perceived "software crisis" at the time. The IEEE Computer Society's Software Engineering Body of Knowledge defines "software engineering" as the application of a systematic, disciplined, quantifiable approach to the development, operation, and maintenance of software, and the study of these approaches; that is, the application of engineering to software. It is the application of Engineering to software because it integrates significant mathematics, computer science and practices whose origins are in Engineering.

Author

Preface

[illegible]

1

Computer Software

CONCEPT

There hardly existed any specific documentation, system design approach and related documents etc. These things were confined to only those who developed hardware systems. Software development plans and designs were confined to only concepts in mind. Even after number of people jumped in this field, because of the lack of proper development strategies, documentations and maintenance plans, the software system that was developed was costlier than before, it took more time to develop the entire system (even sometimes, it was next to impossible to predict the completion date of the system that was under development), the lines of codes were increased to a very large number increasing the complexity of the project/software, as the complexity of the software increased it also increased the number of bugs/problems in the system.

Most of the times the system that was developed, was unusable by the customer because of problems such as late delivery (generally very very very late) and also because of number of bugs, there were no plans to deal with situations where in the system was needed to be maintained, this lead to the situation called 'Software Crisis'. Most of software projects, which were just concepts in brain but had no standard methodologies, practices to follow, experienced failure, causing loss of millions of dollars.

'Software Crisis' was a situation, which made people think seriously about the software development processes, and practices that could be followed to ensure a successful, cost-effective system implementation, which could be delivered on time and used by the customer. People were compelled to think about new ideas of systematic development of software systems.

This approach gave birth to the most crucial part of the software development process, this part constituted the most modern and advanced thinking and even the basics of any project management, it needed the software development process be given an engineering perspective thought. This approach is called as 'Software Engineering'. Standard definition of 'Software Engineering' is 'the application of systematic, disciplined, quantifiable, approach to the development, operation and maintenance of software *i.e.* the application of engineering to software.'

The Software Engineering subject uses a systematic approach towards developing any software project. It shows how systematically and cost-effectively a software project can be handled and successfully completed assuring higher success rates.

Software Engineering includes planning and developing strategies, defining time-lines and following guidelines in order to ensure the successful completion of particular phases, following predefined Software Development Life-Cycles, using documentation plans for follow-ups etc. In order to complete various phases of software development process and providing better support for the system developed.

Software Engineering takes an all-round approach to find out the customer's needs and even it asks customers about their opinions hence proceeding towards development of a desired product. Various methodologies/practices such as 'Waterfall Model', 'Spiral Model' etc. Are developed under Software Engineering which provides guidelines to follow during software development ensuring on time completion of the project.

These approaches help in dividing the software development process into small Tasks/phases such as requirement gathering and analysis, system design phase, coding phase etc. That makes it very much easy to manage the project. These methods/approaches also help in understanding the problems faced (which occur during the system development process and even after the deployment of the system at customer's site) and strategies to be followed to take care of all the problems and providing a strong support for the system developed (for example: the problems with one phase are resolved in the next phase, and after deployment of the product, problems related to the system such as queries, bug that was not yet detected etc. which is called support and maintenance of the system.

SOFTWARE PROGRMMING

Software Engineering is an approach to developing software that attempts to treat it as a formal process more like traditional engineering than the craft that many programmers believe it is. We talk of crafting an application, refining and polishing it, as if it were a wooden sculpture, not a series of logic instructions. Manufacturers cannot build complex life-critical systems like aircraft, nuclear reactor controls, medical systems and expect the software to be thrown together.

They require the whole process to be thoroughly managed, so that budgets can be estimated, staff recruited, and to minimize the risk of failure or expensive mistakes. In safety critical areas such as aviation, space, nuclear power plants, medicine, fire detection systems, and roller coaster rides the cost of failure can be enormous as lives are at risk. A divide by zero error that brings down an aircraft is just not acceptable.

CAD ENGINEERING

Enormous design documents- hundreds or thousands of pages long are produced using C.A.S.E. (Computer Aided Software Engineering) tools then converted into Design Specification documents which are used to design code.

C.A.S.E suffers from the "not quite there yet" syndrome. There are no systems that can take a set of design constraints and requirements then generate code that satisfies all the requirements and constraints. Its far too complex a process. So the available C.A.S.E. systems manage parts of the lifecycle process but not all of it. One distinguishing feature of Software Engineering is the paper trail that it produces.

Designs have to be signed off by Managers and Technical Authorities all the way from top to bottom and the role of Quality Assurance is to check the paper trail. Many Software Engineers would admit that their job is around 70% paperwork and 30% code. It's a costly way to write software and this is why avionics in modern aircraft are so expensive.

BASIC SOFTWARE COMPONENTS

Software can be further divided into seven layers. Firmware can be categorized as part of hardware, part of software, or both. The seven layers of software are (top to bottom): Programmes; System Utilities; Command Shell; System Services; User Interface; Logical Level; and Hardware Level. A Graphics Engine stradles the bottom three layers.

Strictly speaking, only the bottom two levels are the operating system, although even technical persons will often refer to any level other than programmes as part of the operating system (and Microsoft tried to convince the Justice Department that their web browser application is actually a part of their operating system). Because this technical analysis concentrates on servers, Internet Facilities are specifically separated out from the layers.

Human users normally interact with the operating system indirectly, through various programmes (application and system) and command shells (text, graphic, etc.), The operating system provides programmes with services thrrough system programmes and Application Programme Interfaces (APIs).

NETWORK AND INTERNET SERVICES

- Internet
- TCP/IP

- Server choices
- Tuning web servers
- DHCP
- Print serving
- File serving
- FTP
- SAMBA
- Mail Transport Agents (e-mail servers)
- Majordomo
- Application serving

HARDWARE LEVEL OF OPERATING SYSTEM

Basics of Computer Hardware

- Processor
- Arithmetic and logic
- Control
- Main storage
- External storage
- Input/output overview
- Input
- Output

Processors

- CISC
- RISC
- DSP
- Hybrid

Processes and Jobs

- General information
- Linking
- Loading
- Run/execute

Buses

- Kinds of buses
- Bus standards

Memory

- Main storage
- External storage
- Buffers
- Absolute addressing
- Overlay
- Relocatable software
- Demand paging and swapping
- Programme counter relative
- Base pointers
- Indirection, pointers, and handles
- OS memory services

MEMORY MAPS

- PC-DOS and MS-DOS memory map
- MS-DOS TSR memory map
- Mac Plus memory map
- Mac Plus video memory locations
- Mac Plus sound memory locations

Low Memory

PC-DOS and MS-DOS low memory

- BIOS Communication Area
- Reserved
- Inter-Application (User) Communication Area
- DOS Communication Area

Character codes

LOGICAL LEVEL OF OPERATING SYSTEM

- File systems
- Files
- Resource Manager
- Cut and paste

GRAPHICS ENGINE

- Font Management

USER INTERFACE

- Command line user interfaces
- Graphic user interfaces
- Aqua
- Common Desktop Environment
- IRIX Interactive Desktop
- Macintosh Toolbox
- Motif
- Visual User Environment
- Workbench
- XFree86
- Spoken user interfaces
- Screen shots
- Event Management
- Windows
- Controls
- Menus
- Text Display and Editing
- Dialog Boxes
- Alerts

SYSTEM SERVICES

COMMAND SHELL

- Command line command shells
- DCL
- DOS
- JCL
- UNIX shells
- Scripting
- Graphic command shells
- Screen shots

SYSTEM UTILITIES

PROGRAMMES

- Desk Accessories

SOFTWARE CHARACTERISTICS

SOFTWARE REQUIREMENT

- Microsoft Windows 98 SE, Me, NT4 (sp5+), 2000 or XP,
- Word processing software (optional),
- Spell checker (optional),
- Spreadsheet (optional), Microsoft Excel is necessary to generate analysis reports
- Web browser (optional), Internet Explorer 5 or Netscape 6 or above,
- Adobe Acrobat (optional).

HARDWARE REQUIREMENT

- PC compatible computer (Pentium II or compatible),
- CD-ROM Drive,
- SVGA or XGA (1024×768) graphic screen and card,
- Floppy drive (optional, for Ethnos input transfer),
- Printer port (parallel port RS232).

TEXT ANALYSIS

- Minimum size advised for a text: less than 1 page (1 Kb),
- Maximum size advised for a single text: 5,000 pages (50 Mb),
- Average analysis throughput: from 20,000 words/second (Pentium III 733 MHz) to 80,000 words/second (Pentium IV 3.2 GHz, HT) on local Web pages, for a single processor.

SEMANTIC SEARCH ENGINE

- Automatic generation of hierarchical keywords,
- Automatic information filtering (based on a pertinence treshold),
- Massive data analysis and information cartography (text-mining),
- Search improvement for the references (nouns, trademarks and proper names),

- Maximum numbers of text databases: unlimited,
- Average indexing throughput: from 1 Gb/hour (Pentium III 733 Mhz) to 4 Gb/hour (Pentium IV 3.2 GHz, HT) on local Web pages, for a single processor.

FEATURES

- File formats converted by our linguistic softwares (Tropes, Zoom and Index): Adobe Acrobat, ASCII, ANSI, HTML, Macromedia Flash, Microsoft Excel, Microsoft Powerpoint, Microsoft Word, Microsoft WordML (Word XML), RTF, XML, SGML and Macintosh texts
- Automatic extraction of Microsoft Outlook messages via an external utility (Zoom Semantic Search Engine)
- Automatic exportation of the results towards other software (Zoom Semantic Search Engine)
- Indexing engine in batch mode (Acetic Index)
- Win32 Application Programming Interface (Acetic Index)
- Real time XML output interface (Acetic Index)
- Distributed fault tolerant and load-balancing Interface (CORBA, Acetic Index)
- Runtime, operation on Intranet, HTML generation (contact us)
- Some features (for example, very large Text Mining) may require the use of an additional statistics software, of data mining software and/or a RDBMS

SOFTWARE FEATURES

SOFTWARE PRODUCTS

- Successful software
- Provides the required functionality
- Is usable by real (*i.e.* naive) users
- Is predictable, reliable and dependable
- Functions efficiently
- Has a "life-time" (measured in years)
- Provides an appropriate user interface

- Is accompanied by complete documentation
- May have different configurations
- Can be "easily" maintained

SOFTWARE CONSUMER

- Cheap to buy
- Easy to learn
- Easy to use
- Solves the problem
- Reliable
- Powerful
- Fast
- Flexible
- Available

REQUIREMENT OF SOFTWARE PRODUCER

- Cheap to produce
- Well-defined behaviour
- Easy to "sell"
- Easy to maintain
- Reliable
- Easy to use
- Flexible
- Available (quick to produce)

ISSUE OF MEASUREMENT

- The issue is...how to measure these things
- Why measure at all?
- Human subjective perception is notoriously inaccurate (how many shark attacks in the last 200 years?)
- Numbers give us a way of comparing, controlling and predicting
- Measurements give us a way of tracking progress (and rescheduling if necessary)
- Also provide an assessment of product quality
- Measurement is the difference between "craft" and "engineering"

METRIC

- "A quantitative measure of the degree to which a system component or process possesses a given attribute (IEEE)
- Hence, for each metric, we require...
- A measurable property
- A relationship between that property and what we wish to know
- A consistent, formal, validated expression of that relationship
- *For example*: who is the greatest actor of all time?

GOOD METRIC

- Simple and computable
- Persuasive
- Consistent/objective
- Consistent in use of units/dimensions
- Programming language independent
- Gives useful feedback

PROCESS METRICS

- Measures of attributes of a process
- Attributes may relate to people (*e.g.* "person-hours")...
- Or technology (*e.g.* "megaLOCs")...
- Or the product (*e.g.* "total cost to date")

MEASUREMENT

- Effort, time and capital spent on various related activities
- Number of functionalities implemented
- Number of errors remediated (of various severities)
- Number of errors *not* remediated (during development process)
- Conformance to delivery schedule
- Benchmarks (speed, throughput, error-rates, etc)

Hard Measure

- Abstract desiderata

- Usability
- Efficiency
- Reliability
- Maintainability
- Quality

Standard Code of Metrics

- Lines of code (LOC)
- Cyclomatic complexity (McCabe)
- Function/feature points (Albrecht/Jones)

Lines of Code

- A size-oriented metric
- Easy to measure
- Easy to compare
- Easy to differentiate wrt time, cost, etc.
- Programming language dependent (*e.g.* 1 OO-LOC = 3 3GL-LOC = 9 assembler-LOC)
- Meaningless in isolation
- Penalize efficient design and coding

OBJECT-ORIENTED METRICS

- Measures of...
- Classes
- Encapsulation
- Modularity
- Inheritance
- Abstraction

Some Object-oriented Metrics

- Chidamber and Kemerer
- Lorenz and Kidd

Chidamber and Kemerer's

- Class-oriented metrics (*Proc. OOPSLA*)...
- Weighted methods per class (number of methods weighted by static complexity)
- Depth of inheritance tree (number of ancestral classes)

- Number of children (number of immediate subclasses)
- Degree of coupling (how many other classes rely on the class, and vice versa)
- Response (number of public methods)
- Method cohesion (degree to which data members shared by two or more methods)

SOFTWARE CRISIS

Indeed, the problem of trying to write an encyclopedia is very much like writing software. Both running code and a hypertext/encyclopedia are wonderful turn-ons for the brain, and you want more of it the more you see, like a drug. As a user, you want it to do everything, as a customer you don't really want to pay for it, and as a producer you realise how unrealistic the customers are. Requirements will conflict in functionality vs affordability, and in completeness vs timeliness.

DIFFERENT TYPES OF CRISIS

Chronic Software Crisis

By today's definition, a "large" software system is a system that contains more than 50,000 lines of high-level language code. It's those large systems that bring the software crisis to light. If you're familiar with large software development projects, you know that the work is done in teams consisting of project managers, requirements analysts, software engineers, documentation experts, and programmers.

With so many professionals collaborating in an organized manner on a project, what's the problem? Why is it that the team produces fewer than 10 lines of code per day over the average lifetime of the project? And why are sixty errors found per every thousand lines of code? Why is one of every three large projects scrapped before ever being completed? And why is only 1 in 8 finished software projects considered "successful?"

- The cost of owning and maintaining software in the 1980's was twice as expensive as developing the software.
- During the 1990's, the cost of ownership and maintenance increased by 30% over the 1980's.
- In 1995, statistics showed that half of surveyed development projects were operational, but were not considered successful.
- The average software project overshoots its schedule by half.
- Three quarters of all large software products delivered to the customer are failures that are either not used at all, or do not meet the customer's requirements.

Software projects are notoriously behind schedule and over budget. Over the last twenty years many different paradigms have been created in attempt to make software development more predictable and controllable.

While there is no single solution to the crisis, much has been learned that can directly benefit today's software projects.

It appears that the Software Crisis can be boiled down to two basic sources:

1. Software development is seen as a craft, rather than an engineering discipline.
2. The approach to education taken by most higher education institutions encourages that "craft" mentality.

Software Development

Software development today is more of a craft than a science. Developers are certainly talented and skilled, but work like craftsmen, relying on their talents and skills and using techniques that cannot be measured or reproduced. On the other hand, software engineers place emphasis on reproducible, quantifiable techniques–the marks of science. The software industry is still many years away from becoming a mature engineering discipline. Formal software engineering processes exist, but their use is not widespread. A crisis similar to the software crisis is not seen in the hardware industry, where well documented, formal processes are tried and true, and ad hoc hardware development is unheard of. To make matters worse, software technology is constrained by hardware technology. Since hardware develops at a much faster pace than software, software developers are constantly trying to catch up and take advantage of hardware improvements.

Management often encourages ad hoc software development in an attempt to get products out on time for the new hardware architectures. Design, documentation, and evaluation are of secondary importance and are omitted or completed after the fact. However, as the statistics show, the ad hoc approach just doesn't work. Software developers have classically accepted a certain number of errors in their work as inevitable and part of the job. That mindset becomes increasingly unacceptable as software becomes embedded in more and more consumer electronics. Sixty errors per thousand lines of code is unacceptable when the code is embedded in a toaster, automobile, ATM machine or razor (let your imagination run free for a moment).

Computer Science and Product Orientation

Software developers pick up the ad hoc approach to software development early in their computer science education, where they are taught a "product orientation" approach to software development. In the many undergraduate computer science courses I took, the existence of software engineering processes was never even mentioned.

Computer science education does not provide students with the necessary skills to become effective software engineers. They are taught in a way that encourages them to be concerned only with the final outcome of their assignments–whether or not the programme runs, or whether or not it runs efficiently, or whether or not they used the best possible algorithm. Those concerns in themselves are not bad. But on the other hand, they should not be the focus of a project. The focus should be on the complete process from beginning to end and beyond. Product orientation also leads to problems when the student enters the work force–not having seen how processes affect the final outcome, individual programmers tend to think their work from day to day is too "small" to warrant the application of formal methods.

Fully Supported Software

As we have seen, most software projects do not follow a formal process. The result is a product that is poorly designed and documented. Maintenance becomes problematic because without a design and documentation, it's difficult or impossible to predict what sort of effect a simple change might have on other parts of the system. Fortunately there is an awareness of the software crisis, and it has inspired a worldwide movement towards process improvement. Software industry leaders are beginning to see that following a formal software process consistently leads to better quality products, more efficient teams and individuals, reduced costs, and better morale.

Ratings range from Maturity Level 1, which is characterized by ad hoc development and lack of a formal software development process, up to Maturity Level 5, at which an organization not only has a formal process, but also continually refines and improves it. Each maturity level is further broken down into key process areas that indicate the areas an organization should focus on to improve its software process (*e.g.* requirement analysis, defect prevention, or change control).

Level 5 is very difficult to attain. In early 1995, only two projects, one at Motorola and another at Loral (the on-board space shuttle software project), had earned Maturity Level 5. Another study showed that only 2% of reviewed projects rated in the top two Maturity Levels, in spite of many of those projects placing an extreme emphasis on software process improvement.

Customers contracting large projects will naturally seek organizations with high CMM ratings, and that has prompted increasingly more organizations to investigate software process improvement. Mature software is also reusable software. Artisans are not concerned with producing standardized products, and that is a reason why there is so little interchangeability in software components.

Ideally, software would be standardized to such an extent that it could be marketed as a "part", with its own part number and revision, just as though it were a hardware part. The software component interface would be compatible with any other software system. Though it would seem that nothing less than a software development revolution could make that happen, the National Institute of Standards and Technology (NIST) founded the Advanced Technology Programme (ATP), one purpose of which was to encourage the development of standardized software components.

SOFTWARE ENGINEERING

PROCESS

Software engineering process and practices are the structures imposed on development of a software product. There are different models of software process (software lifecycle is a synonym) used in different organizations and industries. RAL has identified three levels of software process for its projects. These levels balance the different needs of different types of projects. Scaling the process to the project is vital to its success, too much process can be as problematic as too little; too much process can slow down a purely R&D exploration, too little process can slow down a large development project with hard deliverables. The levels are briefly identified as follows:

Level 1: R&D

- No software products delivered, pure research
- Minimal software process

Level 2· Research system

- Larger development team, informal software releases
- Moderate software process

Level 3: Delivered system

- Large software development team, formal software releases
- More formal software process

For example, the Juneau, Alaska Winds Project has evolved from a Level 1 to a Level 3 project over multiple years. It started as a purely R&D effort (Level 1), expanded to a field programme in Juneau (Level 2), and is currently running in the field as a Operational Prototype (Level 3).

The software process and software engineering practices have become more formalized and more structured as the project proceeded through the different levels. RAL has evolved a set of software engineering best practices that implement the three software process levels. These include: source code control, nightly code builds, writing reusable code, using different team models, commitment to deadlines, design and code reviews, risk management, bug tracking, software metrics, software configuration management, requirements management.

Software configuration management (SCM) is a step up in formality and reproducibility from source code control and includes controlling and versioning of software releases. Source code control is a software engineering best practice used with RAL Level 2 and Level 3 projects. SCM is a best practice used on a number of RAL Level 3 projects.

DESCRIPTION

Software Engineering Process

The elements of a software engineering process are generally enumerated as:

- Marketing Requirements
- System-Level Design
- Detailed Design
- Implementation
- Integration
- Field Testing
- Support

No element of this process ought to commence before the earlier ones are substantially complete, and whenever a change is made to some element, all dependent elements ought to be reviewed or redone in light of that change. It's possible that a given module will be both specified and implemented before its dependent modules are fully specified – this is called advanced development or research.

It is absolutely essential that every element of the software engineering process include several kinds of *review:* peer review, mentor/management review, and cross-disciplinary review. Software engineering elements (whether documents or source code) must have version numbers and auditable histories. "Checking in" a change to an element should require some form of review, and the depth of the review should correspond directly to the scope of the change.

Marketing Requirements

The first step of a software engineering process is to create a document which describes the target customers and their reason for needing this product, and then goes on to list the features of the product which address these customer needs. The Marketing Requirements Document (MRD) is the battleground where the answer to the question "What should we build, and who will use it?" is decided.

In many failed projects, the MRD was handed down like an inscribed stone tablet from marketing to engineering, who would then gripe endlessly about the laws of physics and about how they couldn't actually build that product since they had no ready supply of Kryptonite or whatever. The MRD is a joint effort, with engineering not only reviewing but also writing a lot of the text.

System-Level Design

This is a high-level description of the product, in terms of "modules" (or sometimes "programmes") and of the interaction between these modules. The goals of this document are first, to gain more confidence that the product could work and could be built, and second, to form a basis for estimating the total amount of work it will take to build it. The system-level design document should also outline the system-level testing plan, in terms of customer needs and whether they would be met by the system design being proposed.

Detailed Design

The detailed design is where every module called out in the system-level design document is described in detail. The interface (command line formats, calling API, externally visible data structures) of each module has to be completely determined at this point, as well as dependencies between modules. Two things that will evolve out of the detailed design is a PERT or GANT chart showing what work has to be done and in what order, and more accurate estimates of the time it will take to complete each module.

Every module needs a unit test plan, which tells the implementor what test cases or what kind of test cases they need to generate in their unit testing in order to verify functionality. Note that there are additional, nonfunctional unit tests which will be discussed later.

Implementation

Every module described in the detailed design document has to be implemented. This includes the small act of coding or programming that is the heart and soul of the software engineering process. It's unfortunate that this small act is sometimes the only part of software engineering that is taught (or learned), since it is also the only part of software engineering which can be effectively self-taught.

A module can be considered implemented when it has been created, tested, and successfully used by some other module (or by the system-level testing process). Creating a module is the old edit-compile-repeat cycle. Module testing includes the unit level functional and regression tests called out by the detailed design, and also performance/stress testing, and code coverage analysis.

Integration

When all modules are nominally complete, system-level

integration can be done. This is where all of the modules move into a single source pool and are compiled and linked and packaged as a system. Integration can be done incrementally, in parallel with the implementation of the various modules, but it cannot authoritatively approach "doneness" until all modules are substantially complete.

Integration includes the development of a system-level test. If the built package has to be able to install itself (which could mean just unpacking a tarball or copying files from a CD-ROM) then there should be an automated way of doing this, either on dedicated crash and burn systems or in containerized/simulated environments. Sometimes, in the middleware arena, the package is just a built source pool, in which case no installation tools will exist and system testing will be done on the as-built pool. Once the system has been installed (if it is installable), the automated system-level testing process should be able to invoke every public command and call every public entry point, with every possible reasonable combination of arguments.

If the system is capable of creating some kind of database, then the automated system-level testing should create one and then use external (separately written) tools to verify the database's integrity. It's possible that the unit tests will serve some of these needs, and all unit tests should be run in sequence during the integration, build, and packaging process.

Field Testing

Field testing usually begins internally. That means employees of the organization that produced the software package will run it on their own computers. This should ultimately include all "production level" systems — desktops, laptops, and servers.

The statement you want to be able to make at the time you ask customers to run a new software system (or a new version of an existing software system) is "we run it ourselves." The software developers should be available for direct technical support during internal field testing.

Ultimately it will be necessary to run the software externally, meaning on customers' (or prospective customers') computers. It's best to pick "friendly" customers for this exercise since it's likely that they will find a lot of defects — even some trivial and obvious ones — simply because their usage patterns and habits are likely to be different from those of your internal users.

The software developers should be close to the front of the escalation path during external field testing. Defects encountered during field testing need to be triaged by senior developers and technical marketers, to determine which ones can be fixed in the documentation, which ones need to be fixed before the current version is released, and which ones can be fixed in the next release (or never).

Support

Software defects encountered either during field testing or after the software has been distributed should be recorded in a tracking system. These defects should ultimately be assigned to a software engineer who will propose a change to either the definition and documentation of the system, or the definition of a module, or to the implementation of a module. These changes should include additions to the unit and/or system-level tests, in the form of a regression test to show the defect and therefore show that it has been fixed (and to keep it from recurring later).

Just as the MRD was a joint venture between engineering and marketing, so it is that support is a joint venture between engineering and customer service. The battlegrounds in this venture are the bug list, the categorization of particular bugs, the maximum number of critical defects in a shippable software release, and so on.

SOFTWARE QUALITY ATTRIBUTE

HIGH QUALITY SOFTWARE

Developing high quality software is hard, especially when the interpretation of term "quality" is patchy based on the environment in which it is used. In order to know if quality has been achieved, or degraded, it has to be measured, but determining what to measure and how is the difficult part. Software Quality Attributes are the benchmarks that describe system's intended behaviour within the environment for which it was built.

The quality attributes provide the means for measuring the fitness and suitability of a product. Software architecture has a profound affect on most qualities in one way or another, and software quality attributes affect architecture. Identifying desired system qualities before a system is built allows system designer to mold a solution (starting with its architecture) to match the desired needs of the system within the context of constraints (available resources, interface with legacy systems, etc). When a designer understands the desired qualities before a system is built, then the likelihood of selecting or creating the right architecture is improved.

STATEMENTS

Both statements are useless as they provide no tangible way of measuring the behaviour of the system. The quality attributes must be described in terms of scenarios, such as "when 100 users initiate 'complete payment' transition, the payment component, under normal circumstances, will process the requests with an average latency of three seconds." This statement, or scenario, allows an architect to make quantifiable arguments about a system.

A scenario defines the source of stimulus (users), the actual stimulus (initiate transaction), the artifact affected (payment component), the environment in which it exists (normal operation), the effect of the action (transaction processed), and the response measure (within three seconds). Writing such detailed statements is only possible when relevant requirements have been identified and an idea of components has been proposed.

QUALITIES

Scenarios help describe the qualities of a system, but they

don't describe how they will be achieved. Architectural tactics describe how a given quality can be achieved. For each quality there may be a large set of tactics available to an architect. It is the architect's job to select the right tactic in light of the needs of the system and the environment.

For example, a performance tactics may include options to develop better processing algorithms, develop a system for parallel processing, or revise event scheduling policy. Whatever tactic is chosen, it must be justified and documented.

SOFTWARE QUALITIES

It would be naïve to claim that the list below is as a complete taxonomy of all software qualities – but it's a solid list of general software qualities compiled from respectable sources. Domain specific systems are likely to have an additional set of qualities in addition to the list below. System qualities can be categorized into four parts: runtime qualities, non-runtime qualities, business qualities, and architecture qualities.

Each of the categories and its associated qualities are briefly described below. Other articles on this site provide more information about each of the software quality attributes listed below, their applicable properties, and the conflicts the qualities.

TYPES OF SOFTARE QUALITIES

It defines six software quality attributes, also called quality characteristics:

1. *Functionality*: Are the required functions available, including interoperabilithy and security
2. *Reliability*: Maturity, fault tolerance and recoverability
3. *Usability*: How easy it is to understand, learn, operate the software system
4. *Efficiency*: Performance and resource behaviour
5. *Maintainability*: How easy is it to modify the software
6. *Portability*: Can the software easily be transferred to another environment, including installability

Product Revision

The product revision perspective identifies quality factors that influence the ability to change the software product, these factors are:

- Maintainability, the ability to find and fix a defect.
- Flexibility, the ability to make changes required as dictated by the business.
- Testability, the ability to Validate the software requirements.

Product Transition

The product transition perspective identifies quality factors that influence the ability to adapt the software to new environments:

- Portability, the ability to transfer the software from one environment to another.
- Reusability, the ease of using existing software components in a different context.
- Interoperability, the extent, or ease, to which software components work together.

Product Operations

The product operations perspective identifies quality factors that influence the extent to which the software fulfils its specification:

- Correctness, the functionality matches the specification.
- Reliability, the extent to which the system fails.
- Efficiency, system resource (including cpu, disk, memory, network) usage.
- Integrity, protection from unauthorized access.
- Usability, ease of use.

2

Model of Software

LIFE CYCLE MODELS

SYSTEM DEVELOPMENT

The Systems Development Life Cycle (SDLC) is a conceptual model used in project management that describes the stages involved in an information system development project from an initial feasibility study through maintenance of the completed application.

Various SDLC methodologies have been developed to guide the processes involved including the waterfall model (the original SDLC method), rapid application development (RAD), joint application development (JAD), the fountain model and the spiral model.

Mostly, several models are combined into some sort of hybrid methodology. Documentation is crucial regardless of the type of model chosen or devised for any application, and is usually done in parallel with the development process.

Some methods work better for specific types of projects, but in the final analysis, the most important factor for the success of a project may be how closely particular plan was followed.

FEASIBILITY

The feasibility study is used to determine if the project should get the go-ahead. If the project is to proceed, the feasibility study will produce a project plan and budget estimates for the future stages of development.

Requirement Analysis and Design

Analysis gathers the requirements for the system. This stage includes a detailed study of the business needs of the organization. Options for changing the business process may be considered. Design focuses on high level design like, what programmes are needed and how are they going to interact, low-level design (how the individual programmes are going to work), interface design (what are the interfaces going to look like) and data design (what data will be required).

During these phases, the software's overall structure is defined. Analysis and Design are very crucial in the whole development cycle. Any glitch in the design phase could be very expensive to solve in the later stage of the software development. Much care is taken during this phase. The logical system of the product is developed in this phase.

Implementation

In this phase the designs are translated into code. Computer programmes are written using a conventional programming language or an application generator. Programming tools like Compilers, Interpreters, Debuggers are used to generate the code. Different high level programming languages like C, C++, Pascal, Java are used for coding.

Testing

In this phase the system is tested. Normally programmes are written as a series of individual modules, these subject to separate and detailed test. The system is then tested as a whole. The separate modules are brought together and tested as a complete system. The system is tested to ensure that interfaces between modules work (integration testing), the system works on the intended platform and with the expected volume of data (volume testing) and that the system does what the user requires (acceptance/beta testing).

Maintenance

Inevitably the system will need maintenance. Software will definitely undergo change once it is delivered to the customer. There are many reasons for the change. Change could happen because of some unexpected input values into the system. In addition, the changes in the system could directly affect the software operations. The software should be developed to accommodate changes that could happen during the post implementation period.

DESCRIPTION

Curtain Raiser

Like any other set of engineering products, software products are also oriented towards the customer. It is either market driven or it drives the market. Customer Satisfaction was the buzzword of the 80's.

Customer Delight is today's buzzword and Customer Ecstasy is the buzzword of the new millennium. Products that are not customer or user friendly have no place in the market although they are engineered using the best technology. The interface of the product is as crucial as the internal technology of the product.

Potential Customers

A market study is made to identify a potential customer's need. This process is also known as market research. Here, the already existing need and the possible and potential needs that are available in a segment of the society are studied carefully. The market study is done based on a lot of assumptions.

Assumptions are the crucial factors in the development or inception of a product's development. Unrealistic assumptions can cause a nosedive in the entire venture. Though assumptions are abstract, there should be a move to develop tangible assumptions to come up with a successful product.

Research and Development

Once the Market Research is carried out, the customer's need is given to the Research and Development division

(R&D) to conceptualize a cost-effective system that could potentially solve the customer's needs in a manner that is better than the one adopted by the competitors at present. Once the conceptual system is developed and tested in a hypothetical environment, the development team takes control of it. The development team adopts one of the software development methodologies that is given below, develops the proposed system, and gives it to the customer.

The Sales and Marketing division starts selling the software to the available customers and simultaneously works to develop a niche segment that could potentially buy the software. In addition, the division also passes the feedback from the customers to the developers and the R&D division to make possible value additions to the product. While developing a software, the company outsources the non-core activities to other companies who specialize in those activities. This accelerates the software development process largely. Some companies work on tie-ups to bring out a highly matured product in a short period.

MODELLING

SYSTEM DEVELOPMENT MODEL

It specifies the relationships between project phases, including transition criteria, feedback mechanisms, milestones, baselines, reviews, and deliverables. Typically, a life cycle model addresses the phases of a software project: requirements phase, design phase, implementation, integration, testing, operations and maintenance. Much of the motivation behind utilizing a life cycle model is to provide structure to avoid the problems of the "undisciplined hacker" or corporate IT bureaucrat (which is probably ten times dangerous then undisciplined hacker). As always, it's a matter of picking the right tool for the job, rather than picking up your hammer and treating everything as a nail.

System/Information Engineering and Modeling

As software is always of a large system (or business),

work begins by establishing the requirements for all system elements and then allocating some subset of these requirements to software. This system view is essential when the software must interface with other elements such as hardware, people and other resources.

System is the basic and very critical requirement for the existence of software in any entity. So if the system is not in place, the system should be engineered and put in place. In some cases, to extract the maximum output, the system should be re-engineered and spruced up. Once the ideal system is engineered or tuned, the development team studies the software requirement for the system.

Software Requirement Analysis

This process is also known as feasibility study. In this phase, the development team visits the customer and studies their system. They investigate the need for possible software automation in the given system. By the end of the feasibility study, the team furnishes a document that holds the different specific recommendations for the candidate system. It also includes the personnel assignments, costs, project schedule, target dates etc....

The requirement gathering process is intensified and focussed specially on software. To understand the nature of the programme(s) to be built, the system engineer or "Analyst" must understand the information domain for the software, as well as required function, behaviour, performance and interfacing. The essential purpose of this phase is to find the need and to define the problem that needs to be solved.

System Analysis and Design

In this phase, the software development process, the software's overall structure and its nuances are defined. In terms of the client/server technology, the number of tiers needed for the package architecture, the database design, the data structure design etc... are all defined in this phase.

A software development model is thus created. Analysis and Design are very crucial in the whole development cycle.

Any glitch in the design phase could be very expensive to solve in the later stage of the software development. Much care is taken during this phase. The logical system of the product is developed in this phase.

Code Generation

The code generation step performs this task. If the design is performed in a detailed manner, code generation can be accomplished without much complication. Progra-mming tools like compilers, interpreters, debuggers etc... are used to generate the code. Different high level programming languages like C, C++, Pascal, Java are used for coding. With respect to the type of application, the right programming language is chosen.

Testing

Once the code is generated, the software programme testing begins. Different testing methodologies are available to unravel the bugs that were committed during the previous phases. Different testing tools and methodologies are already available. Some companies build their own testing tools that are tailor made for their own development operations.

Maintenance

The software will definitely undergo change once it is delivered to the customer. There can be many reasons for this change to occur. Change could happen because of some unexpected input values into the system. In addition, the changes in the system could directly affect the software operations. The software should be developed to accommodate changes that could happen during the post implementation period.

PROTOTYPING MODEL

This is a cyclic version of the linear model. In this model, once the requirement analysis is done and the design for a prototype is made, the development process gets started. Once the prototype is created, it is given to the customer for evaluation. The customer tests the package and gives his/her feed back to the developer who refines the product according to the customer's exact expectation. After a finite number of iterations, the final software package is given to the customer.

In this methodology, the software is evolved as a result of periodic shuttling of information between the customer and deveioper. This is the most popular development model in the contemporary IT industry. Most of the successful software products have been developed using this model - as it is very difficult (even for a whiz kid!) to comprehend all the requirements of a customer in one shot. There are many variations of this model skewed with respect to the project management styles of the companies. New versions of a software product evolve as a result of protutyping.

The goal of prototyping based development is to counter the first two limitations of the waterfall model discussed earlier. The basic idea here is that instead of freezing the requirements before a design or coding can proceed, a throwaway prototype is built to understand the requirements. This prototype is developed based on the currently known requirements. Development of the prototype obviously undergoes design, coding and testing.

But each of these phases is not done very formally or thoroughly. By using this prototype, the client can get an "actual feel" of the system, since the interactions with prototype can enable the client to better understand the requirements of the desired system. Prototyping is an attractive idea for complicated and large systems for which there is no manual process or existing system to help determining the requirements.

The basic reason for little common use of prototyping is the cost involved in this built-it-twice approach. However, some argue that prototyping need not be very costly and can actually reduce the overall development cost. The prototype are usually not complete systems and many of the details are not built in the prototype.

The goal is to provide a system with overall functionality. In addition, the cost of testing and writing detailed documents are reduced. These factors helps to reduce the cost of developing the prototype. On the other hand, the experience of developing the prototype will very useful for developers when developing the final system. This experience helps to reduce the cost of development of the final system and results in a more reliable and better designed system.

Advantages of Prototyping

Creating software using the prototype model also has its benefits. One of the key advantages a prototype modeled software has is the time frame of development. Instead of concentrating on documentation, more effort is placed in creating the actual software. This way, the actual software could be released in advance.

The work on prototype models could also be spread to others since there are practically no stages of work in thismodel. Everyone has to work on the same thing and at the same time, reducing man hours in creating a software. The work will even be faster and efficient if developers will collaborate more regarding the status of a specific function and develop the necessary adjustments in time for the integration.

Another advantage of having a prototype modeled software is that the software is created using lots of user feedbacks. In every prototype created, users could give their honest opinion about the software. If something is unfavorable, it can be changed. Slowly the programme is created with the customer in mind.

- Users are actively involved in the development
- It provides a better system to users, as users have natural tendency to change their mind in specifying requirements and this method of developing systems supports this user tendency.
- Since in this methodology a working model of the system is provided, the users get a better understanding of the system being developed.
- Errors can be detected much earlier as the system is mode side by side.

- Quicker user feedback is available leading to better solutions.

Disadvantages

Implementing the prototype model for creating software has disadvantages. Since its being built out of concept, most of the models presented in the early stage are not complete. Usually they lack flaws that developers still need to work on them again and again.

Since the prototype changes from time to time, it's a nightmare to create a document for this software. There are many things that are removed, changed and added in a single update of the prototype and documenting each of them has been proven difficult.

There is also a great temptation for most developers to create a prototype and stick to it even though it has flaws. Since prototypes are not yet complete software programmes, there is always a possibility of a designer flaw. When flawed software is implemented, it could mean losses of important resources.

Lastly, integration could be very difficult for a prototype model. This often happens when other programmes are already stable. The prototype software is released and integrated to the company's suite of software. But if there's something wrong the prototype, changes are required not only with the software. It's also possible that the stable software should be changed in order for them to be integrated properly.

Prototype Models Types

There are four types of Prototype Models based on their development planning: the Patch-Up Prototype, Nonoperational Prototype, First-of-a-Series Prototype and Selected Features Prototype.

Patch Up Prototype

This type of Prototype Model encourages cooperation of different developers. Each developer will work on a specific part of the programme. After everyone has done their part, the programme will be integrated with each other resulting in a whole new programme. Since everyone is working on a different field, Patch Up Prototype is a fast development model. If each developer is highly skilled, there is no need to overlap in a specific function of work. This type of software development model only needs a strong project manager who can monitor the development of the programme. The manager will control the work flow and ensure there is no overlapping of functions among different developers.

Non-Operational Prototype

A non-operational prototype model is used when only a certain part of the programme should be updated. Although it's not a fully operational programme, the specific part of the programme will work or could be tested as planned. The main software or prototype is not affected at all as the dummy programme is applied with the application. Each developer who is assigned with different stages will have to work with the dummy prototype.

This prototype is usually implemented when certain problems in a specific part of the programme arises. Since the software could be in a prototype mode for a very long time, changing and maintenance of specific parts is very important. Slowly it has become a smart way of creating software by introducing small functions of the software.

First of a Series Prototype

Known as a beta version, this Prototype Model could be very efficient if properly launched. In all beta versions, the software is launched and even introduced to the public for testing. It's fully functional software but the aim of being in beta version is to as for feedbacks, suggestions or even practicing the firewall and security of the software.

It could be very successful if the First of a Series Prototype is properly done. But if the programme is half heartedly done, only aiming for additional concept, it will be susceptible to different hacks, ultimately backfiring and destroying the prototype.

Selected Features Prototype

This is another form of releasing software in beta version. However, instead of giving the public the full version of the software in beta, only selected features or limited access to some important tools in the programme is introduced. Selected Features Prototype is applied to software that are part of a bigger suite of programmes. Those released are independent of the suite but the full version should integrate with other software. This is usually done to test the independent feature of the software.

RAPID APPLICATION DEVELOPMENT

The RAD model is a "high speed" adaptation of the linear sequential model in which rapid development is achieved by using a component-based construction approach. Used primarily for information systems applications, the RAD approach encompasses the following phases:

Business Modeling

The information flow among business functions is modeled in a way that answers the following questions:

- What information drives the business process?
- What information is generated?
- Who generates it?
- Where does the information go?
- Who processes it?

Data Modeling

The information flow defined as part of the business modeling phase is refined into a set of data objects that are needed to support the business. The characteristic (called attributes) of each object is identified and the relationships between these objects are defined.

Process Modeling

The data objects defined in the data-modeling phase are

transformed to achieve the information flow necessary to implement a business function. Processing the descriptions are created for adding, modifying, deleting, or retrieving a data object.

Application Generation

The RAD model assumes the use of the RAD tools like VB, VC++, Delphi etc... rather than creating software using conventional third generation programming languages. The RAD model works to reuse existing programme components (when possible) or create reusable components (when necessary). In all cases, automated tools are used to facilitate construction of the software.

Testing and Turnover

Since the RAD process emphasizes reuse, many of the programme components have already been tested. This minimizes the testing and development time.

COMPONENT ASSEMBLY MODEL

Object technologies provide the technical framework for a component-based process model for software engineering. The object oriented paradigm emphasizes the creation of classes that encapsulate both data and the algorithm that are used to manipulate the data. If properly designed and implemented, object oriented classes are reusable across different applicationsand computer based system architectures.

Component Assembly Model leads to software reusability. The integration/assembly of the already existing software components accelerate the development process. Nowadays many component libraries are available on the Internet. If the right components are chosen, the integration aspect is made much simpler.

All these different software development models have their own advantages and disadvantages. Nevertheless, in the contemporary commercial software evelopment world, the fusion of all these methodologies is incorporated. Timing is very crucial in software development. If a delay happens in the development phase, the market could be taken over by the competitor. Also if a 'bug' filled product is launched in a short period of time (quicker than the competitors), it may affect the reputation of the company. So, there should be a tradeoff between the development time and the quality of the product. Customers don't expect a bug free product but they expect a user-friendly product.

SOFTWARE LIFE CYCLE MODELS

WATERFALL MODEL

The least flexible of the life cycle models. Still it is well suited to projects which have a well defined architecture and established user interface and performance requirements. The waterfall model *does* work for certain problem domains, notably those where the requirements are well understood in advance and unlikely to change significantly over the course of development. Software products are oriented towards customers like any other engineering products. It is either driver by market or it drives the market. Customer Satisfaction was the main aim in the 1980's. Customer Delight is today's logo and Customer Ecstasy is the new buzzword of the new millennium. Products which are not customer oriented have no place in the market although they are designed using the best technology. The front end of the product is as crucial as the internal technology of the product.

A market study is necessary to identify a potential customer's need. This process is also called as market research. The already existing need and the possible future needs that are combined together for study. A lot of assumptions are made during market study. Assumptions are the very important factors in the development or start of a product's development.

Advantages

- Simple and easy to use.
- Easy to manage due to the rigidity of the model –

each phase has specific deliverables and a review process.

- Phases are processed and completed one at a time.
- Works well for smaller projects where requirements are very well understood.

Disadvantages

- Adjusting scope during the life cycle can kill a project
- No working software is produced until late during the life cycle.
- High amounts of risk and uncertainty.
- Poor model for complex and object-oriented projects.
- Poor model for long and ongoing projects.
- Poor model where requirements are at a moderate to high risk of changing.

EXTREME PROGRAMMING (XP)

Is the latest incarnation of Waterfall model and is the most recent software fad. Most postulates of Extreme programming are pure fantasy. It has been well known for a long time that *big bang* or waterfall models don't work well on projects with complex or shifting requirements. The same is true for XP. Too many shops implement XP as an excuse for not understanding the user requirements. XP try improve classic waterfall model by trying to start coding as early as possible but without creating a full-fledged prototype as the first stage. In this sense it can be considered to be variant of evolutionary prototyping (see below). Often catch phase "Emergent design" is used instead of evolutionary prototyping.

It also introduces a very questionable idea of pair programming as an attempt to improve extremely poor communication between developers typical for large projects. While communication in large projects is really critical and attempts to improve it usually pay well, "pair programming" is a questionable strategy.

There are two main problems here:

1 In a way it can be classified as a hidden attempt to

create one good programmer out of two mediocre. But in reality it is creating one mediocre programmer from two or one good. No senior developer is going to put up with some jerk sitting on his lap asking questions about every line. It just prevents the level of concentration needed for high quality coding. Microsoft's idea of having a tester for each programmer is more realistic: one developer writes tests.

2 The actual code to be tested. This forces each of them to communicate and because tester has different priorities then developer such communication brings the developer a new and different perspective on his code, which really improves quality. This combination of different perspectives is a really neat idea as you can see from the stream of Microsoft Office products and operating systems.

SPIRAL MODEL

The spiral model is a variant of "dialectical spiral" and as such provides useful insights into the life cycle of the system. Can be considered as a generalization of the prototyping model. That why it is usually implemented as a variant of prototyping model with the first iteration being a prototype.

The spiral model is similar to the incremental model, with more emphases placed on risk analysis. The spiral model has four phases: Planning, Risk Analysis, Engineering and Evaluation.

A software project repeatedly passes through these phases in iterations (called Spirals in this model). The baseline spiral, starting in the planning phase, requirements are gathered and risk is assessed.

Each subsequent spirals builds on the baseline spiral. Requirements are gathered during the planning phase. In the risk analysis phase, a process is undertaken to identify risk and alternate solutions. A prototype is produced at the end of the risk analysis phase. Software is produced in the engineering phase, along with testing at the end of the phase.

Advantages

- High amount of risk analysis
- Good for large and mission-critical projects.
- Software is produced early in the software life cycle.

Disadvantages

- Can be a costly model to use.
- Risk analysis requires highly specific expertise.
- Project's success is highly dependent on the risk analysis phase.
- Doesn't work well for smaller projects.

EVOLUTIONARY PROTOTYPING MODEL

This is kind of mix of Waterfall model and prototyping. Presuppose gradual refinement of the prototype until a usable product emerge. Might be suitable in projects where the main problem is user interface requirements, but internal architecture is relatively well established and static. In this case system first is coded in a scripting language and then gradually critical components are rewritten in the lower language.

OSS DEVELOPMENT MODEL

It is the latest variant of evolutionary prototype model. The "waterfall model" was probably the first published model and as a specific model for military it was not as naive as some proponents of other models suggest. The model was developed to help cope with the increasing complexity of aerospace products. The waterfall model followed a documentation driven paradigm.

Prototyping model was probably the first realistic of early models because many aspects of the syst4m are unclear until a working prototype is developed. A better model, the "spiral model" was suggested by Boehm in 1985. The spiral model is a variant of "dialectical spiral" and as such provides useful insights into the life cycle of the system. But it also presuppose unlimited resources for the project. No organization can perform more then a couple iterations during the initial development of the system. the first iteration is usually called prototype. Prototype based development requires more talented managers and good planning while waterfall model works (or does not work) with bad or stupid managers works just fine as the success in this model is more determined by the nature of the task in hand then any organizational circumstances.

Like always humans are flexible and programmer in waterfall model can use guerilla methods of enforcing a sound architecture as manager is actually a hostage of the model and cannot afford to look back and re-implement anything substantial. Because the life cycle steps are described in very general terms, the models are adaptable and their implementation details will vary among different organizations.

The spiral model is the most general. Most life cycle models can in fact be derived as special instances of the spiral model. Organizations may mix and match different life cycle models to develop a model more tailored to their products and capabilities.

There is nothing wrong about using waterfall model for some components of the complex project that are relatively well understood and straightforward. But mixing and matching definitely needs a certain level of software management talent.

V-SHAPED MODEL

Just like the waterfall model, the V-Shaped life cycle is a sequential path of execution of processes. Each phase must be completed before the next phase begins. Testing is emphasized in this model more so than the waterfall model though. The testing procedures are developed early in the life cycle before any coding is done, during each of the phases preceding implementation.

Requirements begin the life cycle model just like the waterfall model. Before development is started, a system test plan is created. The test plan focuses on meeting the functionality specified in the requirements gathering.

The high-level design phase focuses on system architecture and design. An integration test plan is created in this phase as well in order to test the pieces of the software systems ability to work together. The low-level design phase is where the actual software components are designed, and unit tests are created in this phase as well. The implementation phase is, again, where all coding takes place.

Advantages

- Simple and easy to use.
- Each phase has specific deliverables.
- Higher chance of success over the waterfall model due to the development of test plans early on during the life cycle.
- Works well for small projects where requirements are easily understood.

Disadvantages

- Very rigid, like the waterfall model.
- Little flexibility and adjusting scope is difficult and expensive.
- Software is developed during the implementation phase, so no early prototypes of the software are produced.
- Model doesn't provide a clear path for problems found during testing phases.

INCREMENTAL MODEL

The incremental model is an intuitive approach to the waterfall model. Multiple development cycles take place here, making the life cycle a "multi-waterfall" cycle. Cycles are divided up into smaller, more easily managed iterations.

Each iteration passes through the requirements, design, implementation and testing phases. A working version of software is produced during the first iteration, so you have working software early on during the software life cycle. Subsequent iterations build on the initial software produced during the first iteration.

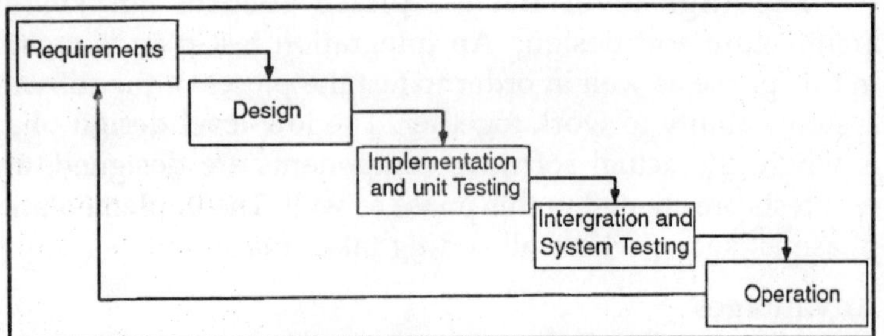

Fig. Incremental Life Cycle Model.

Advantages

- Generates working software quickly and early during the software life cycle.
- More flexible – less costly to change scope and requirements.
- Easier to test and debug during a smaller iteration.
- Easier to manage risk because risky pieces are identified and handled during its iteration.
- Each iteration is an easily managed milestone.

Disadvantages

- Each phase of an iteration is rigid and do not overlap each other.
- Problems may arise pertaining to system architecture because not all requirements are gathered up front for the entire software life cycle.

3

Role of Software Requirements Specifications

SRS DOCUMENTS

The SRS document itself states in precise and explicit language those functions and capabilities a software system (*i.e.*, a software application, an eCommerce Web site, and so on) must provide, as well as states any required constraints by which the system must abide. The SRS also functions as a blueprint for completing a project with as little cost growth as possible. The SRS is often referred to as the "parent" document because all subsequent project management documents, such as design specifications, statements of work, software architecture specifications, testing and validation plans, and documentation plans, are related to it. It's important to note that an SRS contains functional and nonfunctional requirements only; it doesn't offer design suggestions, possible solutions to technology or business issues, or any other information other than what the development team understands the customer's system requirements to be.

A well-designed, well-written SRS accomplishes four major goals:

- It provides feedback to the customer. An SRS is the customer's assurance that the development organization understands the issues or problems to be solved and the software behaviour necessary to address those problems. Therefore, the SRS should be written in natural language (versus a formal language, explained later in this article), in an unambiguous manner that may also include charts, tables, data flow diagrams, decision tables, and so on.

- It decomposes the problem into component parts. The simple act of writing down software requirements in a well-designed format organizes information, places borders around the problem, solidifies ideas, and helps break down the problem into its component parts in an orderly fashion.
- It serves as an input to the design specification. As mentioned previously, the SRS serves as the parent document to subsequent documents, such as the software design specification and statement of work. Therefore, the SRS must contain sufficient detail in the functional system requirements so that a design solution can be devised.
- It serves as a product validation check. The SRS also serves as the parent document for testing and validation strategies that will be applied to the requirements for verification.

SOFTWARE REQUIREMENTS SPECIFICATIONS

Unfortunately, much of the time, systems architects and programmers write SRSs with little (if any) help from the technical communications organization. And when that assistance is provided, it's often limited to an edit of the final draft just prior to going out the door. Having technical writers involved throughout the entire SRS development process can offer several benefits:

- Technical writers are skilled information gatherers, ideal for eliciting and articulating customer requirements. The presence of a technical writer on the requirements-gathering team helps balance the type and amount of information extracted from customers, which can help improve the SRS.
- Technical writers can better assess and plan documentation projects and better meet customer document needs. Working on SRSs provides technical writers with an opportunity for learning about

customer needs firsthand—early in the product development process.

- Technical writers know how to determine the questions that are of concern to the user or customer regarding ease of use and usability. Technical writers can then take that knowledge and apply it not only to the specification and documentation development, but also to user interface development, to help ensure the UI (User Interface) models the customer requirements.
- Technical writers, involved early and often in the process, can become an information resource throughout the process, rather than an information gatherer at the end of the process.

SRS TEMPLATE

There's not a "standard specification template" for all projects in all industries because the individual requirements that populate an SRS are unique not only from company to company, but also from project to project within any one company. The key is to select an existing template or specification to begin with, and then adapt it to meet your needs.

SAMPLE SRS OUTLINE

Introduction

- Purpose
- Document conventions
- Intended audience
- Additional information
- Contact information/SRS team members
- References

Overall Description

- Product perspective
- Product functions
- User classes and characteristics
- Operating environment

- User environment
- Design/implementation constraints
- Assumptions and dependencies

External Interface Requirements

- User interfaces
- Hardware interfaces
- Software interfaces
- Communication protocols and interfaces

System Features

- System feature A
- Description and priority
- Action/result
- Functional requirements
- System feature B

Other Nonfunctional Requirements

- Performance requirements
- Safety requirements
- Security requirements
- Software quality attributes
- Project documentation
- User documentation

Other Requirements

- *Appendix A*: Terminology/Glossary/Definitions list
- *Appendix B*: To be determined

Shows a more detailed SRS outline, showing the structure of an SRS template.

Sample of a More Detailed SRS Outline

- Scope
  - *Identification*: Identify the system and the software to which this document applies, including, as applicable, identification number(s), title(s), abbreviation(s), version number(s), and release number(s).

- *System overview*: State the purpose of the system or subsystem to which this document applies.
- *Document overview*: Summarize the purpose and contents of this document.

  This document comprises six sections:
  1. Scope
  2. Referenced documents
  3. Requirements
  4. Qualification provisions
  5. Requirements traceability
  6. Notes

     Describe any security or privacy considerations associated with its use.

- Referenced Documents
  - Project documents.
  - Identify the project management system documents here.
  - Other documents.
  - Precedence.
  - Source of documents.
- *Requirements*: This section shall be divided into paragraphs to specify the Computer Software Configuration Item (CSCI) requirements, that is, those characteristics of the CSCI that are conditions for its acceptance. CSCI requirements are software requirements generated to satisfy the system requirements allocated to this CSCI. Each requirement shall be assigned a project-unique identifier to support testing and traceability and shall be stated in such a way that an objective test can be defined for it.
  - Required states and modes.
  - CSCI capability requirements.
  - CSCI external interface requirements.
  - CSCI internal interface requirements.
  - CSCI internal data requirements.
  - Adaptation requirements.
  - Safety requirements.

  - Security and privacy requirements.
  - CSCI environment requirements.
  - Computer resource requirements.
  - Software quality factors.
  - Design and implementation constraints.
  - Personnel requirements.
  - Training-related requirements.
  - Logistics-related requirements.
  - Other requirements.
  - Packaging requirements.
  - Precedence and criticality requirements.
- Qualification Provisions
  - To be determined.
- Requirements Traceability
  - To be determined.

SOFTWARE REQUIREMENTS SPECIFICATION

There are many good definitions of System and Software Requirements Specifications that will provide us a good basis upon which we can both define a great specification and help us identify deficiencies in our past efforts. There is also a lot of great stuff on the web about writing good specifications. The problem is not lack of knowledge about how to create a correctly formatted specification or even what should go into the specification. The problem is that we don't follow the definitions out there.

We have to keep in mind that the goal is not to create great specifications but to create great products and great software. Can you create a great product without a great specification? Absolutely! You can also make your first million through the lottery – but why take your chances? Systems and software these days are so complex that to embark on the design before knowing what you are going to build is foolish and risky.

The IEEE is an excellent source for definitions of System and Software Specifications. As designers of real-time, embedded system software, we use IEEE STD 830-1998 as the basis for all of our Software Specifications unless specifically requested by our clients. Essential to having a great Software Specification is having a great System Specification. The equivalent IEEE standard for that is IEEE STD 1233-1998. However, for most purposes in smaller systems, the same templates can be used for both.

BENEFITS OF SRS

Establish the basis for agreement between the customers and the suppliers on what the software product is to do. The complete description of the functions to be performed by the software specified in the SRS will assist the potential users to determine if the software specified meets their needs or how the software must be modified to meet their needs

Reduce the development effort. The preparation of the SRS forces the various concerned groups in the customer's organization to consider rigorously all of the requirements before design begins and reduces later redesign, recoding, and retesting. Careful review of the requirements in the SRS can reveal omissions, misunderstandings, and inconsistencies early in the development cycle when these problems are easier to correct.

Provide a basis for estimating costs and schedules. The description of the product to be developed as given in the SRS is a realistic basis for estimating project costs and can be used to obtain approval for bids or price estimates. Provide a baseline for validation and verification. Organizations can develop their validation and Verification plans much more productively from a good SRS. As a part of the development contract, the SRS provides a baseline against which compliance can be measured.

Facilitate transfer. The SRS makes it easier to transfer the software product to new users or new machines. Customers thus find it easier to transfer the software to other parts of their organization, and suppliers find it easier to transfer it to new customers.

Serve as a basis for enhancement. Because the SRS discusses the product but not the project that developed it, the SRS serves as a basis for later enhancement of the finished product. The SRS may need to be altered, but it does provide a foundation for continued production evaluation.

CHARACTERISTICS

An SRS should be:

- Correct
- Unambiguous
- Complete
- Consistent
- Ranked for importance and/or stability
- Verifiable
- Modifiable
- Traceable
  - *Correct*: This is like motherhood and apple pie. Of course you want the specification to be correct. No one writes a specification that they know is incorrect. We like to say - "Correct and Ever Correcting." The discipline is keeping the specification up to date when you find things that are not correct.
  - *Unambiguous*: An SRS is unambiguous if, and only if, every requirement stated therein has only one interpretation. Again, easier said than done. Spending time on this area prior to releasing the SRS can be a waste of time. But as you find ambiguities - fix them.
  - *Complete*: A simple judge of this is that is should be all that is needed by the software designers to create the software.
  - *Consistent*: The SRS should be consistent within itself and consistent to its reference documents. If you call an input "Start and Stop" in one place, don't call it "Start/Stop" in another.
  - *Ranked for Importance*: Very often a new system has requirements that are really marketing wish lists. Some may not be achievable. It is useful provide this information in the SRS.
  - *Verifiable*: Don't put in requirements like - "It

should provide the user a fast response." Another of my favorites is - "The system should never crash." Instead, provide a quantitative requirement like: "Every key stroke should provide a user response within 100 milliseconds."

SYSTEM AND SPECIFICATION

Important issues are not defined up front and Mechanical, Electronic and Software designers do not really know what their requirements are:

- Define the functions of the system
- Define the Hardware/ Software Functional Partitioning
- Define the Performance Specification
- Define the Hardware/ Software Performance Partitioning
- Define Safety Requirements
- Define the User Interface (A good user's manual is often an overlooked part of the System specification. Many of our customers haven't even considered that this is the right time to write the user's manual.)
- Provide Installation Drawings/Instructions.
- Provide Interface Control Drawings (ICD's, External I/O)

One job of the System specification is to define the full functionality of the system. In many systems we work on, some functionality is performed in hardware and some in software. It is the job of the System specification to define the full functionality and like the performance requirements, to set in motion the trade-offs and preliminary design studies to allocate these functions to the different disciplines (mechanical, electrical, software).

Another function of the System specification is to specify performance. For example, if the System is required to move a mechanism to a particular position accurate to a repeatability of ± 1 millimeter, that is a System's requirement. Some portion of that repeatability specification will belong to the mechanical hardware, some to the servo amplifier and electronics and some to the software. It is the job of the System specification to provide that requirement and to set in motion the partitioning between mechanical hardware, electronics, and software.

Very often the System specification will leave this partitioning until later when you learn more about the system and certain factors are traded off (For example, if we do this in software we would need to run the processor clock at 40 mHz.

However, if we did this function in hardware, we could run the processor clock at 12 mHz). However, for all practical purposes, most of the systems we are involved with in small to medium size companies, combine the software and the systems documents. This is done primarily because most of the complexity is in the software. When the hardware is used to meet a functional requirement, it often is something that the software wants to be well documented.

Very often, the software is called upon to meet the system requirement with the hardware you have. Very often, there is not a systems department to drive the project and the software engineers become the systems engineers. For small projects, this is workable even if not ideal. In this case, the specification should make clear which requirements are software, which are hardware, and which are mechanical.

DESIGN AND REQUIREMENT

SRS should not include any design requirements. However, this is a difficult discipline. For example, because of the partitioning and the particular RTOS you are using, and the particular hardware you are using, you may require that no task use more than 1 ms of processing prior to releasing control back to the RTOS.

Although that may be a true requirement and it involves software and should be tested – it is truly a design requirement and should be included in the Software Design Document or in the Source code. Consider the target audience for each specification to identify what goes into what documents.

MARKETING/PRODUCT MANAGEMENT

Creates a product specification and gives it to Systems. It should define everything Systems needs to specify the product

SYSTEMS/SOFTWARE

Creates a Software Specification and gives it to Software. It should define everything Software needs to develop the software. Thus, the SRS should define everything explicitly or (preferably) by reference that software needs to develop the software. References should include the version number of the target document. Also, consider using master document tools which allow you to include other documents and easily access the full requirements.

REQUIREMENT ENGINEERING PROCESS

Based on assessed user needs, the SAF User Requirements are established and implemented into a Technical Specification and Design baseline, in line with scientific assessments and plans.

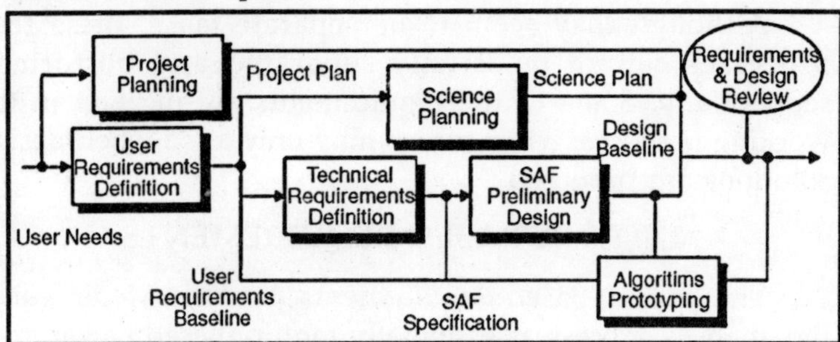

Software requirements engineering is the process of determining what is to be produced in a software system. In developing a complex software system, the requirements engineering process has the widely recognized goal of determining the needs for, and the intended external behaviour, of a system design.

This process is regarded as one of the most important parts of building a software system: " The hardest single part of building a software system is deciding what to build. No other part of the conceptual work is as difficult a establishing the detailed technical requirements, including all the interfaces to people, to machines, and to other software systems.

Tracing the emergence of significant ideas in software development over the years, one can observe that in the '60s the attention was on coding, in the '70s on design and in the '80s on specification. However, in the process of requirements engineering it is often difficult to state the real 'what' level of a system because one person's 'how' may be another person's 'what' and conversely. In this perspective, the requirements engineer faces a complex problem, in meeting the needs of the customer and at the same time meeting the needs of the designer.

The four specific steps in software requirements engineering are:

1. Requirements elicitation
2. Requirements analysis
3. Requirements specification
4. Requirements validation

Although they seem to be separate tasks, these four processes cannot be strictly separated and performed sequentially. Some of the requirements are implicit in the working practices, while others may only arise when design solutions are proposed.

INQUIRY BASED REQUIREMENTS

The Inquiry-Based Requirements Analysis Model views the analysis process as essentially inquiry-based "a series of questions and answers designed to pinpoint where information needs come from and when". The Inquiry Cycle Model, a "formal structure for describing discussion about requirements", addresses the case of mass-market-driven product development, for which there may be no clear customer authority.

The term used in this model is "stakeholder", anyone who shares information about the system, its implementation constraints or problem domain. The model consists of an integration of three phases, where the stakeholders write down their proposed requirements, challenge them by attaching typed annotations and then refine the requirements when change requests are approved.

These requirements are derived from many sources and in many formats, hence a tremendous amount of complex raw data comprise the source material for a given system."AMORE is interested in modeling those vast amounts of raw source material as requirements, and provides access to knowledge about the problem domain, as well as tools for the capture, modeling, analysis and manipulation of raw requirements data.

USER-DEVELOPMENT INTERACTION

The most important aspect of user-development interaction is the mutual learning and cooperation among them. Some methodologies assume that the transfer of knowledge between users and designers can be achieved in the environment of a meeting room. At the same time, other methodologies (*e.g.* PD) foster the full collaboration of stakeholders through a process where users are directly faced with the designers' work situation and conversely, and by the end of the elicitation process everyone learned about real needs of users and technical possibilities.

In this context, success in meeting the real needs of the software system is contingent upon the ability of users to clearly specify what their requirements are. For this reason, requirements definition needs close interaction between developers and end-users of the software.

It is critical that requirements engineering tools must support collaborative development of the software requirements negotiation. Requirements definition should be an iterative process where, through reflection and experience, users become familiar with the technology and developers become familiar with the work. For example, scenarios, prototypes or mock-ups which provide the opportunity for the users to "experience" the new technology and for the developers to "experience" the work practice.

TEAM ROOMS

The groupware system called Tearooms provides an electronic equivalent of a team room for groups that are either co-located or at a distance. More about Tearooms as a Group Kit application may be found in Roseman and Greenberg. It is implemented using an extended version of the groupware toolkit GroupKit. Facilities offered by the GroupKit's Application Programming Interface are preserved in Team Rooms. This enabled the developers to move the existing GroupKit applications to TeamRooms and rapidly create new ones. It combines the rich applications and interfaces found in the existing real-time groupware applications, providing a persistent work space suitable for both synchronous and asynchronous collaboration. It encapsulates both structured and unstructured work through its applications and also takes into account individual and group work.

Apples are special-purpose applications, designated for more specific needs of a group. Team Rooms supports any type of application which can be constructed in Group Kit, such as meeting tools, drawing tools, text editors, card games and so on. When a user starts up the system, he or she is prompted for a user name and a password. If he is among the work group permitted to use the system, he or she will be connected to the Team Rooms central server.

ELICITATION

Using an elicitation method can help in producing a consistent and complete set of security requirements. However, brainstorming and elicitation methods used for ordinary functional (end-user) requirements usually are not oriented towards security requirements and do not result in a consistent and complete set of security requirements. The resulting system is likely to have fewer security exposures when security requirements are elicited in a systematic way.

Elicitation Evaluation Criteria

The following are example evaluation criteria that may be useful in selecting an elicitation method, but certainly there are other criteria that you could use. The main point is to use criteria and to have a common understanding of what they mean.

- *Adaptability*: The method can be used to generate requirements in multiple environments. For example, the elicitation method works equally as well with a software product that is near completion as with a project in the planning stages.
- *Computer-aided software engineering (CASE) tool*: The method includes a CASE tool. (The Software Engineering Institute defines a CASE tool as "a computer-based product aimed at supporting one or more software engineering activities within a software development process")
- *Stakeholder acceptance*: The stakeholders are likely to agree to the elicitation method in analyzing their requirements. For example, the method isn't too invasive in a business environment.
- *Easy implementation*: The elicitation method isn't overly complex and can be properly executed easily.
- *Graphical output*: The method produces readily understandable visual artifacts.
- *Quick implementation*: The requirements engineers and stakeholders can fully execute the elicitation method in a reasonable length of time.
- *Shallow learning curve*: The requirements engineers and stakeholders can fully comprehend the elicitation method within a reasonable length of time.

DATA FLOW DIAGRAMS

INTRODUCTION

A data flow diagram (DFD) is a significant modeling technique for analyzing and constructing information processes. DFD literally means an illustration that explains the course or movement of information in a process. DFD illustrates this flow of information in a process based on the inputs and outputs. A DFD can be referred to as a Process Model. Additionally, a DFD can be utilized to visualize data processing or a structured design. A DFD illustrates technical or business processes with the help of the external data stored, the data flowing from a process to another, and the results. A designer usually draws a context-level DFD showing the relationship between the entities inside and outside of a system as one single step. This basic DFD can be then disintegrated to a lower level diagram demonstrating smaller steps exhibiting details of the system that is being modeled.

USES

The technique starts with an overall picture of the business and continues by analyzing each of the functional areas of interest. This analysis can be carried out to precisely the level of detail required. The technique exploits a method called top-down expansion to conduct the analysis in a targeted way.

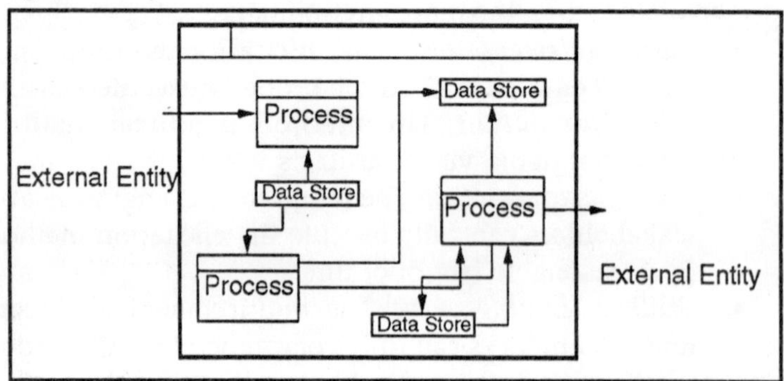

The result is a series of diagrams that represent the business activities in a way that is clear and easy to communicate. A business model comprises one or more data flow diagrams (also known as business process diagrams). Initially a context diagram is drawn, which is a simple representation of the entire system under investigation. This is followed by a level 1 diagram; which provides an overview of the major functional areas of the business. Don't worry about the symbols at this stage, these are explained shortly. Using the context diagram together with additional information from the area of interest, the level 1 diagram can then be drawn.

The level 1 diagram identifies the major business processes at a high level and any of these processes can then be analysed further - giving rise to a corresponding level 2 business process diagram. This process of more detailed analysis can then continue ýÿC through level 3, 4 and so on. However, most investigations will stop at level 2 and it is very unusual to go beyond a level 3 diagram.

Identifying the existing business processes, using a technique like data flow diagrams, is an essential precursor to business process re-engineering, migration to new technology, or refinement of an existing business process. However, the level of detail required will depend on the type of change being considered.

The process model is typically used in structured analysis and design methods. Also called a data flow diagram (DFD), it shows the flow of information through a system. Each process transforms inputs into outputs.

PROCESS

The process shows a part of the system that transforms inputs into outputs; that is, it shows how one or more inputs are changed into outputs. Some systems analysts prefer to use an oval or a rectangle with rounded edges, as shown in Figure below; still others prefer to use a rectangle, as shown in Figure. The differences between these three shapes are purely cosmetic, though it is obviously important to use the same shape consistently to represent all the functions in the system. Throughout the rest of this book, we will use the circle or bubble.

In some cases, the process will contain the name of a person or a group of people (*e.g.*, a department or a division of an organization), or a computer, or a mechanical device. That is, the process sometimes describes who or what is carrying out the process, rather than describing what the process is.

The Flow

A flow is represented graphically by an arrow into or out

of a process. The flow is used to describe the movement of chunks, or packets of information from one part of the system to another part. For most of the systems that you model as a systems analyst, the flows will indeed represent data, that is, bits, characters, messages, floating point numbers, and the various other kinds of information that computers can deal with. But DFDs can also be used to model systems other than automated, computerized systems; we may choose, for example, to use a DFD to model an assembly line in which there are no computerized components.

In such a case, the packets or chunks carried by the flows will typically be physical materials; an example is shown in Figure below. For many complex, real-world systems, the DFD will show the flow of materials and data.

The flows in Figures are *named*. The name represents the meaning of the packet that moves along the flow. A corollary of this is that the flow carries only one type of packet, as indicated by the flow name. The systems analyst should not name a dataflow Apples and organes and widgets and various other thing.

However, we will see in Part III, that there are exceptions to this convention: it is sometimes useful to consolidate several elementary dataflow into a consolidated flow. Thus, one might see a single dataflow labeled vegetables instead of several different dataflow labeled potatoes, brussel sprouts, and peas. whether data (or material) are moving into or out of a process (or doing both). The flow shown in Figure, for example, clearly shows that a telephone number is being sent into the process labeled Validate Phone Number.

Dataflows can diverge and converge in a DFD; conceptually, this is somewhat like a major river splitting into smaller tributaries, or tributaries joining together. However, this has a special meaning in a typical DFD in which packets of data are moving through the system: in the case of a diverging flow, it means that duplicate copies of a packet of data are being sent to different parts of the system, or that a complex packet of data is being split into several more elementary data packets, each of which is being sent to different parts of the system, or that the dataflow pipeline carries items with different values (*e.g.*, vegetables whose values may be "potato," "brussel sprout," or "lima bean") that are being separated. Conversely, in the case of a converging flow, it means that several elementary packets of data are joining together to form more complex, aggregate packets of data.

The Terminator

The next component of the DFD is a *terminator*; it is graphically represented as a rectangle, as shown in Figure. Terminators represent external entities with which the system communicates. Typically, a terminator is a person or a group of people, for example, an outside organization or government agency, or a group or department that is *within* the same company or organization, but *outside*the control of the system being modeled.

In some cases, a terminator may be another system, for example, some other computer system with which your system will communicate.

Accounting Department

Fig. Graphical Representation of a Terminator.

There are three important things that we must remember about terminators:

1. They are *outside* the system we are modeling; the flows connecting the terminators to various processes (or stores) in our system represent the interface between our system and the outside world.
2. As a consequence, it is evident that neither the systems analyst nor the systems designer are in a position to change the contents of a terminator or the way the terminator works. In the language of several classic textbooks on structured analysis, the terminator is outside the domain of change. What

this means is that the systems analyst is modeling a system with the intention of allowing the systems designer a considerable amount of flexibility and freedom to choose the best (or most efficient, or most reliable, etc.) implementation possible.

3. Any relationship that exists *between* terminators will not be shown in the DFD model. There may indeed be several such relationships, but, by definition, those relationships are not part of the system we are studying. Conversely, if there *are*relationships between the terminators, and if it is essential for the systems analyst to model those requirements in order to properly document the requirements of the system, then, by definition, the terminators are actually part of the system and should be modeled as processes.

ENTITY RELATIONSHIP DIAGRAMS

Introduction

An entity can be thought of as a class of data. Each entity has a name, a definition, a type. In addition, each entity has a set of attributes that describe the various characteristics of the entity. Each attribute also has a name, a definition, a type and constraints. The attribute types are text, numeric, binary and date types. Field and attributes are different name for the same thing. Entity and table are different name for the same thing. In the context of relationship diagrams, the words entity and attributes are used. In the context of physical database work, the words table and field are used.

An Entity-Relationship (E-R) Diagram (or E-R Model) visually depicts an organization's entities, the entities' relationships to each other, and the business rules (*i.e.*, cardinality and dependency) associated with the relationships. The E-R Diagram is the picture used to represent and test the knowledge obtained from Data Modelling.

The output of Data Modelling includes:

- E-R Diagram,

- Descriptions of entities and their relationships,
- Dttributes and their descriptions,
- Edit rules,
- Business rules,
- Volumetrics.

The last step in creating entity relationship diagrams is the specification of the relationships among the entities. Just as every object in the real world has some kind of relationship to one or more objects so too the entities in a database are related to other entities.

The nature of relationships between entities is usually implied in the very definition of the entity. Despite the obviousness of these relationships, it is important to review all entities and specify how they relate to each other.

There are at least three types of relationships possible:

1. One to one, where one entity corresponds to exactly another entity. For example, a table about patient's death has a one to one relationship with the table "Person."
2. One to many, where one instance of one entity can be repeatedly used by another. For example the look up table Gender may be repeatedly used in the table "Patient."
3. Many to many where one instance of both entities can be repeatedly used by another. For example, tables "Patient" and "Clinician" have many to many relationships as a clinician may have many patient and a patient may have many clinicians.

Sometimes, the relationship between two entities is not clear. The most common cause is that a third entity is missing. This often occurs when two entity have many to many relationship. For example, the entity Patient and the entity Clinician have, as mentioned earlier, many to many relationship. It is difficult to show these relationships inside a database in a way that can easily be manipulated.

An alternative is to show a new table that links these two tables to each other and has one to many relationship to each of the tables. For example, we can make a new table called Visit. Within a visit a patients is diagnosed. Both the patients and the clinicians identity are kept in the visit table. The Visit table has one to many relationship with either patient or clinician table. Sometimes, as we specify the relationships among entities, a new entity must be defined.

Linkages between entities are part of the business rules that databases should capture. In our example, the business rule for the linkage between a Clinician and a Patient is that a clinician may have zero, one, or, more patients.

The business rule for the linkage between the Patient and the Clinician is that a patient may have one, or, more clinicians. Note that these are the business rules that someone may have specified. In a different information system someone could decide that a patient can only have one clinician at a time, or that the number of clinicians dealing with a patient must always be 3, or some other similar rule. The important point is that entities can be linked to each other, and that the nature of the linkage is part of the business rules of the system.

In Access, a database, The line shows the relationship between the two tables and the shared field shows the nature of the relationship. The arrow shows if the relationship is one to many, with the many side shown by the direction of the arrow. As with the specification of the entities discussed at the beginning of this lecture, the documentation of the relationships is part of the logical information model. The format for documenting the linkages among entities includes the name of both entities, the verb phrase that describes the semantics of the linkage and the cardinality of the linkage (*i.e.* whether one to one, one to many or many to many). The statement of the cardinality can be made plain English. All relationships must be documented before proceeding to the physical design of the database.

Components of Entity-Relationship Diagram

Entities

An entity is a person, place, thing, event, or concept of interest to the business or organization about which data is likely to be kept. For example, in a school environment possible entities might be Student, Instructor, and Class.

Entity type refers to a generic class of things such as Company. Entity is the short form of entity-type. Entity occurrence refers to specific instances or examples of a type. For example, one occurrence of the entity Car is Chevrolet Cavalier. An entity usually has attributes (*i.e.*, data elements) that further describe it. Each attribute is a characteristic of the entity. An entity must possess a set of one or more attributes that uniquely identify it (called a primary key).

Identifying entities is the first step in Data Modelling. Start by gathering existing information about the organization. Use documentation that describes the information and functions of the subject area being analysed, and interview subject matter specialists (*i.e.*, end-users). Derive the preliminary entity-relationship diagram from the information gathered by identifying objects (*i.e.*, entities) for which information is kept. Entities are easy to find. Look for the people, places, things, organizations, concepts, and events that an organization needs to capture, store, or retrieve information about.

Types of Entities

Different types of entities are required to provide a complete and accurate representation of an organization's data and to enable the analyst to use the Entity-Relationship Diagram as a starting point for physical database design.

Types of entities include:

- Fundamental where the entity is a base entity that depends on no other for its existence. A fundamental entity has a primary key that is independent of any other entity and is typically composed of a single attribute. Fundamental entities are real-world, tangible objects, such as, Employee, Customer, or Product.
- Attributive where the entity depends on another for its existence, for example, Employee Hobby depends

on Employee. An attributive entity depends on another entity for parts of its primary key. It can result from breaking out a repeating group, the first rule of normalization, or from an optional attribute.
- Associative where the entity describes a connection between two entities with an otherwise many-to-many relationship, for example, assignment of Employee to Project (an Employee can be assigned to more than one Project and a Project can be assigned to more than one Employee). If information exists about the relationship, this information is kept in an associative entity. For example, the number of hours the Employee worked on a particular Project is an attribute of the relationship between Employee and Project, not of either Employee or Project. An associative entity is uniquely identified by concatenating the primary keys of the two entities it connects.

The common data elements are put in the supertype entity and the specific data elements are placed with the subtype to which they apply. For example, Employee (supertype) may contain three subtypes, Permanent Employee, Part-time Employee, and Temporary Employee.

All data elements of the supertype must apply to all subtypes. Each subtype contains the same key as the supertype.

Relationships between an entity supertype and its subtypes are always described as "is a." For example, Employee is a Permanent Employee, Employee is a Part-time Employee.

Identifying Entity Supertypes/Subtypes

Entity supertypes/subtypes involve classes of entities that are truly different, but at the same time, significantly similar.

When identifying supertypes/subtypes, look for:

- Entity types that have the same attributes,
- Entity types that participate in the same relationships,
- Occurrences of an entity that do not participate in

all the relationships in which the entity type participates,

- Occurrences of an entity that do not have all the attributes that the entity type has.

CATEGORIES OF ENTITIES

There are different general categories of entities:

- Physical entities are tangible and easily understood. They generally fall into one of the following categories:
- People, for example, doctor, patient, employee, customer,
- Property, for example, equipment, land and buildings, furniture and fixtures, supplies,
- Products, such as goods and services.
- Conceptual entities are not tangible and are less easily understood. They are often defined in terms of other entity-types.

  They generally fall into one of the following categories:
  - organizations, for example, corporation, church, government,
  - agreements, for example, lease, warranty, mortgage,
  - abstractions, such as strategy and blueprint.
  - Event/State entities are typically incidents that happen. They are very abstract and are often modelled in terms of other entity-types as anassociative entity. Examples of events are purchase, negotiation, service call, and deposit. Examples of states are ownership, enrollment, and employment.

Imposter Entities

When an Entity is not an Entity

There are a number of things that may appear to be entities about which facts are kept, but which should not be defined as such.

These include:

- Processes,
- Calculations,
- Reports,
- Facts about entities.

Processes

Processes may actually perform actions on entities but are not, themselves, entities. Examples are:

- Payroll deduction,
- Budgeting (an action on an organization unit).

Calculations

Calculations are derived from the attributes of an entity. *Examples are*:

- Inventory level,
- Average age,
- Net worth.

Reports

Reports present facts about one or more entities. *Examples are*:

- Project schedule,
- Income statement.

Facts About Entities

Facts about entities describe characteristics of an entity and should be modelled as attributes. *Examples are*:

- Telephone number,
- Date of hire.

Attributes Define Entities

Collectively, attributes define an entity. An attribute is meaningless by itself. For example, date of birth comes from the context of the entity to which it is assigned, for example, date of birth of an employee. Attributes are not shown on the Entity-Relationship Model but are recorded in the underlying data dictionary which contains the definitions of attributes for all entities and relationships identified in the model. An attribute should not have facts recorded about it. In practice, however, there are exceptions.

For example, you might wish to show address as an attribute of Customer. Address is not significant enough to be modelled as an entity in its own right and would typically be shown as an attribute of Customer. However, at the detailed level, it may itself have attributes such as an indicator for mailing address or home address.Attributes do not have to be recognized and defined during the early stages of entity definition. Entity definition is an iterative process, and it is unlikely that a completely satisfactory Entity-Relationship Model will be obtained on the first iteration.

Identifying Attributes

To identify entity attributes, examine:

- All external entities from the Context Diagram,
- The data flows passed by the external entities,
- Existing automated data,
- Each entity (*i.e.*, generate a list of entity attributes that describe the entity).

Attributes Versus Data Elements

Attributes have a looser description than data elements. For instance, whereas an attribute may have only a descriptive name, a data element needs:

- A size and range,
- A format and length,
- An accurate and detailed description,
- valid values,
- Defined edit rules.

Some attributes may be converted into many data elements.

For instance, the attribute "address" may become four data elements representing:

1. Street Address,
2. City/Town,
3. State/Province,

4. Postal or Zip Code.

Additional data elements may also be defined as a result of customer requirements. For example, the customer may require a list of all companies by county. For the purposes of Data Modelling, attributes and data elements are often considered identical because attributes in the data model typically become data elements in the database.

Relationships

A relationship is an association that exists between two entities. For example, Instructor teaches Class or Student attends Class. Most relationships can also be stated inversely. For example, Class is taught by Instructor. The relationships on an Entity-Relationship Diagram are represented by lines drawn between the entities involved in the association. The name of the relationship is placed either above, below, or beside the line.

DECISION TABLE

A decision is a choice about a "course of action". A course of action may include many individual actions. A decision may becharacterized on a continuum from unstructured to structured.

UNSTRUCTURED DECISIONS

Unstructured decisions are generally one-time propositions taken in emergent situations, *i.e.* the set ofconditions are unique and there are no fixed rules for the course of action totake based on the conditions. The possible courses of action need not be finite.Making an unstructured decision is therefore heuristic.

Automating suchdecisions involves the use of Decision Support Systems, which attempt to obtainand organize as much relevant information as possible for presentation to thedecision maker. The decision maker then applies whatever heuristics he considers appropriate to come up with a course of action.

STRUCTURED DECISIONS

Structured decisions are predictable, *i.e.* given a particular set of conditions, the course of action to be taken is clear and definable. Thechoice is which actions to take among a predefined, finite collection ofactions. Making a structured decision is therefore algorithmic. There are threecommon methods of expressing these algorithms.

STRUCTURED ENGLISH

Structured English is an attempt to allow the use of natural language, stripped of ambiguity, to express actions to be taken under particular conditions.

This is accomplished by:

- Choosing a simple subset of natural language verbs and nouns, and
- Defining constructs to express
- Sequence
- Selection
- And iteration

If this stripping of ambiguity is sufficiently rigorous, the resulting definition defines an executable programming language. This was the approach taken in the creation of the original procedural computer language compilers in the 50s and 60s. These definitions were (and remain) so complex that programmers required months and even years of training to acquire competence in the syntax and semantics of the definition. This made it almost impossible to combine knowledge of the business domain and technical proficiency in the programming language in one individual.

Less rigorous non-executable Structured English definitions are known as *pseudocode* and are used as analytical tools by analysts to create an intermediate specification. This specification is passed to programmers who translate it into actual compiler-compliant code. This extra step results in added expense both because of extra specialist personnel and because of the inevitable miscommunications and errors involved in an intermediate translation.

DECISION TREES

A decision tree is a graphic tool that represents conditions and their resulting actions. It consists of a directed acyclic graph (rooted tree) in which the non-terminal edges represent a set of conditions evaluated sequentially from the root. A node is a decision point where a condition is evaluated. The terminal edges (leaves) represent actions.

Decision trees are a useful tool for expressing complex decision variables in a format conducive to human visualization. Software that directly manipulates decision trees is available, but tends to be limited to highly technical scientific specialties like astronomy or DNA sequence analysis and requires a high degree of technical sophistication to use.

DECISION TABLES FEATURES

A decision table is a two-dimensional matrix with one row for each possible action and one row for each relevant condition and one column for each combination of condition states. A decision table can very concisely and rigorously show complex conditions and their resulting actions while remaining comprehensible to a human reader.

The first set of rows indicates the possible actions that may be taken. An "X" in an action row shows that the action will be taken under the condition states indicated in the column. In a vicariate decision table, conditions are binary, restricting condition evaluations to "yes" and "no".

This results in a number of columns equal to 2. This can quickly result in a huge number of columns as the number of conditions rise. Fortunately, it is unusual that every combination of conditions results in a different action.

In Figure, the use of the "-", or "don't care" notation is illustrated. This means that the condition in that row does not affect the action to be taken. Looking at the first column, we see that no action will be taken no matter the state of the last two conditions as long as the first condition is false.

Each "don't care" reduces the number of columns necessary and increases the comprehensibility of the table. In this example the $2^3 = 8$ possible combinations are reduced to 4. The most common tool for the creation of decision tables is spreadsheet software, such as Microsoft Excel. Although this is really quite sophisticated software, it is cheap, readily available, and has a large base of trained users. Because of the ubiquity and sophistication of this software, itis quite easy to create additional software that can read decision tables created in the spreadsheet, understand the semantics therein contained, and take action to implement the logic expressed in the table.

SRS DOCUMENT

INTRODUCTION

An SRS is basically an organization's understanding (in writing) of a customer or potential client's system requirements and dependencies at a particular point in time (usually) prior to any actual design or development work. It's a two-way insurance policy that assures that both the client and the organization understand the other's requirements from that perspective at a given point in time.

The SRS document itself states in precise and explicit language those functions and capabilities a software system (*i.e.*, a software application, an ecommerce Web site, and so on) must provide, as well as states any required constraints by which the system must abide. The SRS also functions as a blueprint for completing a project with as little cost growth as possible.

The SRS is often referred to as the "parent" document because all subsequent project management documents, such as design specifications, statements of work, software architecture specifications, testing and validation plans, and documentation plans, are related to it.

It's important to note that an SRS contains functional and nonfunctional requirements only; it doesn't offer design suggestions, possible solutions to technology or business issues, or any other information other than what the development team understands the customer's system requirements to be.

PREPARATION OF AN SRS DOCUMENT

Introduction

Purpose of this Document

This document specifies the software requirements for the XXX system. This document includes functional and non-functional user requirements, that were gathered in the requirement analysis phase.

Scope of This Document

The scope of this document includes an overview of the XXX system, detailed information about the requirements, including functional requirements, interface requirements, performance requirements, non-functional requirements and additional constraints of the system.

Definitions, Acronyms and Abbreviations

- *SRS*: Software Requirement Specification
- *User:* A person who will be using the system for its intended purpose
- *Will:* Indicates a prediction or description of intent
- *Shall:* Indicates a binding prediction
- Etc.

Business Context

The XXX company has as it's main mission to provide XXXXXX to consumers. The Mission Statement of the company is: SSSS The goals of the organization are: SSSSS

General Description

Product Perspective

The system will be developed using XX, XXX, and XXX.

Product Functions

The product developed will provide an easy access to XXXX for consumers to order products.

The major functions of the system are:

- Provide products online to customers
- Provide payment options
- Etc.

User Characteristics

The users of the system are customers ordering products from their home or office computer. These users have a basic knowledge of computers, but may need help navigating through on-line ordering.

General Constraints

- The cost constraint includes ordering additional hardware to run the new system
- No current web-site
- Security must be upgraded for on-line purchasing

Assumptions

- The system will run on a XXX platform
- The processor must be XXX
- The hardware for the clients must be provided by the client
- Etc.

Requirements

Functional Requirements

The user should be able to order all products on-line through the designed web site; make a payment (billed); receive an order confirmation and shipping date.

Login by Customer

The system should allow the customer to login under a secure system. A new user should be allowed to enter new information.

Place Order by Customer

The system should allow the customer to place an order on-line for the products they want.

Introduction

The system should be able to verify the orders placed and confirm if the order placed is available in the warehouse.

Inputs

- Customer's list of desired products
- Customer detailed information for ordering and shipping

Processing

Customers will be validated upon entering the system. Orders will be verified as to product number, availability. Orders will be updated into the database. An electronic bill will be generated for the customer real-time. The customer will be provided different methods for payment including credit card or on-line check.

After accepting payment, verification of payment will be sent to bank centre for processing. After receiving confirmation, this will be transmitted to customer and date for shipping will be calculated and displayed.

IEEE STANDARDS FOR SRS DOCUMENT

RELATIONSHIP OF IEEE SRS CATEGORIES TO THIS DOCUMENT

Introduction (basically the same as here)

- Purpose
- Scope (of Project)
- Definitions, acronyms, and abbreviations (called Glossary here)
- References
- Overview (of Document)

Overall Description

- *Product perspective*: System Environment here
- *Product functions*: Requirements Definition here
- *User characteristics*: User Interface Requirements here

- *Constraints*: Non-Functional Requirements here
- *Assumptions and dependencies*: Non-Functional Requirements here
- *Requirements subsets*: Requirements Evolution here

Specific Requirements- Requirements Specification here

The Software Requirements Specification (SRS) must have the following contents (preferably with the section numbering used here)

Purpose

Clearly state the purpose of this *document* and its intended audiences. Note that this subsection does not describe the *project*.

An example from the Testing Assistant is as follows: The purpose of this document is to present an overall description and listing of the functionality of The Testing Assistant *for Regression Testing*. It will explain the scope of the project as well as describe the system environment.

This document will also include an easily traceable means by which the user can trace each functionality's brief description to its full description.

Also included is a user interface specification whereby the user can demonstrate interface standards to be used in designing the system. Furthermore, considerations regarding non-functional requirements and system evolution are addressed.

Scope of Project

Overview the project briefly. Tell the name of the product to be created. Describe the need, context, and rationale for the system. Discuss how it fits into the overall business or strategic objectives of the organization. Describe previous versions of the software (if any) and the relationship with the proposed version. The Proposal is an ideal starting point for this section. The explicit functionality of the project is described below.

An example from the Testing Assistant is as follows: The

Testing Assistant *for Regression Testing* will act as an aid for the test recording procedures. The system consists of a series of forms where Test Plan Designers and Unit Testers can input relevant testing information about a new system in development. These two users represent separate classes and each will interact with the system differently.

The Test Plan Designers initially interact with the system. They provide persistent data to the system such as the names of the units, their dependencies, and the references to test process and test data. The Unit Testers provide the transient data to the system such as the names of testers, date of tests, and finally the results of the actual tests.

The Testing Assistant *for Regression Testing* will provide a software developer with a distinct advantage. By providing a tester with a user-friendly interface for inputting this information, The Testing Assistant will allow the tester to focus his/her time on the testing process rather than the tedious task of recording testing data. The greatest value of the system will be in its ability to assist in regression testing. This product will realise the most efficient ordering for carrying out the testing process. Lastly, the system will create reports for status checks, testing results, and an overall evaluation of the testing effort.

Glossary

Define the technical terms used in this document. Do not assume the experience or expertise of the reader. Each type of reader will have a technical vocabulary not necessarily shared by other readers.

References

List here any references to other documents cited anywhere in this document including references to related project documents. This is usually the only Bibliography in the document.

At the beginning, the Proposal is often the only other document. As the project progresses, the design and testing documents and the user manual will be added. When the complete Proposal has been subsumed into this document, a reference to the Proposal is only kept if there is some reason for the proposal to be a maintained document.

Overview of Document

Describe the contents and organization of the rest of *this document*. Since there is already a Table of Contents, this overview will be less formal but more informative. Describe the two basic remaining sections, the Overall Description and the Requirements Specification.

Overall Description

This section gives the context and an overview of the functionality of the project. It is used to establish a context for both the informal requirements definition and for the technical requirement specifications in the next chapter. It needs to be readable by the user of the project so that s/he can be assured that the correct project is being designed. (Braude refers to the user descriptions as the C-Requirements for Customer Requirements.)

System Environment

Called the system's context in the *Domain* Model by Jacobson, *et al*, *System Model* by Sommerville and *Product Perspective* by IEEE This describes the relationship between the system, its components and the external environment of the system. The purpose of this diagram is to clearly show what is part of your system and what is not part of your system. If it is a stand-alone single-user system, that information is noted here.

Use the UML to create labeled actor icons for each user class. Create actor icons for each class of user. Create actor icons for each external system with which your system will interface. An external clock that sends periodic messages to the system is an actor, for example. Create entities for (the parts of) your system to provide a clear explanation of the environment of your system. Use lines to show which units are related and which are not. Label these relationships. In this section, provide descriptions of the external interfaces (represented by actors). It would have accompanying text such as Aside from the University Database (Banner) system, the Registration Forecast System will rely on a remote web server while being run from a client browser. In this section, we describe this controlled environment. The administrator begins a *Generate Reports* session, and a file concerning the requirements of each major in the form of a database tree is loaded into a temporary database on the web server.

The system loads Student and Class Data files from the University Database when reports are to be generated. Evening school student data is gathered by examining each student file with a matching school field, and passing over the rest. The necessary fields are downloaded to the web server and loaded into the temporary database as well. The system will then have all required data, and can begin to generate its reports.

Functional Requirements Definition

Provide a detailed *overview* of the services provided to the user. Organize this part in a manner that is easy for the user to understand. It must be cross-referenced to the following chapter (Requirements Specification) where these functions are repeated in full detail. The cross-referencing must be explicit. There is no guarantee that the next section will have a similar organization.

A use case here that is an apparently simple use case as shown to the user may require more than one detailed use case in the next section in order to consider all paths. Do not rely on a numbering scheme such as used for the sections of this document for reference purposes because if one part is renumbered, the other must then be made consistent.

A better scheme is to provide an *identification* name or coded number to each use case in each section and to use the same identification (with extensions) in the next section. The cross-references must be correct. Use meaningful names in Verb-Noun format with very specific verbs and nouns.

User Interface Specification

*An example from the Testing Assistant is as follows:*The user interfaces for The Testing Assistant are simple Microsoft Access forms. These forms will make use of radio buttons, toggle buttons, text boxes, pull-down menus and other familiar Windows features.

The users of the system are Test Plan Designers and Unit Testers and will need little training for the system, as they are familiar with databases and filling out forms. There will be three report formats available for generation at the user's request. These reports are the Test Summary Report, the Test Item Transmittal Report, and The Test Items Remaining Report.

- *Test Items Transmittal Report:* Will identify test items; contains information on current status and can be generated at user's request at any time but usually after all test units have been entered into the system and before testing is carried out.
- *Test Items Remaining/Items Retest Report:* Will identify those test units which have not been tested and their corresponding dependencies or will identify those items which need to be retested and their corresponding dependencies.
- *Test Summary Report*: Will give an evaluation of the entire testing effort, usually run when all units have been entered into the system, testing is carried out, and the results have been entered.

4

Software Testing

INTRODUCTION

Software Testing is not considered to be part of the Project Management approach. More often, it is defined within the methodology being used or in a specific testing methodology. However, most Project Managers have to deal with technology development and all should wish to test their solutions before moving into live operations. There are many approaches to software testing that attempt to control the quality of the testing process to yield useful information about the quality of the software being tested.Although most testing research is concentrated on finding effective testing techniques, it is also important to make software that can be effectively tested.

It is suggested in that software is testable if faults are likely to cause failure, since then those faults are most likely to be detected by failure during testing. Several programming techniques are suggested to raise testability, such as minimizing variable reuse and maximizing output parameters.

In it is noted that although having faults cause failure is good during testing, it is bad after delivery. For a more intuitive testability property, it is best to maximize the probability of faults being detected during testing while minimizing the probability of faults causing failure after delivery. Several programming techniques are suggested to raise testability, including assertions that observe the internal state of the software during testing but do not affect the specified output, and multiple version development in which any disagreement between versions can be reported during testing but a majority voting mechanism helps reduce the likelihood of incorrect output after delivery. Since both of those techniques are frequently used to help construct reliable systems in practice, this version of testability may capture a significant factor in software development.

For large systems, many errors are often found at the beginning of the testing process, with the observed error rate decreasing as errors are fixed in the software. When the observed error rate during testing approaches zero, statistical techniques are often used to determine a reasonable point to stop testing. This approach has two significant weaknesses. First, the testing effort cannot be predicted in advance, since it is a function of the intermediate results of the testing effort itself. A related problem is that the testing schedule can expire long before the error rate drops to an acceptable level.

Second, and perhaps more importantly, the statistical model only predicts the estimated error rate for the underlying test case distribution being used during the testing process. It may have little or no connection to the likelihood of errors manifesting once the system is delivered or to the total number of errors present in the software.

Another common approach to testing is based on requirements analysis. A requirements specification is converted into test cases, which are then executed so that testing verifies system behaviour for at least one test case within the scope of each requirement. Although this approach is an important part of a comprehensive testing effort, it is certainly not a complete solution.

Even setting aside the fact that requirements documents are notoriously error-prone, requirements are written at a much higher level of abstraction than code. This means that there is much more detail in the code than the requirement, so a test case developed from a requirement tends to exercise only a small fraction of the software that implements that requirement. Testing only at the requirements level may miss many sources of error in the software itself.

The structured testing methodology falls into another category, the white box (or code-based, or glass box) testing approach. In white box testing, the software implementation itself is used to guide testing. A common white box testing criterion is to execute every executable statement during testing, and verify that the output is correct for all tests.

In the more rigorous branch coverage approach, every decision outcome must be executed during testing. Structured testing is still more rigorous, requiring that each decision outcome be tested independently. A fundamental strength that all white box testing strategies share is that the entire software implementation is taken into account during testing, which facilitates error detection even when the software specification is vague or incomplete.

A corresponding weakness is that if the software does not implement one or more requirements, white box testing may not detect the resultant errors of omission. Therefore, both white box and requirements-based testing are important to an effective testing process. The rest of this document deals exclusively with white box testing, concentrating on the structured testing methodology.

OBJECTIVES

It is common to think of testing as a technical issue - something that is done for technology developments. It is good practice, however, to test all elements of all solutions, whether or not technology is involved. Maybe "test" is not a good word to use. We need to be confident that every element of the solution is ready for operational use.

Here are some examples, starting with some common technical issues but moving onto critical business issues:

- Does the computer application work acceptably?
- Can the network cope with the volumes of transactions and data?
- Do we have adequate provisions for backup, recovery, and disaster recovery of the systems?
- Will the disaster recovery process work, eg staff awareness, instructions, facilities, re-routing telephone

numbers, availability of office equipment, stationery, downtime, loss of transactions in progress, etc?
- Can the workforce cope with additional workloads during cutover and early live operation?
- Do the staff have sufficient knowledge and capability to operate the new processes?
- Are the new processes documented accurately in a usable manner and accessible to the staff?
- Have our customers understood the changes that will affect them?
- Will the new product and service offerings be a commercial success?

BUILDING A SOLID

The main goal of formal testing is to produce a sound, logically valid proof that the results meet desired levels of confidence. Testing must be conducted in a carefully controlled manner to achieve this. A great deal of testing is normally conducted as part of the development process - testing components of the solution as they are built to ensure they meet their specifications. This is a valuable and valid process, but it does not form part of the formal proof of the solution. Until development is completed there is no guarantee that components have been stabilised. There is also no independent verification that they met the overall needs in the context of the overall solution.

As well as providing a reasonable degree of confidence prior to formal testing, the informal tests can provide useful material and preparation for the subsequent formal tests. They lay a foundation that is the staring point for formal testing. Testing a complex solution cannot usually be achieved in a single step. Normally the work is broken down into manageable pieces.

For example, you might:

- Start by testing the various functions of the solution in isolation. Validate in full detail everything they are supposed to do. Check plausible alternative scenarios as well as the normal situations, for example, a sale might be cancelled, a payment might be rejected, an item might be out of stock. Do not check the implausible, for example, a negative quantity if it is impossible to enter it as a negative value (that is more a job for the developers to consider during their unit testing).

- When all the functions in a particular process have been validated in detail, test them together. This time you are looking for the correct passage of information and transactions throughout the entire end-to-end process. You do not need to repeat the detailed tests you did before. You are only looking at issues that involve the combinations of separate functions.
- When all the processes have been validated you can test the full system. Again, you do not repeat earlier tests. Only focus on issues that involve the overall operation of the system.
- Finally, when you have confidence in the new system, test how it behaves when connected to other systems and external parties.

TYPES OF TESTING

UNIT TESTING

Unit testing validates in detail each component that was developed. It is typically the developer's point of view - does it conform to the specification. It ignores whether that component works in the context of the completed system.

USER TESTING

User testing, or business testing, looks at the results from a business/ user perspective. Does the final product do the things we want it to do? Do all the individual features work properly?

TECHNICAL TESTING AND TUNING

Technical testing and tuning examines the capability of the solution to be operated safely, efficiently and dependably at normal and peak levels of usage. It is concerned with the inner operational workings and procedures. It does not concern itself with whether it meets the users' functional needs, but it is concerned about the demands they will place upon it.

Testing Data

There is an art to creating good test data. Having a complete, fictitious world in which to follow realistic storylines is a good way to test out the various business scenarios. Remember that all the sub-plots of the story have to co-exist. You will need to follow normal transactions alongside all the abnormal situations - amendments, cancellations, failures, mis-matches.

You will also want to simulate the passage of time. Follow the scenarios throughout their natural lifecycle and beyond into consequences such as management reporting and accounting. Good test data requires good preparation. The scenarios should be planned in advance.

They should be constructed to explore every aspect of the business solution in a logical manner. Expected results should be predicted alongside the test scenarios so that you are not dependent on the judgement of the tester.

- Paint the backdrops
- Tell a story
- Divide the story into acts and scenes
- Any good story has twists and turns
- Many misadventures will befall our hero
- But the hero will always find a way to escape and recover

DATA TESING

The test data is intended to validate the correct functionality of the solution. But where is that correct baseline defined. Consider these possibilities as shown:

Baseline	Comments
Original Project Description	Shows the original intentions but is unlikely to contain enough detail and

	will probably not have been kept up to date as ideas changed.
Requirements Definition or Functional Specification	In theory these are definitive statements of what the business needs. Again, they may not contain sufficient detail and may not have been kept up to date. In some contractual procurement scenarios, these may have been defined to be the sole definition of the requirements that the developers must meet.
Systems or Technical Specification	Typically these have been developed to high degree of detail and have been maintained. One drawback is that they may be the developer's interpretation of the business needs. Testing against these will not detect errors in that interpretation.
Business users' current interpretation of their needs	Sometimes tests are defined independently of the original specifications to represent the current business needs. This may be a good test of the suitability of the end-result, but it is unlikely to match the precise details of the developed solution.
Maintained and agreed definition of requirements	Ideally, there will be a definitive statement of currently agreed requirements. As understanding of the business needs evolved and detailed designs were produced, this source will have been updated to show precisely what the solution should do. Disadvantages may be that it has been a moving target and there may be no comparison to what was originally requested.

TEST TOOLS

Many test tools are available these days. They offer control, speed, and repeatability of tests. They are particularly useful for testing scenarios that require high volumes of transactions such as peak-volume network loading. Repeatability is useful for running re-tests after problems have been solved and regression testing where a component of the solution has been changed and it is necessary to validate that other functionality has not been affected. The disadvantages of test tools are the time and cost. Preparation of test data has to be exhaustive and correct. The tools themselves can represent a significant cost.

REGRESSION TESTING

Regression means going back. With testing processes we mean that you need to repeat previously successful tests any time there is a chance that subsequent changes could have affected an aspect of the solution.The testing process involved building a sequence of tests, many of which stood upon the successful results of earlier tests. If a component of the solution has been changed, all other components which relied upon it might have been affected. Similarly, all tests that relied on an earlier test might no long be valid. Consider carefully which solution and testing components need to be re-validated. One consequence of this issue is that changes during the testing process are bad news. There will always be errors and changes during the testing, but it might be better to defer the correction of some minor problems to make better overall progress.

A seemingly innocuous example with a big hidden catch is when a software supplier suggests that a problem you are experiencing would be solved by moving to their next software release in which the problem has been fixed. Moving to a new release probably means that every test you did to date is now invalidated and will have to be repeated.

USER ACCEPTANCE TESTING

User Acceptance Testing (UAT) is a common name for the type of testing that forms the basis for the business accepting the solution from its developers (whether internal or external). It is a common requirement in many organisations and in many contracts. There are two drawbacks

- it might not be very reliable and it might be a waste of effort. In fact, you might get a better solution, faster and cheaper if you do not do it. The developers will need to conduct exhaustive methodical tests regardless of the need for independent User Acceptance Tests. Best quality will be achieved if they include the business and users in these tests to make sure they have not misunderstood the business needs.

If, therefore, the developers' formal testing is done with full participation of the business and with the responsible user managers having prime authority over the content, review and sign-off of the tests, the requirement for user acceptance can be met in a single phase of testing instead of two different phases. Conversely, where the business is left to define and conduct its own independent testing, it is common to find that they do not have the methodical, comprehensive approach of the developers. The reliability of the tests is often questionable. A single, combined phase of systems testing and User Acceptance Tests can produce the best results in the shortest time. Consider whether it is appropriate and permissible in your circumstances.

SOFTWARE COMPLEXITY MEASUREMENT

Software complexity is one branch of software metrics that is focused on direct measurement of software attributes, as opposed to indirect software measures such as project milestone status and reported system failures. There are hundreds of software complexity measures, ranging from the simple, such as source lines of code, to the esoteric, such as the number of variable definition/usage associations.

An important criterion for metrics selection is uniformity of application, also known as "open reengineering." The reason "open systems" are so popular for commercial software applications is that the user is guaranteed a certain level of interoperability-the applications work together in a common framework, and applications can be ported across hardware platforms with minimal impact. The open reengineering concept is similar in that the abstract models used to represent software systems should be as independent as possible of implementation characteristics such as source code formatting and programming language. The objective is to be able to set complexity standards and interpret the resultant numbers uniformly across projects and languages.

A particular complexity value should mean the same thing whether it was calculated from source code written in Ada, C, FORTRAN, or some other language. The most basic complexity measure, the number of lines of code, does not meet the open reengineering criterion, since it is extremely sensitive to programming language, coding style, and textual formatting of the source code. The cyclomatic complexity measure, which measures the amount of decision logic in a source code function, does meet the open reengineering criterion. It is completely independent of text formatting and is nearly independent of programming language since the same fundamental decision structures are available and uniformly used in all procedural programming languages.

Ideally, complexity measures should have both descriptive and prescriptive components. Descriptive measures identify software that is error-prone, hard to understand, hard to modify, hard to test, and so on. Prescriptive measures identify operational steps to help control software, for example splitting complex modules into several simpler ones, or indicating the amount of testing that should be performed on given modules.

COMPLEXITY AND TESTING

There is a strong connection between complexity and testing, and the structured testing methodology makes this connection explicit. First, complexity is a common source of error in software. This is true in both an abstract and a concrete sense. In the abstract sense, complexity beyond a certain point defeats the human mind's ability to perform accurate symbolic manipulations, and errors result.

The same psychological factors that limit people's ability to do mental manipulations of more than the infamous "7 +/ - 2" objects simultaneously apply to software. Structured programming techniques can push this barrier further away, but not eliminate it entirely. In the concrete sense, numerous studies and general industry experience have shown that the cyclomatic complexity measure correlates with errors in software modules. Other factors being equal, the more complex a module is, the more likely it is to contain errors. Also, beyond a certain threshold of complexity, the likelihood that a module contains errors increases sharply. Also the complexity can be used directly to allocate testing effort by leveraging the connection between complexity and error to concentrate testing effort on the most error-prone software.

TESTING OBJECTIVES

First, define a comprehensive set of tests to build the solid testing "wall". Every requirement and plausible scenario should be covered - with no gaps and, preferably, with no overlaps or duplication. Each test may be described initially in terms of its objective, for example, an objective might be "to test that a cancelled order reverses all transaction data, works orders, stock positions and financial postings". Identify who is responsible for conducting this test and name the relevant user manager who is to approve the definition, review and sign-off of the test. At a later stage, you might add scheduling and sequencing information.

TEST

When the list of test objectives has been reviewed and agreed, detail the test scenario and steps, for example:

Test Definition Form

Ref
Test Objectives
Date of Tests
Sub Ref
Test Steps
Expected Results
Tick or Incident Control Reference

- Note stock level for item XYZ
- Note credit available for customer CUS01
- Create order #1234 for quantity 1 of item XYZ at price £100 for customer CUS01
- Check stock level for item XYZ
- Check credit available for customer CUS01
- Cancel order #1234
- Check stock level for item XYZ
  Check credit available for customer CUS01
- etc

Alongside these steps, write the expected results - ie how the tester will know that it worked as expected. For example:

- 100
- £ 1000
- Order confirmation message confirms quantity 1 of item XYZ at price £100 for customer CUS01
- 99
- £900
- Order cancellation message confirms quantity 1 of item XYZ at price £100 for customer CUS01
- 100
- £1000
- etc

The remainder of this form is used as a checklist for running the test. For each step the tester either ticks the step to note that it worked or creates an test incident control record. In this approach, we do not allow any other action. In other approaches a variety of other actions might be taken in an attempt to avoid noting the failure. Although this might seem desirable, the lack of control can be dangerous and counter-productive.

Encourage the expectation and belief that the purpose of a tester is to find discrepancies and that registering them is a good thing. In fact, you will find a majority of the problems are faults in the test scripts rather than the actual solution.

TEST CONTROL LOG

Progress will be tracked in a test control log. At any point in the process it should be clear what the status is for each test, along with the various incidents that were reported.

TEST INCIDENT CONTROL

For each discrepancy in the testing a test incident control form notes the details and tracks any remedial action.

TEST INCIDENT CONTROL LOG

Test incidents are logged and tracked to completion.

TEST SIGNOFF

When a test is completed, it should be reviewed and formally signed-off by the test leader, the responsible user manager and anyone else who is been identified as an authoritative reviewer.

In some cases you might note that a test was not entirely satisfactory although the problems were not sufficiently severe that you would wish to delay completing the tests or releasing the system. You should record what future action is required to remedy this problem.

TYPES OF TESTING

Consider which of these would be appropriate in your circumstances.

Note also that these types may have different characteristics when applied to different aspects of the overall solution. For example, you could pilot a new computer system, a training course or a new workgroup structure.

Specific methodologies will use their own terminology. You should note that several expressions can mean more than one thing. The best example here is "Conference Room Pilot" where we list five different usages we have heard, each at a different stage in the lifecycle.

Type: Conference Room Pilot

Comments:

- Trying out possible software solutions as part of the selection process. The name comes from the concept that the interested parties shut themselves into a single room to simulate the conduct of business operations.

- Testing possible systems solutions by simulating business operations. This is essentially a form of design.
- Testing developed solutions by simulating live operations.
- Demonstrating operations and ascertaining business/ user acceptability by simulating live usage of the completed system.
- Live running of a small part of the overall business on the new system to test it under real conditions before transferring the remainder of the enterprise to the new system.

Type: Configuration Testing
Comments:

- Testing that the configuration of packaged software meets the business needs prior to formal testing.

*Type:*Data Load/ Data Conversion Tests
Comments:

- Tests that data prepared for the new system is acceptable, for example, controls, comparisons with pre-converted data, integrity checking of linked records, validation of standard fields. Data may have been converted or loaded manually.

Type: Data Purification/ Integrity/ Quality
Comments:

- Review by the end-user departments that the operational data they hold is complete and correct. This exercise will often be conducted over a period of several months prior to data conversion for the new system. The data review might be supported by computer systems that highlight incomplete data and inconsistencies.

*Type:*Disaster Recovery Testing
Comments:

- Test the ability to re-instate the systems using off-site data and resources.

- Test the overall disaster recovery procedures and facilities from a business perspective.
  Type: Fallback Testing
  Comments:
- *Fallback Testing*: Test the contingency plan for reverting to the old system or to an alternative emergency solution (eg manual operation) in the event of a failure of the new system.
  Type: Informal tests
  Comments:
- Trying out ideas as a design aid.
- Checking that a developed component is fit to be released for formal testing.
  Type: Integration Testing
  Comments:
- Test of the sharing or transfer of transactions and data between the technical solution and all related systems.
- Overall testing of the business solution in conjunction with all other related operations and systems.
  Type: Link Test
  Comments:
- Test input, output and shared data are correctly transferred between associated programmes and databases.
  Type: Live Pilot
  Comments:
- Live running of a small part of the overall business on the new system to test it under real conditions before transferring the remainder of the enterprise to the new system.
  Type: Model Office or Simulated Live Running
  Comments:
- Informal testing where users try out the system as if it were real, testing that the processes, procedures, and operational support operate correctly and work in harmony using simulated normal work and volumes.

Type: Module Tests
Comments:

- Test that a developed module meets its technical specification.

Type: Operational Acceptance Testing
Comments:

- Formal tests to satisfy the IT operations department that the developed system is of adequate quality to enter the live environment and go into live production.

Type: Operations Testing
Comments:

- Testing of technical operational procedures such as start-up, shut-down, batch processing, special stationery handling, output handling, controls, error recovery, system backup and recovery procedures etc.

Type: Parallel Pilot
Comments:

- Test running of a small part of the overall business on the new system to test it under real conditions. Differs from Parallel Running in that not all input need be duplicated with the existing system and there is no attempt to reconcile the overall results between the two systems in a controlled manner.

Type: Parallel Running
Comments:

- Form of testing whereby the results on the new system are compared with identical real data passing through the old systems. This is normally achieved by duplicating the transactions for a specific time period and reconciling the results with the existing system. Very often it is not possible to get parallel results because the new system is not a duplicate copy of the old one. Where it is possible, parallel running may require a great deal of user effort to do things in duplicate and to reconcile the results.

Type: Pilot

Comments::

- Completion and live usage of a solution such that it can be tried out in a limited part of the organisation or marketplace. It is intended as a proof of concept. The eventual solution will probably be developed further or modified to take advantage of the lessons learned.

Type: Programme Tests

Comments:

- Test that a developed programme meets its technical specification.

Type: Prototyping

Comments:

- Development of a limited technical model of a component that can be used as a design tool to validate the concept. A prototype may use technology or techniques that are of no use beyond the prototyping work (eg screens simulated using PowerPoint).
- Development of the technical solution in stages such that each degree of refinement can be validated before moving to the next stage.
- The configuration of packaged software to apply the organisation's requirements and validate that they are properly addressed. When completed, the configured version will be the complete version ready for testing.

Type: Regression testing

Comments:

- Returning to earlier tests after a change has been made, both to check that the change was correct and to ensure no unforeseen impact has occurred. This is vital to maintain the integrity of prior testing during formalised, controlled testing. During formal testing, the environment should be designed to allow reversion and repeats. Timescales should assume a number of repeat cycles will be required.

- Re-testing a system following changes such as bug fixes or upgrades. Ideally, the original tests will have been preserved and be relatively easy to repeat and reconcile.

  Type: Security Testing

  Comments:

- Test overall protection from unauthorised access or usage. It should include physical access, access through external network links, firewalls, improper access by internal users, encryption, trusted third-parties, electronic emissions of physical and wireless networks, etc.
- Testing the mapping of individual users' access to specific functions, data and authorisation levels.

  Type: System Testing

  Comments:

- Main formal test of the overall technical solution.
- Main formal test of the functionality of an overall solution.

  Type: Tiger Team Attack

  Comments:

- Attempt to break through security measures by specialist external team.

  Type: Unit Testing

  Comments:

- Formal Tests applied to each "unit" of functionality within the system.

  Type: User Acceptance Testing

  Comments:

- Testing of the full solution by the business/ users to validate that it operates correctly and meets requirements. The implication is that this is the point at which the business agrees to take the solution as produced by the developers (whether internal or external).

  Type:

  Comments:

- Volume Testing/ Load Testing Creating sufficient hit

rates, network loading, transactions and data volumes to simulate normal and peak loads thus verifying that response times and processing times will be satisfactory and that file sizes are sufficiently large. This also gives a firm basis for effective scheduling, operational capacity and tuning requirements.

SOFTWARE TESTING OBJECTIVES

INTRODUCTION

Establishing Software testing Objectives is a critical part of planning the Software testing process. Defining testing objectives is also one of the most difficult test planning activities. It is difficult because humans frequently do not have a clear idea of what they want to do until they begin to do it.

This means the best laid test plans change during test process execution. This is a problem without a solution, but there are some actions testers can take which will improve test planning. The establishment of clear testing objectives goes a long way towards offsetting future execution problems. Before the tester can do this s/he must understand what we mean by the word objective.

An objective is a testing "goal." It is a statement of what the tester wants to accomplish when implementing a specific testing activity. Each testing activity may have several objectives and there are two levels of objective specification.

A test plan should contain both high-level general objectives in the overview section, and specific low-level "provable" objectives for each particular type of testing being implemented. The latter kind being operational goals for specific testing tasks. A good set of operational objectives can intuitively explain why we are executing a particular step in the testing process.

INPUTS

- System Requirements Document
- Software Design Description Document

- Risk Score Analysis Results (Task II.II)

Three methods can be used to specify test objectives. The first is brainstorming. The test team uses "creative" interaction to construct a list of test objectives. The second approach is to identify "key" System functions. Next, specify test objectives for each function. The third method is to identify business transactions and base objectives on them. This can also be thought of as Scenario-based as business cycles could be used to drive the process.

OUTPUT

Statement of Test Objectives - The statement of the test objectives is really a statement of the test requirements. It can be created using any word processing package or spread sheet. It can also be implemented with automated testing tools. As an example, in SQA's Manager product the test objects/requirements are input as a test requirements hierarchy and are stored in the test repository. Each branch within the requirements tree can have sub-branches, and sub-branches can also have sub-branches. SQA is only one example. Other automated testing tools will have their own type of test objectives/requirements documentation.

COMPLETION CRITERIA

A completion criterion is the standard by which a test objective is measured. Completion criteria can be either quantitative or qualitative. The important point is that the test team must some how be able to determine when a test objective has been satisfied. One or more completion criteria must be specified for each test objective.

OUTPUT

Statement of Objective Completion Criteria - The important consideration is that each requirement and how it is validated is documented. Test requirements are completely useless unless they can be satisfied. Important test metrics that should be calculated and reported are the percentage of test requirements that have be covered by test cases, and the percentage of test requirements that have been successfully validated. The statement of objective completion criteria does not have to be a separate document. It can simply be an addendum to the statement of test objectives. For example, if using SQA's Manager product, The description field that is included for each requirement could contain a statement of the requirement's validation rule(s). The test objectives should be prioritized based on the risk analysis findings.

Priority should be assigned using this scale:

- *High:* Most important tests: must be executed
- *Medium:* Second-level objectives: should be executed only after high-priority tests
- *Low:* Least important: should be tested last and only if there is enough time
- *High and Medium:* test objectives should be assigned more resources than Low priority objectives.
- *Output:* Prioritized Test Objectives
- *Manual:* Test objectives should be implemented manually in the form of quality checklists, with one or more checklist items satisfying a specific objective. (Single checklist items can also satisfy more than one objective, as is the case for the date field objectives).
- *Automated:* Test objectives should be translated into an appropriate form for the automated test tool being used. For example, when using SQA TeamTest Test Manager a test requirements hierarchy would be created. Automated test requirements would be stored in the tool's test repository and would be used as the basis for constructing automated test scripts.

TEST APPROACH

INCLUSIONS

The contents of this release are as follows:

Phase 1 Deliverables

- New and revised Transaction Processing with automated support

- New Customer Query Processes and systems
- Revised Inter-Office Audit process
- Relocate Exceptions to Head Office
- New centralised Agency Management system
- Revised Query Management process
- Revised Retrievals process
- New International Reconciliation process
- New Account Reconciliation process

EXCLUSIONS

When the scope of each Phase has been agreed and signed off, no further inclusions will be considered for inclusion in this release, except:

- Where there is the express permission and agreement of the Business Analyst and the System Test Controller;
- Where the changes/inclusions will not require significant effort on behalf of the test team (*i.e.* requiring extra preparation - new test conditions etc.) and will not adversely affect the test schedule.

Specific Exclusions

- Cash management is not included in this phase
- Sign On/Sign Off functions are excluded - this will be addressed by existing processes
- The existing Special Order facility will not be replaced
- Foreign Currency Transactions
- International Data Exchanges
- Accounting or reporting of Euro transactions

TESTING PROCESS

- Organise Project involves creating a System Test Plan, Schedule and Test Approach, and requesting/ assigning resources.
- Design/Build System Test involves identifying Test Cycles, Test Cases, Entrance and Exit Criteria, Expected Results, etc. In general, test conditions/

expected results will be identified by the Test Team in conjunction with the Project Business Analyst or Business Expert. The Test Team will then identify Test Cases and the Data required. The Test conditions are derived from the Business Design and the Transaction Requirements Documents

- Design/Build Test Procedures includes setting up procedures such as Error Management systems and Status reporting, and setting up the data tables for the Automated Testing Tool.
- Build Test Environment includes requesting/building hardware, software and data set-ups.
- Execute Project Integration Test - See Section 3 - Test Phases and Cycles
- Execute Operations Acceptance Test - See Section 3 - Test Phases and Cycles
- Signoff - Signoff happens when all pre-defined exit criteria have been achieved. See Section 2.4.

Exclusions

SQA will not deal directly with the business design regarding any design/ functional issues/ queries. The development team is the supplier to SQA - if design/ functional issues arise they should be resolved by the development team and its suppliers.

TESTING SCOPE

Outlined below are the main test types that will be performed for this release. All system test plans and conditions will be developed from the functional specification and the requirements catalogue.

Functional Testing

The objective of this test is to ensure that each element of the application meets the functional requirements of the business as outlined in the:

- Requirements Catalogue
- Business Design Specification

- Year 2000 Development Standards
- Other functional documents produced during the course of the project *i.e.* resolution to issues/change requests/feedback.

This stage will also include Validation Testing - which is intensive testing of the new Front end fields and screens. Windows GUI Standards; valid, invalid and limit data input; screen and field look and appearance, and overall consistency with the rest of the application.

The third stage includes Specific Functional testing - these are low-level tests which aim to test the individual processes and data flows.

Integration Testing

This test proves that all areas of the system interface with each other correctly and that there are no gaps in the data flow. Final Integration Test proves that system works as integrated unit when all the fixes are complete.

Business (User) Acceptance Test

This test, which is planned and executed by the Business Representative(s), ensures that the system operates in the manner expected, and any supporting material such as procedures, forms etc. are accurate and suitable for the purpose intended. It is high level testing, ensuring that there are no gaps in functionality.

Performance Testing

These tests ensure that the system provides acceptable response times.

Regression Testing

A Regression test will be performed after the release of each Phase to ensure that:

- There is no impact on previously released software, and
- to ensure that there is an increase in the functionality and stability of the software.

The regression testing will be automated using the automated testing tool.

Bash and Multi-User Testing

Multi-user testing will attempt to prove that it is possible for an acceptable number of users to work with the system at the same time. The object of Bash testing is an ad-hoc attempt to break the system.

Technical Testing

Technical Testing will be the responsibility of the Development Team.

Operations Acceptance Testing (OAT)

This phase of testing is to be performed by the Systems Installation and Support group, prior to implementing the system in a live site. The SIS team will define their own testing criteria, and carry out the tests.

SYSTEM TEST ENTRANCE/EXIT CRITERIA

Entrance Criteria

The Entrance Criteria specified by the system test controller, should be fulfilled before System Test can commence. In the event, that any criterion has not been achieved, the System Test may commence if Business Team and Test Controller are in full agreement that the risk is manageable.

- All developed code must be unit tested. Unit and Link Testing must be completed and signed off by development team.
- System Test plans must be signed off by Business Analyst and Test Controller.
- All human resources must be assigned and in place.
- All test hardware and environments must be in place, and free for System test use.
- The Acceptance Tests must be completed, with a pass rate of not less than 80%.

Acceptance Tests

25 test cases will be performed for the acceptance tests. To achieve the acceptance criteria 20 of the 25 cases should be completed successfully - *i.e.* a pass rate of 80% must be achieved before the software will be accepted for System Test proper to start. This means that any errors found during acceptance testing should not prevent the completion of 80% of the acceptance test applications.

Resumption Criteria

In the event that system testing is suspended resumption criteria will be specified and testing will not re-commence until the software reaches these criteria.

Exit Criteria

The Exit Criteria detailed below must be achieved before the Phase 1 software can be recommended for promotion to Operations Acceptance status. Furthermore, I recommend that there be *a minimum 2 days effort Final Integration testing AFTER the final fix/change has been retested.*

- All High Priority errors from System Test must be fixed and tested
- If any medium or low-priority errors are outstanding - the implementation risk must be signed off as acceptable by Business Analyst and Business Expert
- Project Integration Test must be signed off by Test Controller and Business Analyst.
- Business Acceptance Test must be signed off by Business Expert.

NEED FOR SOFTWARE TESTING

A primary purpose for testing is to detect software failures so that defects may be uncovered and corrected. The scope of software testing often includes examination of code as well as execution of that code in various environments and conditions as well as examining the quality aspects of code: does it do what it is supposed to do and do what it needs to do. We test software because developers are unable to build defect free software. If the development processes were perfect, meaning no defects were produced, testing would not be necessary. Testing by the individual who developed the work has not proven to be a substitute to building and following a detailed test plan.

The disadvantages of a person checking their own work using their own documentation are as follows:

- Misunderstandings will not be detected, because the checker will assume that what the other individual heard from him was correct.
- Improper use of the development process may not be detected because the individual may not understand the process.
- The individual may be "blinded" into accepting erroneous system specifications and coding because he falls into the same trap during testing that led to the introduction of the defect in the first place.
- Information services people are optimistic in their ability to do defect-free work and thus sometimes underestimate the need for extensive testing.
- Without a formal division between development and test, an individual may be tempted to improve the system structure and documentation, rather than allocate that time and effort to the test.

Testing unveils design defects as well as data defects of any product. All testing focuses on discovering and eliminating defects or variances from what is expected.

Testers need to identify these two types of defects:

1. *Variance from Specifications*: A defect from the perspective of the builder of the product.
2. *Variance from what is Desired*: A defect from a user (or customer) perspective.

BACKGROUND AND OBJECTIVES

Software testing is an integral and important activity in every software development environment. Software seems to have has permeated almost every equipment that we use in our daily lives. Companies that produce embedded systems for use in health care, transportation, and other critical segments of our society have embraced model based software testing by integrating them into their development environments.

- Software Testing is designed to establish that the software is working satisfactorily as per the requirements.
- Software Testing is a process designed to prove that the programme is error free.
- Software The job of testing is to certify that the software does its job correctly and can be used in production.

Because, with these as the guidelines, one would tend to operate the system in a normal manner to see if it works and one would unconsciously choose such normal/correct test data as would prevent the system from failing. Besides, it is any way not possible to certify that a software has no errors, simply because it is almost impossible to detect all errors. In a way, we can say that software testing is basically a task of locating errors. From the objective point of view, testing can be done in two ways:

Positive Testing

Operate application or software as it should be operated. Use proper variety of test data, including data values at boundries to test if it fails.

Check actual test results with the expected and see:

- Does it behave normally?
- Are results correct?
- Does the software function correctly?

Negative Testing

Test for abnormal operations. Test with illegal/ abnormal test data. Intentionally attempt to make things go wrong and to discover/ detect and see

- Does the system fail/ crash?
- Does the programme do what it should not?
- Does it fail to do what it should?

Positive view of Negative Testing

The job of testing is to discover errors before the user does. A good tester is one who is successfull in making the system fail. Mentality of the tester has to be destructive – opposite to that of the creator/ developer which should be constructive.

This chapter is designed to enable a clear understanding and knowledge of the foundations, techniques, and tools in the area of software testing and its practice in the industry. The course will prepare students to be leaders in software testing. Whether you are a developer or a tester, you must test software. This course is a unique opportunity to learn strengths and weaknesses of a variety of software testing techniques.

Applications of testing techniques in health care industry (*e.g.* pacemaker), nuclear industry (*e.g.* plant control), aerospace industry (*e.g.* Mars Polar Lander), security (*e.g.* smart card), automobile industry (*e.g.* automotive control systems), and others will be considered.

The chapter will focus on:

- Test process and continuous quality improvement
- Test generation from requirements
- Modeling techniques: UML: FSM and Statecharts, Combinatorial design; and others.
- Test generation from models.
- Test adequacy assessment.
- Industrial applications.

Discussion oriented lectures by the instructor, in-class group presentations by teams, laboratory exercises using advanced testing tools, and invited talks by experts from the industry will be the primary mechanisms for learning and the dissemination of knowledge.

CHAPTER DESCRIPTION

Fundamentals of software testing; software test proces and continuous quality improvement; Test generation using finite state models, Combinatorial design, and others; Test adequacy assessment using black box and white box criteria;

Industrial applications of model based testing. Students will be required to form small teams of three or four, preferably interdisciplinary, and make presentations to the class.The work of each team will be reviewed by the instructor and other teams.

UNIT TESTING

These type of tests are usually written by developers as they work on code (white-box style), to ensure that the specific function is working as expected. One function might have multiple tests, to catch corner cases or other branches in the code. Unit testing alone cannot verify the functionality of a piece of software, but rather is used to assure that the building blocks the software uses work independently of each other.

TESTING IN SOFTWARE

Unit testing is a software development process in which the smallest testable parts of an application, called units, are individually and independently scrutinized for proper operation.This testing mode is a component of software development that takes a meticulous approach to building a product by means of continual testing and revision.

Once all of the units in a programme have been found to be working in the most efficient and error-free manner possible, larger components of the programme can be evaluated by means of integration testing. Unit testing must be done with an awareness that it may not be possible to test a unit for every input scenario that will occur when the programme is run in a real-world environment.

RULES

- Write the test first
- Never write a test that succeeds the first time
- Start with the null case, or something that doesn't work
- Don't be afraid of doing something trivial to make the test work
- Loose coupling and testability go hand in hand

- Use mock objects. A mock object is an object that pretends to be a particular type, but is really just a sink, recording the methods that have been called on it
- A test is not a pure unit test if: It talks to the database
  - It communicates across the network
  - It touches the file system
  - It can't run at the same time as any of your other unit tests
  - You have to do special things to your environment (such as editing config files) to run it. Tests that do these things should be kept aside from the regular unit test suit to run the test cases faster whenever we make changes.

Unit testing deals with testing a unit as a whole. This would test the interaction of many functions but confine the test within one unit. The exact scope of a unit is left to interpretation. Supporting test code, sometimes called scaffolding, may be necessary to support an individual test. This type of testing is driven by the architecture and implementation teams. This focus is also called black-box testing because only the details of the interface are visible to the test. Limits that are global to a unit are tested here.

In the construction industry, scaffolding is a temporary, easy to assemble and disassemble, frame placed around a building to facilitate the construction of the building. The construction workers first build the scaffolding and then the building. Later the scaffolding is removed, exposing the completed building. Similarly, in software testing, one particular test may need some supporting software.

This software establishes an environment around the test. Only when this environment is established can a correct evaluation of the test take place. The scaffolding software may establish state and values for data structures as well as providing dummy external functions for the test. Different scaffolding software may be needed from one test to another test. Scaffolding software rarely is considered part of the system.

Sometimes the scaffolding software becomes larger than the system software being tested. Usually the scaffolding software is not of the same quality as the system software and frequently is quite fragile. A small change in the test may lead to much larger changes in the scaffolding.

Internal and unit testing can be automated with the help of coverage tools. A coverage tool analyses the source code and generates a test that will execute every alternative thread of execution. It is still up to the programmer to combine these test into meaningful cases to validate the result of each thread of execution. Typically, the coverage tool is used in a slightly different way.

First the coverage tool is used to augment the source by placing informational prints after each line of code. Then the testing suite is executed generating an audit trail. This audit trail is analysed and reports the per cent of the total system code executed during the test suite. If the coverage is high and the untested source lines are of low impact to the system's overall quality, then no more additional tests are required.

The idea behind unit testing is elegant and simple, but can be expanded to enable sophisticated series of tests for code validation and regression testing. A unit test is strictly something that 'exercises' or runs the code under test. Many developers manually perform unit testing on a regular basis in the course of working on a segment of code. In other words, it can be as simple as *'I know the code should perform this task when I supply this input; I'll try it and see what happens.'* If it doesn't behave as expected, the developer would likely modify the code and repeat this iterative process until it works.

The problem with doing this manually is that it can easily overlook large ranges of values or different combinations of inputs and it offers no insight into how much of the code was actually executed during testing. Additionally, it does not help us with the important task of proving to someone else that it worked and that it worked *correctly*.

The cost and time required is compounded by the reality that one round of testing is rarely enough; besides fixing bugs, any changes that are made to code later in the development process may require additional investment of time and resources to ensure it's working properly.

Large projects typically augment manual procedures with tools such as the Framework to automate and improve this process. Automation mitigates risk of undetected errors, saves costs by detecting problems early, and saves time by keeping developers focused on the task of writing the software, instead of performing the tests themselves.

The idea behind unit testing is that once you have a unit that you think works, you set up a test case where you specify some input to the unit and compare the result of your unit with your expected result. You know about the expected result, because you know what your unit is doing (or you should know it).

Well, you better know what your unit is supposed to do, or else you should not do programming in the first place...;) Then you run the tests and the CakePHP/«insert your framework here» test suite tells you if they passed or if not, with some graceful message where the error occurred.

Now you have that testcase. Now you add testcases for t h a t input and this one. The advantage of this is that once you wrote the tests down they are there (cool, huh?) and you can hold on to them. There is no need anymore for you to open the browser and test everything manually again when you change your system. Instead, you add functionality, run the automated unit tests again, if they pass you are good to go, if they don't pass you broke something. Well, what if you broke something but your tests don't catch it? That's something that UT cannot do for you. You must make sure you have a good test coverage

Typically, the order of the running of the tests should not matter. There might be special cases, but in well over 90% it does not. This should also be your goal, too, to have two different problems if two test cases fail. Keep them all isolated and you will sleep well. For most tests there is also not much configuration to be done. You specify the input, your expected result, crank the handle and evaluate how well you have done.

You should typically be able to group tests together, too. When you run these groups you can get a good overview over large components of your system.

TESTING PHASE

The first test in the development process is the unit test. The source code is normally divided into modules, which in turn are divided into smaller units called units. These units have specific behaviour. The test done on these units of code is called unit test. Unit test depends upon the language on which the project is developed. Unit tests ensure that each unique path of the project performs accurately to the documented specifications and contains clearly defined inputs and expected results.

Table. The Testing Phase: Improve Quality.

Phase	Deliverable
Testing	Regression Test
	Internal Testing
	Unit Testing
	Application Testing
	Stress Testing

Simply stated, quality is very important. Many companies have not learned that quality is important and deliver more claimed functionality but at a lower quality level. It is much easier to explain to a customer why there is a missing feature than to explain to a customer why the product lacks quality. A customer satisfied with the quality of a product will remain loyal and wait for new functionality in the next version. Quality is a distinguishing attribute of a system indicating the degree of excellence.

In many software engineering methodologies, the testing phase is a separate phase which is performed by a different team after the implementation is completed. There is merit in this approach; it is hard to see one's own mistakes, and a fresh eye can discover obvious errors much faster than the person who has read and re-read the material many times. Unfortunately, delegating testing to another team leads to a slack attitude regarding quality by the implementation team. Alternatively, another approach is to delegate testing to the the whole organization. If the teams are to be known as craftsmen, then the teams should be responsible for establishing high quality across all phases. Sometimes, an attitude change must take place to guarantee quality.

Regardless if testing is done after-the-fact or continuously, testing is usually based on a regression technique split into several major focuses, namely internal, unit,application, and stress.The testing technique is from the perspective of the system provider.

Because it is nearly impossible to duplicate every possible customer's environment and because systems are released with yet-to-be-discovered errors, the customer plays an important, though reluctant, role in testing. As will be established later in the thesis, in the Water Sluice methodology this is accomplished in the alpha and beta release of the system.

USES

Forget for a moment that there is something called XP (Extreme Programming) that coined the Unit Test term. The most of the projects developed today are always under tight development schedules and usually have only its developers as the tester of their code. By writing the unit tests themselves they can have a head start towards bug-free and quality code.

One will argue that if the developer is writing all the unit tests, it is quite possible to get the set of unit tests that are passable, because these unit tests are developed based either on the foreknowledge of application code or the assumptions made in the application code. However, do not be fooled with this, imagine what will happen if developer decides to change the application, her old test cases will break. That will force her to either re-think her changes or re-write the unit tests.

The application architect or analyst can write all the unit test cases upfront (Not what XP recommend, but we are not worried about it) and test the developed code against these cases and functionalities. The advantage is well defined deliverable for the developer and more quantifiable progress. A developer can also use this to disciple their work habits *e.g.* she can write a set of unit test that she wants to accomplish in a days work. Once tests ready, she can start developing the application and check her progress against the unit test. Now she has a metre to check her progress.

NUNIT FRAMEWORK

NUnit framework is port of JUnit framework from java and Extreme Programming (XP). This is an open source product. You can download it from http://www.nunit.org. The NUnit framework is developed from ground up to make use of.NET framework functionalities. It uses an Attribute based programming model. It loads test assemblies in separate application domain hence we can test an application without restarting the NUnit test tools. The NUnit further watches a file/assembly change events and reload it as soon as they are changed. With these features in hand a developer can perform develop and test cycles sides by side.

Before we dig deeper, we should understand what NUnit Framework is not:

- It is not Automated GUI tester.
- It is not a scripting language, all test are written in.NET supported language *e.g.* C#, VC, VB.NET, J# etc.
- It is not a benchmark tool.
- Passing the entire unit test suite does not mean software is production ready.

IMPLEMENTING THE TEST

You can write the test anywhere you like, for example:

- A test method in application code class, you can use #if-#endif directives to include/exclude the code.
- A test class in application assembly, or
- A separate test assembly.

5

Quality Assurance

ROLE

Quality Assurance makes sure the project will be completed based on the previously agreed specifications, standards and functionality required without defects and possible problems. It monitors and tries to improve the development process from the beginning of the project to ensure this. It is oriented to "prevention".

CONCEPTS

- Quality is conformance to product requirements and should be free.
- Quality is achieved through prevention of defects.
- Quality control is aimed at finding problems as early as possible and fixing them.
- Doing things right the first time is the performance standard which results in zero defects and saves the expenses of doing things over.
- *The expense of quality is nonconformance* to product requirements
- Quality is what distinguishes a good company from a great one.
- Quality is meeting or exceeding our customer's needs and requirements.
- Software Quality is measureable.
- Quality is continuous improvement.
- The quality of a software product comes from the quality of the process used to create it.

- Quality is the Entire Company's Business
- Our Quality network testing products help make our customers successful.

VERIFICATION AND VALIDATION

A perfect software product is built when every step is taken with full consideration that 'A right product is developed in a right manner'. 'Software Verification and Validation' is one such model, which helps the system designers and test engineers to confirm that a right product is build right way throughout the development process and improve the quality of the software product.

'Verification and Validation Model' makes it sure that, certain rules are followed at the time of development of a software product and also makes it sure that the product that is developed fulfills the required specifications. This reduces the risk associated with any software project up to certain level by helping in detection and correction of errors and mistakes, which are unknowingly done during the development process.

Verification and Validation (V&V) is a series of technical and managerial activities performed by someone other than the developer of a system to improve the quality and reliability of the system and assure the developed product satisfies the user's operational needs. Verification is the assurance that the products of a particular development phase are consistent with the requirements of that phase and preceding phase(s), while validation is the assurance that the final product meets system requirements.

VERIFICATION

The standard definition of Verification goes like this: "Are we building the product RIGHT?" *i.e.* Verification is a process that makes it sure that the software product is developed the right way. The software should confirm to its predefined specifications, as the product development goes through different stages, an analysis is done to ensure that all required specifications are met.

Methods and techniques used in the Verification and Validation shall be designed carefully, the planning of which starts right from the beginning of the development process. The Verification part of 'Verification and Validation Model' comes before Validation, which incorporates Software inspections, reviews, audits, walkthroughs, buddy checks etc. in each phase of verification (every phase of Verification is a phase of the Testing Life Cycle) During the Verification, the work product (the ready part of the Software being developed and various documentations) is reviewed/examined personally by one ore more persons in order to find and point out the defects in it. This process helps in prevention of potential bugs, which may cause in failure of the project.

Verification Terms

Inspection

Inspection involves a team of about 3-6 people, led by a leader, which formally reviews the documents and work product during various phases of the product development life cycle. The work product and related documents are presented in front of the inspection team, the member of which carry different interpretations of the presentation. The bugs that are detected during the inspection are communicated to the next level in order to take care of them.

Walkthroughs

Walkthrough can be considered same as inspection without formal preparation (of any presentation or documentations). During the walkthrough meeting, the presenter/author introduces the material to all the participants in order to make them familiar with it. Even when the walkthroughs can help in finding potential bugs, they are used for knowledge sharing or communication purpose.

Buddy Checks

This is the simplest type of review activity used to find out bugs in a work product during the verification. In buddy check, one person goes through the documents prepared by another person in order to find out if that person has made mistake(s) *i.e.* to find out bugs which the author couldn't find previously.

VALIDATION

Validation is a process of finding out if the product being built is right? *i.e.* whatever the software product is being developed, it should do what the user expects it to do. The software product should functionally do what it is supposed to, it should satisfy all the functional requirements set by the user. Validation is done during or at the end of the development process in order to determine whether the product satisfies specified requirements.

Validation and Verification processes go hand in hand, but visibly Validation process starts after Verification process ends (after coding of the product ends). Each Verification activity (such as Requirement Specification Verification, Functional design Verification etc.) has its corresponding Validation activity (such as Functional Validation/Testing, Code Validation/Testing, System/Integration Validation etc.). All types of testing methods are basically carried out during the Validation process. Test plan, test suits and test cases are developed, which are used during the various phases of Validation process.

The phases involved in Validation process are: Code Validation/Testing, Integration Validation/Integration Testing, Functional Validation/Functional Testing, and System/User Acceptance Testing/Validation.

Validation Process Terms

Code Validation/Testing

Developers as well as testers do the code validation. Unit Code Validation or Unit Testing is a type of testing, which the developers conduct in order to find out any bug in the code unit/module developed by them. Code testing other than Unit Testing can be done by testers or developers.

Integration Validation/Testing

Integration testing is carried out in order to find out if different (two or more) units/modules co-ordinate properly. This test helps in finding out if there is any defect in the interface between different modules.

Functional Validation/Testing

This type of testing is carried out in order to find if the system meets the functional requirements. In this type of testing, the system is validated for its functional behaviour. Functional testing does not deal with internal coding of the project, in stead, it checks if the system behaves as per the expectations.

User Acceptance Testing or System Validation

In this type of testing, the developed product is handed over to the user/paid testers in order to test it in real time scenario. The product is validated to find out if it works according to the system specifications and satisfies all the user requirements.

As the user/paid testers use the software, it may happen that bugs that are yet undiscovered, come up, which are communicated to the developers to be fixed. This helps in improvement of the final product.

SQA PLANS

PURPOSE

The purpose of this plan is to specify how Software Quality Assurance (SQA) will be performed during the process. SQA personnel will both ensure that software maintenance is performed according to the process described in the Generic Process Architecture document and help to improve and refine the process.

By doing so, SQA personnel will help to improve the overall quality of software products. This plan describes the SQA activities to be performed and defines a set of standardized techniques for performing those activities.

DOCUMENTATION

The documents identified in Table are generated during the software maintenance process. The table specifies both the inspection procedures, during which a document will be checked for accuracy, and the criteria against which the document will be checked.

Table. Governing Documentation.

Documents	Inspection	Criteria
Analysis Report	Analysis Report Inspection	Analysis Report Standard
Implementation Report	Implementation Inspection	Coding Standards, Unit Test Standard, and TCL Style Guide

STANDARDS, PRACTICES AND CONVENTIONS

The following table lists all standards, practices, and conventions used in the process and identifies when SQA personnel will apply them:

Table. Process Standards

Standard, Practice, or Convention	Inspection Type	Cell
Analysis Report Standard	Analysis Report Inspection	303
Coding Standard	Implementation Inspection	505
Unit Test Standard	Implementation Inspection	505
TCL Style Guide	Implementation Inspection	505

TISK PROCESS CHECKLIST

It is the responsibility of SQA to ensure that the TISK Process Checklist is properly updated. SQA will inform the responsible parties if they have neglected to complete the appropriate sections of the checklist.

TRAINING

Initial SQA training may be conducted by SQA personnel early in each project cycle. This training will consist of a lecture that describes SQA activities and an inspection simulation. Follow on SQA training will be conducted prior to each inspection as needed. This training will consist of a review of inspection procedures by the SQA inspection moderator with inspection team members.

INFORMAL WALK-THROUGHS

The objective of the walk-through is to evaluate the product and eliminate as many defects, omissions, and deviations from standards as possible before proceeding to a formal inspection. A walk-through is an informal procedure performed by a software engineer other than the author. All of the review procedures for a walk-through may be done via E-mail.

The following actions occur during a walk-through:

- The Author of the product or the lead software engineer selects a software engineer/reviewer to perform the walk-through.
- The SE/Reviewer will review the product for completeness, accuracy, and compliance with standards and good practice.
- The SE/Reviewer will report any defects found to the author.
- The Author will correct and resolve all noted defects.
- The SE/Reviewer will update the TISK Process Checklist to confirm completion of the walk-through.
- The Author will notify SQA when the walk-through is complete.
- SQA will verify that the TISK Process Checklist has been updated.

INSPECTION PROCESS

Inspections are used to increase software quality and improve productivity and manageability of the development process. The inspection process follows a specific set of steps which define what will be inspected, when it will be inspected, who will do the inspection, what data will be collected, and what follow-up actions must be taken. Inspections are conducted for Analysis Reports and Implementation. Implementation inspections may be done incrementally as development progresses and need not be delayed until the product is finished. The overall inspection process is as follows:

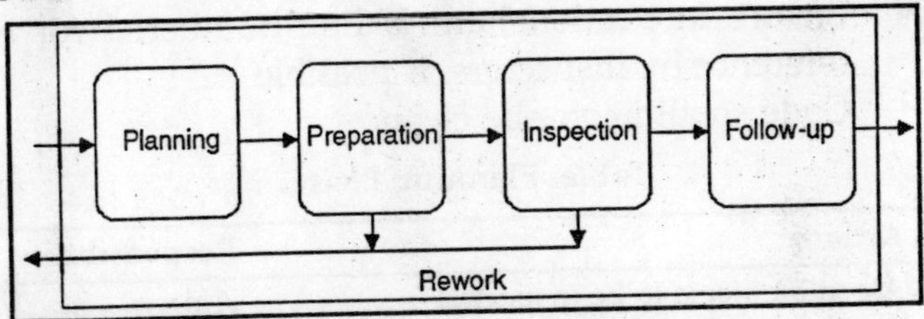

Fig. Inspection Process

The purpose of the Inspection Process is to formally review the product and identify defects. The author of the product to be inspected notifies the Project Coordinator (PC) that the product is complete and ready for inspection.

Table. Inspection Phases

Actions	Responsibility
Planning	Author/Moderator
Preparation	Moderator
Inspection	Moderator
Follow-up	Moderator/Author

Once the inspection is complete, the appropriate Inspection Checklist (Appendix A) will be used to validate the inspection. The moderator certifies that all necessary actions of the inspection are complete. The Inspection Report and combined Defect Log are created and filed in the TISK directory as a result of the inspection process.

Planning Phase

The purpose of the Planning Phase is to ensure that the product to be inspected is properly prepared. The author assembles all software elements necessary for the inspection in the TISK directory to allow easy access for the entire inspection team. The author then notifies the Project Coordinator (PC) that the TISK is ready for inspection. Notification may be in the form of an E-mail message or phone call to the PC.

Minimum criteria, if applicable, shall include:

- Spelling and grammar checked
- Compliant with standards
- Ensure inspection item is line numbered for easy reference by inspectors, if possible
- Code should compile clean

Table. Planning Phase.

Actions	Responsibility
Assemble items to be inspected	Author
Select moderator from SQA group	PC
Review inspection items for completeness	Moderator
Select and notify inspection team	PC
Assign roles	PC
Schedule inspection	Moderator

The moderator certifies that the product to be inspected is complete, the team is selected and notified, and all scheduling actions are accomplished. The outputs for this phase include the assembled product to be inspected, the Defect Log form and the appropriate inspection checklist (Appendix A), if applicable. Inspection forms may be downloaded from the Forms directory.

Preparation Phase

The purpose of the Preparation Phase is to ensure that the team conducting the inspection is properly prepared. Each member of the inspection team is provided access to the product to be inspected.

Table. Preparation Phase

Actions	Responsibility
Review all items to be inspected	Inspectors
Record identified defects on	Inspectors

individual Defect Log.	
Record inspection preparation times on individual Defect Log.	Inspectors
Send copy of individual Defect Log to moderator 48 hours prior to inspection meeting.	Inspectors
One day prior to the inspection, notify PC and Client (by E-mail) of any Inspectors who failed to provide a Defect Log	Moderator
Combine all individual Defect Logs in a logical order to present during the inspection meeting	Moderator
Disperse the combined Defect Log to all inspection participants for review 24 hours prior to the meeting.	Moderator

Inspection Meeting

The purpose of the Inspection Meeting is to formally review the product and the identified defects.

Table. Inspection Meeting

Actions	Responsibility
Review rules for inspections (Appendix A).	Moderator
Confirm and record inspection preparation times.	Moderator
Systematically review the product being inspected	Reader
Present and clarify defects identified.	Inspectors
Note the status of each defect as agreed upon by the inspection team and categorize valid defects	Recorder
Determine results of the inspection	Moderator
Determine estimated rework effort and completion date	Author
Notify PC of inspection results	Moderator

Follow-up

The purpose of the Follow-up is to ensure that any

previous inspection defects have been corrected or resolved and that the inspection is accurately documented in the inspection report. All inspectors should agree that the list of defects is resolved or additional corrective actions identified to resolve concerns.

SOFTWARE QUALITY FRAMEWORK

- *Introduction*: Software Quality Process Framework
  - Process is oriented around key architectural principles.
  - Must be practical and feasible
  - Must support the ability to implement reliability, repeatability, predictability
  - Must be designed for phased component implemention(s)
  - Must have the capability of being improved over time
  - Must be scalable across wide variety of industries/ project types
  - Must be independent of technology base at the highest level
- *Architectural Relationships*: Software Quality Process Framework
  - Technical Environments
  - Windows (Win 2K, Win XP, Vista) - Browsers (Internet Explorer,
  - AS/400/ Legacy (Firefox, Opera)
  - Data Mart - Network

The Framework can accommodate known and projected projects yet remains independent of the technical environments so that the Framework can be enhanced over time. Guiding Principles Methods Techniques Practices White Papers Standards Templates Quantify Quality Facilitate Quality Monitor Performance Verify Quality Tools Technologies Sub- Processes Key Processes... Manage Quality

- *Architecture*: Methods – Software Quality Process Framework Methods Techniques Practices White Papers Standards Templates Quantify Quality

Facilitate Quality Monitor Performance Verify Quality Tools Technologies Sub- Processes Key Processes... Manage Quality Proven methods that are Quality focused and are integrated into the overall SDLC (*e.g.*, Keyword Driven Testing, Causal Analysis, Fagan Inspection Process) Guiding Principles

- *Architecture*: Techniques – Software Quality Process Framework Guiding Principles Specific techniques that are used during the process of assuring the quality of applications, systems, or products Proven methods that are Quality focused and are integrated into the overall SDLC (*e.g.*, Keyword Driven Testing, Causal Analysis, Fagan Inspection Process) Methods Techniques Practices White Papers Standards Templates Quantify Quality Facilitate Quality Monitor Performance Verify Quality Tools Technologies Sub- Processes Key Processes... Manage Quality
- *Architecture*: Practices — Software Quality Process Framework Guiding Principles " Good practices" that have been developed in-company along with industry "Best Practices" Proven methods that are Quality focused and are integrated into the overall SDLC (*e.g.*, Keyword Driven Testing, Causal Analysis, Fagan Inspection Process) Specific techniques that are used during the process of assuring the quality of applications, systems, or products Methods Techniques Practices White Papers Standards Templates Quantify Quality Facilitate Quality Monitor Performance Verify Quality Tools Technologies Sub- Processes Key Processes... Manage Quality
- *Architecture*: White Papers — Software Quality Process Framework Guiding Principles Authoritative reports used to educate or help people make decisions " Good practices" that have been developed in-company along with industry "Best Practices"

Proven methods that are Quality focused and are integrated into the overall SDLC (*e.g.*, Keyword Driven Testing, Causal Analysis, Fagan Inspection Process) Specific techniques that are used during the process of assuring the quality of applications, systems, or products Methods Techniques Practices White Papers Standards Templates Quantify Quality Facilitate Quality Monitor Performance Verify Quality Tools Technologies Sub- Processes Key Processes... Manage Quality

- *Architecture*: Standards — Software Quality Process Framework Guiding Principles Industry, company, or corporate standards for adherence Authoritative reports used to educate or help people make decisions " Good practices" that have been developed in-company along with industry "Best Practices" Proven methods that are Quality focused and are integrated into the overall SDLC (*e.g.*, Keyword Driven Testing, Causal Analysis, Fagan Inspection Process) Specific techniques that are used during the process of assuring the quality of applications, systems, or products Methods Techniques Practices White Papers Standards Templates Quantify Quality Facilitate Quality Monitor Performance Verify Quality Tools Technologies Sub- Processes Key Processes.. Manage Quality
- *Architecture*: Templates — Software Quality Process Framework Guiding Principles Specific templates for documenting or developing test assets Industry, company, or corporate standards for adherence Authoritative reports used to educate or help people make decisions " Good practices" that have been developed in-company along with industry "Best Practices" Proven methods that are Quality focused and are integrated into the overall SDLC (*e.g.*, Keyword Driven Testing, Causal Analysis, Fagan Inspection Process) Specific techniques that are used during the process of assuring the quality of

applications, systems, or products Methods Techniques Practices White Papers Standards Templates Quantify Quality Facilitate Quality Monitor Performance Verify Quality Tools Technologies Sub- Processes Key Processes... Manage Quality

- *Architecture*: Sub-Processes — Software Quality Process Framework Guiding Principles Breakdown of activities that comprise a key process Methods Techniques Practices White Papers Standards Templates Quantify Quality Facilitate Quality Monitor Performance Verify Quality Tools Technologies Sub- Processes Key Processes... Manage Quality
- *Architecture*: Tools — Software Quality Process Framework Guiding Principles Tools used within the Quality Assurance process (*e.g.*, Mercury Quality Centre, Mercury Performance Centre) Methods Techniques Practices White Papers Standards Templates Quantify Quality Facilitate Quality Monitor Performance Verify Quality Tools Technologies Sub- Processes Key Processes... Manage Quality
- *Architecture*: Technologies — Software Quality Process Framework Guiding Principles Tools used within the Quality Assurance process (*e.g.*, Mercury Quality Centre, Mercury Performance Centre) Specialized technologies used (*e.g.*, fault injection testing, monitoring, security testing) Methods Techniques Practices White Papers Standards Templates Quantify Quality Facilitate Quality Monitor Performance Verify Quality Tools Technologies Sub- Processes Key Processes... Manage Quality
- *Architecture*: Guiding Principles — Software Quality Process Framework Guiding Principles
  - Guiding Principles — Examples
  - *Theme* 1: The Quality Assurance function will be

involved in every identified software development life cycle (SDLC) phase to provide appropriate consulting, advise, support, and quality oversight

- *Theme* 2: Requirements-based Quality Assurance testing activities are based on accurate, correct, and testable requirements
- *Theme* 3: Continuous process improvement will provide renewed and constant value to the company
- *Theme* 4: Automated testing with a high ROI will be exploited
- *Theme* 5: Software quality will be gauged by facts and data (metrics and measurements) rather than perception
- *Theme* 6: The long term goal is to move from defect detection to defect prevention

Methods Techniques Practices White Papers Standards Templates Quantify Quality Facilitate Quality Monitor Performance Verify Quality Tools Technologies Sub- Processes Key Processes... Manage Quality

- *Architecture*: Key Processes — Software Quality Process Framework Guiding Principles
  - Comprehensive collection of top level key process areas that provide for Quality focus
  - Heart of overall Framework
  - Provides a collection point for sub-processes, methods, techniques, practices, white papers, tools, and technologies

Methods Techniques Practices White Papers Standards Templates Quantify Quality Facilitate Quality Monitor Performance Verify Quality Tools Technologies Sub- Processes Key Processes... Manage Quality

ISO 9000 MODEL

ISO 9000 is a set of international standards of quality management that have become increasingly popular for large and small companies alike. "ISO is grounded on the 'conformance to specification' definition of quality, " wrote Francis Buttle in the *International Journal of Quality and Reliability Management.* "The standards specify how management operations shall be conducted.

ISO 9000's purpose is to ensure that suppliers design, create, and deliver products and services which meet predetermined standards; in other words, its goal is to prevent non-conformity." Used by both manufacturing and service firms, ISO 9000 had been adopted by more than 100 nations as their national quality management/quality assurance standard by the end of 1997.

This quality standard was first introduced in 1987 by the International Organization for Standards (ISO) in hopes of establishing an international definition of the essential characteristics and language of a quality system for all businesses, irrespective of industry or geographic location. Initially, it was used almost exclusively by large companies, but by the mid-1990s, increasing numbers of small-and mid-sized companies had embraced ISO 9000 as well.

ISO 9000 QUALITY MANAGEMENT SYSTEMS

The standards of ISO 9000 detail 20 requirements for an organization's quality management system in the following areas:

- Management Responsibility
- Quality System
- Order Entry
- Design Control
- Document and Data Control
- Purchasing
- Control of Customer Supplied Products
- Product Identification and Tractability
- Process Control
- Inspection and Testing Control of Inspection, Measuring, and Test Equipment
- Inspection and Test Status
- Control of Nonconforming Products
- Corrective and Preventive Action
- Handling, Storage, Packaging, and Delivery

- Control of Quality Records
- Internal Quality Audits
- Training
- Servicing
- Statistical Techniques

MODELS OF ISO 9000

The ISO 9000 quality standards are broken down into three model sets—ISO 9001, ISO 9002, and ISO 9003. Each of these models, noted *Industrial Management* contributors Stanislav Karapetrovic, Divakar Rajamani, and Walter Willborn, "stipulate a number of requirements on which an organization's quality system can be assessed by an external party (registrar)" in accordance with the ISO's quality system audits standard. "A quality system, " they added, "involves organizational structure, processes, and documented procedures constituted towards achieving quality objectives."

Each of the three sets concentrates on a different quality area. ISO 9001 is the most wide-ranging, for it specifies the various operating requirements in such areas as product design and development, production, installation, and servicing. ISO 9002 is concerned with quality assurance at the production and installation stages.

ISO 9003 covers testing and inspections. As Karapetrovic, Rajamani, and Willborn noted, "if the minimum requirements are met [for the above operating areas], a registrar accredited by a national accreditation institution issues a certificate of compliance and the organization's quality system becomes ISO 9001, 9002, or 9003 registered."

It is worth noting that certification is handed out for individual quality systems, not companies; this means that one company may hold more than one ISO 9000 registration. Moreover, Harvey R. Meyer pointed out in *Nation's Business* that "the standards do not certify the quality of a product or service. Rather, they attest that a company has fully documented its quality-control processes and consistently adheres to them. If that's done, quality products and services generally follow."

In addition to ISO 9000, two related quality standards emerged in American industries in the late 1990s. ISO 14000, also known as the Environmental Management Systems Standards, is intended to combine environmental management systems with the ISO 9000 quality system.

The second system, QS9000 is an adaptation of ISO 9000 to meet the specific needs of the "big three" American automobile manufacturers—Ford, General Motors, and Daimler Chrysler. Both systems were expected to have a substantial impact on U.S. companies.

ADVANTAGES OF ISO 9000

The advantages associated with ISO 9000 certification are numerous, as both business analysts and business owners will attest. These benefits, which can impact nearly all corners of a company, range from increased stature to bottom-line operational savings.

They include:

- *Increased marketability*: Nearly all observers agree that ISO 9000 registration provides businesses with markedly heightened credibility with current and prospective clients alike. Basically, it proves that the company is dedicated to providing quality to its customers, which is no small advantage whether the company is negotiating with a long-time customer or endeavoring to pry a potentially lucrative customer away from a competitor. This benefit manifests itself not only in increased customer retention, but also in increased customer acquisition and heightened ability to enter into new markets; indeed, ISO 9000 registration has been cited as being of particular value for small and mid-sized businesses hoping to establish a presence in international markets.
- *Reduced operational expenses*: Sometimes lost in the many discussions of ISO 9000's public relations cache is the fact that the rigorous registration process often exposes significant shortcomings in various

operational areas. When these problems are brought to light, the company can take the appropriate steps to improve its processes. These improved efficiencies can help companies garner savings in both time and money. "The cost of scrap, rework, returns, and the employee time spent analyzing and troubleshooting various products are all considerably reduced by initiating the discipline of ISO 9000, " confirmed Richard B. Wright in *Industrial Distribution.*

- *Better management control*: The ISO 9000 registration process requires so much documentation and self-assessment that many businesses that undergo its rigors cite increased understanding of the company's overall direction and processes as a significant benefit.
- *Increased customer satisfaction*: Since the ISO 9000 certification process almost inevitably uncovers areas in which final product quality can be improved, such efforts often bring about higher levels of customer satisfaction. In addition, by seeking and securing ISO 9000 certification, companies can provide their clients with the opportunity to tout their suppliers' dedication to quality in their own business dealings.
- *Improved internal communication:* The ISO 9000 certification process's emphasis on self-analysis and operations management issues encourages various internal areas or departments of companies to interact with one another in hopes of gaining a more complete understanding of the needs and desires of their internal customers.
- *Improved customer service*: The process of securing ISO 9000 registration often serves to refocus company priorities on pleasing their customers in all respects, including customer service areas. It also helps heighten awareness of quality issues among employees.
- *Reduction of product-liability risks*: Many business

experts contend that companies that achieve ISO 9000 certification are less likely to be hit with product liability lawsuits, etc., because of the quality of their processes.

- *Attractiveness to investors*: Business consultants and small business owners alike agree that ISO-9000 certification can be a potent tool in securing funding from venture capital firms.

DISADVANTAGES OF ISO 9000

Despite the many advantages associated with ISO 9000, however, business owners and consultants caution companies to research the rigorous certification process before committing resources to it. Following is a list of potential hurdles for entrepreneurs to study before committing to an initiative to gain ISO 9000 certification:

- Owners and managers do not have an adequate understanding of the ISO 9000 certification process or of the quality standards themselves: Some business owners have been known to direct their company's resources towards ISO 9000 registration, only to find that their incomplete understanding of the process and its requirements results in wasted time and effort.
- *Funding for establishing the quality system is inadequate*: Critics of ISO 9000 contend that achieving certification can be a very costly process, especially for smaller firms. Indeed, according to a 1996 *Quality Systems Update* survey, the average cost of ISO certification for small firms (those registering less than $11 million in annual sales) was $71, 000.
- *Heavy emphasis on documentation*: The ISO 9000 certification process relies heavily on documentation of internal operating procedures in many areas, and as Meyer stated, "many say ISO's exacting documentation requirements gobble up time. Indeed, there are horror stories about companies losing substantial business because a documentation

obsession redirected their priorities." According to *Nation's Business,* small business owners need to find an appropriate balance between ISO documentation requirements, which are admittedly "one is ISO 9000's hallmarks, " and attending to the fundamental business of running a company: "Strike a balance among obsessively writing down every employee's task, offering training for the work, and letting common sense dictate how a task is to be performed."

- *Length of the process*: Business executives and owners familiar with the ISO 9000 registration process warn that it is a process that takes many months to complete. The 1996 *Quality Systems Update* survey indicated that it took businesses an average of 15 months to move from the early stages of the process to passage of the final audit, and that processes of 18-20 months or even longer were not that uncommon.

SEI-CMM MODEL

INTRODUCTION

According to the Carnegie Mellon University Software Engineering Institute, CMM is a common-sense application of software or business process management and quality improvement concepts to software development and maintenance. Its a community-developed guide for evolving towards a culture of engineering excellence, model for organizational improvement.

The underlying structure for reliable and consistent software process assessments and software capability evaluations. The Capability Maturity Model for Software (CMM) is a framework that describes the key elements of an effective software process.

There are CMMs for non software processes as well, such as Business Process Management (BPM). The CMM describes an evolutionary improvement path from an ad hoc, immature process to a mature, disciplined process. The CMM covers practices for planning, engineering, and managing software development and maintenance. When followed, these key practices improve the ability of organizations to meet goals for cost, schedule, functionality, and product quality.

The*CMM* establishes a yardstick against which it is possible to judge, in a repeatable way, the maturity of an organization's software process and compare it to the state of the practice of the industry. The CMM can also be used by an organization to plan improvements to its software process. It also reflects the needs of individuals performing software process, improvement, software process assessments, or software capability evaluations; is documented; and is publicly available. The CMM defines five levels of process capability, each of which represents an evolutionary plateau towards a disciplined, measured, and continuously improving software process.

The Initial Level

At the Initial level (Level 1) few, if any, organized processes exist. Each developer utilizes whatever methods or techniques strike his or her fancy. The situation is sometimes described as chaotic and ad hoc. Software quality is more a matter of chance, and is highly dependent on the capabilities of specific individuals within the organization.

The Repeatable Level

To reach Level 2, a software development organization must put into place basic project management practices. This includes the capability to estimate the size of the software to be produced, estimate resources to execute the project, and track progress against these estimates.

Also included is the implementation of software configuration management and quality assurance practices, the capability to effectively manage the requirements definition process, and the capability to manage subcontractors (if applicable). This level is referred to as the Repeatable level; the organization has mastered tasks previously learned. The organization is still highly dependent on individuals for the success of a project. In times of stress, the organization tends to revert back to behaving as a Level 1 organization.

The Defined Level

Level 3 is characterized as the Defined level. At this level, the organization has defined and established the software development and maintenance practices specific to the types of applications they produce. They have put into place a set of standards and procedures to codify these practices, and the organization follows them consistently. Training in these practices is provided. Peer reviews are performed as in-process evaluations of product quality. Integrated project management exists. The organization is no longer highly dependent on key individuals; the process belongs to the organization, not to individuals. At times of stress, the Level 3 practices are not abandoned.

The Managed Level

At Level 3 and below, the primary focus is on product quality. At Level 4 and above, the primary focus shifts to process quality (although some amount of attention is paid to process quality below Level 4). To reach Level 4, the Managed level, the organization focuses on establishing a set of process measures and uses them to initiate corrective actions. Once these measures have been established, the organization is ready to begin to use them to implement continuous process improvement.

The Optimizing Level

At Level 5, the Optimizing level, these measures are not only being used to improve existing processes, but also to evaluate candidate new processes. They are also being used as the basis for determining the efficacy of introducing new technologies into the organization.

Using the CMM

How can the CMM help your organization? There are

three key roles the CMM plays. First, the CMM helps build an understanding of software process by describing the practices that contribute to a level of process maturity. The second role of the CMM is to provide a consistent basis for conducting appraisals of software processes.

The CMM defines a scale for measuring process maturity, thus allowing an organization to accurately compare its process capability to that of another organization. ISO is using the CMM in its efforts to develop international standards for software process assessments.

The CMM's third key role is to serve as a blueprint for software process improvement. The CMM can help an organization focus on the areas it must address in order to advance to the next level of maturity. Today, leading software organizations are adopting the CMM as their core strategy for improving quality and productivity.

6

Software Design

TECHNIQUES

Object oriented techniques have been around for some time, but this exploding popularity seems a bit unusual. Why the sudden interest? All kinds of explanations have been offered. In truth, there is probably no single reason. Probably, a combination of factors has finally reached critical mass and things are taking off. Nevertheless, it seems that C++ itself is a major factor in this latest phase of the software revolution. Again, there are probably a number of reasons why, but I want to suggest an answer from a slightly different perspective: C++ has become popular because it makes it easier to design software and programme at the same time.

If source code is a software design, then actually building software is done by compilers and linkers. We often refer to the process of compiling and linking a complete software system as "doing a build". The capital investment in software construction equipment is low all it really takes is a computer, an editor, a compiler, and a linker.

Once a build environment is available, then actually doing a software build just takes a little time. Compiling a 50,000 line C++ programme may seem to take forever, but how long would it take to build a hardware system that had a design of the same complexity as 50,000 lines of C++.

Another consequence of considering source code as software design is the fact that a software design is relatively easy to create, at least in the mechanical sense. Writing (*i.e.,* designing) a typical software module of 50 to 100 lines of code is usually only a couple of day's effort (getting it fully debugged is another story, but more on that later).

It is tempting to ask if there is any other engineering discipline that can produce designs of such complexity as software in such a short time, but first we have to figure out how to measure and compare complexity. Nevertheless, it is obvious that software designs get very large rather quickly.

ELEMENTS

The design process can be described as the process of choosing a representation of a solution from a set of alternatives, given the constraints towards a set of goals. It can be divided in two phases: diversification and convergence. The diversification is the phase of generating alternatives. Not necessarily documents describing a possible solution, but, at least, on the designer's mind.

These alternatives are the solution candidates and are generated/obtained from knowledge, catalogs, or previous experience. During the convergence phase, the designer chooses the alternative (or the combination of alternatives) that meets the intended goals.

The alternative selected will be the solution, which will meet the constraints imposed by the problem domain. The solution then may be described using some representation. The representation chosen must fit its purpose: describe the solution and the process to build the artifact that reaches the intended goals.

GOALS

Design begins with a need. If something is to be designed, though to be built, it is because the outcome of the design process will fulfill this need. In Software Engineering, the necessity starts from a customer who specifies what are her needs and therefore what are the goals to be achieved with the software system to be designed.

So, the goal of the design process is to achieve a solution that will solve the customer's needs. In software design, goals are also referred to as requirements. Software design is mainly concerned on two types of requirements: functional and nonfunctional requirements. A functional requirement specifies the functionality that a system will exhibit. In other words, *what* the system is to perform according to the customer. For example, a functional requirement for a sorting programme is to provide the ability to sort integers.

Another example could be related to a software system that manages the inventory of a movie rental store. If we were to enumerate the functional requirements of a system like this, among them would be: the ability to search for a movie by its keywords, the ability to perform a movie rental, the ability to perform a movie return, and many others.

On the other hand, a nonfunctional requirement specifies properties or characteristics that a software system must exhibit other than the observable behaviour. Specifically, it is concerned on *how* the software will function. Back to our sorting programme example, a nonfunctional requirement is the customer's concern with the running time of the sorting function (*e.g.*, it is acceptable that the sorting algorithm execution time has the growth rate of $O(n\log n)$, where n is the size of the input).

If we are talking about the movie rental store software, one nonfunctional requirement can be described as exposing some system's functions, such as the search for movie by its keywords, to be accessible via browser to its users.

As nonfunctional requirements play an important role on software architecture, we may return to them in the chapter on Nonfunctional Requirements, where they will exemplified, described, and categorized in detail, as well they will be correlated to their imposers, the system's stakeholders.

CONSTRAINTS

A design product must be feasible. Considering this, a design constraint is the rule, requirement, relation, convention, or principle that define the context of design, in order to achieve a feasible design product.

Smith and Browne gave a detailed description of the role of constraints on design It is important to know that constraints are related to goals, and sometimes they can even be exchanged.

However, in order to differentiate them, it is also important to understand that are not only the goals that rule what is to be designed. In other words, a software system may have clear goals, but its design, or some possibilities of it, may not be feasible because of its constraints.

In order to grasp the role of constraints in design, let us consider two examples. In the first example, despite the software system has a clear goal, its design is not feasible due to some of its constraints. In the second, a software system also has a clear goal, but just a clear design possibility is constrained.

First, consider that a customer describes a simple goal to be achieved by a system: it must be able to decide whether its input, a description of another programme, finishes running or not. An inexperienced software designer might even try to find a design possibility for this requirement – but this would be in vain.

There is a theoretical constraint in computer science, widely known as the halting problem, which forbids a programme to decide whether or not another programme halts after its execution, thus not allowing achieving a solution. So, a design was not allowed due to its constra-ints even with a clear stated goal.

ALTERNATIVES

A design alternative is a possibility of solution. Since design problems often have multiple solutions, since design problems often have multiple solutions, the designer is expected to generate multiple design alternatives for a single problem.

We must understand that the designer, after understanding the problem's goals and constraints, has two concerns: the alternative generation and the solution election among the alternatives. Alternative generation poses the real challenge for a designer. Unlike decision problems area where decision alternatives are known or can be discovered through search methods, design alternatives must be created. This creation process then must be controlled by design enabling techniques, and designer's experiential knowledge and creative imagination. The solution election is simply the choice of one of the alternatives that, according to the designer, will best solve the problem. This choice must be made employing reasoned analysis and experience. The following subsections better explain solutions and their representations.

REPRESENTATIONS

Representations are the language of design. Although the true product of design is a representation for artifact construct, representing the solution is not the only purpose of representation. It also supports the design process. This support happens by allowing communication between stakeholders and by serving as a record of commitments.

A design representation allows communication because it turns alternatives into manipulable products, so they can be described, analysed, and discussed not only by their author but also by others. Please observe that there are multiple dimensions to be represented on a single software design alternative.

These dimensions may comprise runtime behaviour, structure, and relation between logical entities to physical entities just to name a few. These dimensions are often exhibited on different types of representations, which later we will name them views. In order to illustrate design representations, let us present two dimensions of our sorting programme example by using two different representations. The first representation, Figure 1, shows the structure from a design possibility of our example using Unified Modeling Language. Observing this representation, we see how the solution was decomposed, how each class of the structure relates to each other, or even see what points could be replaced by ready-made components, which must implement the same interfaces specified on the representation. Also, we can have the notion of how much space is needed to perform the algorithm.

Merge Sort Pseudocode:

```
function mergesort(m)
     var list left, right
     if length(m) = 1
          return m
     else
          middle = length(m) / 2
          for each x in m up to middle
               add x to left
          for each x in m after middle
               add x to right
          left = mergesort(left)
          right = mergesort(right)
          result = merge(left, right)
          return result
function merge(left,right)
    var list result
    while length(left)>0 and length(right)>0
          if first(left) = first(right)
               append first(left) to result
               left = rest(left)
          else
               append first(right) to result
               right = rest(right)
     if length(left) > 0
          append left to result
     if length(right) > 0
          append right to result
     return result
```

Both representations show important aspects of a system's design, nevertheless one involved on its development might be interested on aspects other than its structure or algorithm asymptotic analysis. As a matter of fact, other representations might be wanted for other purposes and it is the role of the design process to provide them.

SOLUTIONS

A design solution is nothing more than a description

enabling system construction that uses one or many representations in order to expose sufficient details. Its characteristics are listed in the following paragraphs. Design solutions mirror the problem complexity, usually having many attributes and interrelationships. We can observe this characteristic, for example, when designing a solution for managing the inventory of a DVD rental store. Whatever the solution is, it must contain attributes such as movies, DVDs, clients, and genres, which will represent the elements inherent to the problem.

However, this is not enough. It must also contain relations such as "a client can rent one or more DVDs", "a movie have one or more genres", or "a DVD must contain one or more movies", which will behave just like the relations on the problem domain. Consequently, when many different attributes have different interrelationships between themselves, complexity emerges.

It is difficult to validate design solutions. The complexity of the solution renders many points of possible validation against design goals. The very problem resides on how well the design goals are described. Usually, only high-level goals are specified for very complex problems, so validation is hardened.

ARCHITECTURAL DESIGN PRINCIPLES

Design principles are not necessarily right or wrong but should be an accurate reflection of the fundamentals that guide decision making in an enterprise. The following should therefore not be seen as design principles fixed in concrete but rather as examples of business principles. Best practice is to define the design principle in terms of its Benefits and rationale as well as the implication to the enterprise and the counter argument expressing the potential negative impact of the design principle.

DESIGN PRINCIPLE

Description

All management information and business intelligence

will be sourced from a single consolidated source of information

Benefits

- A central source of management information will provide the enterprise with a wide breath of reporting and analysis without being constraint by the organisations functional structuring.
- Users will become used to a single interface to management information allowing managers to become familiar with the infrastructure and extracting maximum benefit from all information available in the organisation.
- The central information will eliminate contradicting information sources and ensure accurate reporting of current affairs and identification of issues and opportunities.
- Increase the flexibility and manageability of providing information rapidly and effectively to support business decisions.
- Use best of breed analytic functionality to support management decision making
- Increased security in managing access to The enterprise's management information

Implications

- Information must be sourced to the central information infrastructure from all the various operational applications as close to real time as possible
- No additional analytical modules are required for transactional applications.
- The interface to management information and training should be rolled out to all decision makers to effectively access information.

Counter Argument

- The central management information might not be

adequate in situations where real time analytics of transactional information is needed

- Information in the central information source might not be structured for a specific requirement and the development time might be too long to provide the information in time for a once off request.
- The assumption cannot be made that a single tool will satisfy all the information requirements. The information infrastructure will therefore consist of a variety of integrated tools.

INTERNATIONALISATION

Description

Information must be structured for global deployment in various cultures and support multi-currency, multi-language and multi platforms

Benefits

- Flexibility to enter into other global markets
- Consistency of being able to deploy a proven business model and then adapt to local conditions

Implications

- Applications should be much more flexible to accommodate differences defined by different countries
- Current applications should be evaluated in terms of internationalisation requirements.

Counter Argument

- Applications designated for use locally in South-Africa only does not have to comply to the internationalisation principle
- The enterprise might strategise to enter only into markets that have a certain set of international commonality which make the rigid application of this principle unnecessary

- It might be too expensive to change or replace legacy systems to adhere to the internationalisation requirement.

SINGLE CONTACT DATABASE

Description

A single contact database for all business contacts *e.g.* policyholders, intermediaries and service providers

Benefits

- A central source of information to manage relationships effectively
- Have a more comprehensive view of interrelationships between business contacts.
- More effective marketing campaign design and management

Implication

- High levels of data integration with transactional systems updating contact information.
- Transactional systems updating information must be assigned with levels of trust.
- Central contact information should not.complicate functional requirements to only view specific relationships.

Counter Argument

- Some functional units might not want to share contact information for the fear that it might be used wrongly or out of context by other parts of the organisation.

SINGLE POINT OF AUTHENTICATION

Description

Access for to information should be constraint through a single point of authentication infrastructure

Benefits

- Improved security of information

Implication

- Central management of user access to information.

Counter Argument

- The current infrastructure might not be mature enough to implement the principle.

DATA QUALITY MEASUREMENT

Description

Data quality will be measured both in quantitative and qualitative terms eg. Audit procedures and Data quality questionnaires

Benefits

- Improved data quality
- Accurate usage of data
- Improved management information
- Increased operational efficiency

Implication

- Bi-annually measure data through with a data quality survey
- Audit data ownership procedures annually
- Build in data quality measures into applications
- Connect data quality results with performance incentives

Counter Argument

- Regular audits and subjective measurement techniques *e.g.* surveys might be time consuming.

FORMALISED DATA EXCHANGE/ENRICHMENT

Description

All data exchange/enrichment activities are managed and

approved by the appointed data strategist and the exchange of information must be subjected to a standardised methodology for information exchange/enrichment.

Benefits

- Control costs associated with data exchange and enrichment
- Protect operational data
- Improve data quality and value
- Data sharing to allow for better detection of fraud

Implication

- Development of a formal policy and methodology for data exchange and enrichment
- Data strategist must be responsible for approving data exchange/enrichment efforts and minimise cost.
- Identification and management of organisations that can enrich and/or validate the enterprise data.

Counter Argument

- The formalised methodology should not become a constraint to enrich and improve data quality.
- The enterprise might not always be in a position to demand compliance from external parties to comply with data sharing standards.
- Current lack of industry standards might make it difficult to implement the principle.

CENTRAL REPOSITORY OF DATA NAMING STANDARDS

Description

Data names and field content must be standardised through a central reference repository and must be accessible to the business *e.g.* Street rather than str. is used to reference a street.

Benefits

- Consistency of information across all business processes

- Usability of information increases across the organisation.

Implication

- Alignment of all applications to support the standardised naming standards

Counter Argument

- Difficulty to implement naming standardisation in some applications

ALIGN INFORMATION REQUIREMENTS WITH DATA MODEL

Description

All information requirements must be aligned with the corporate data model before requesting changes to the information architecture:

Benefits

- Integrity of transactional data model stays in tact.
- Prevent duplication of information.

Implication

- The corporate data model must be maintained to be up to date at all times.
- In any application development life cycle it is a condition to align the application with the corporate data model.

Counter Argument

Data owners might not understand the data model to update it with changes.

INFORMATION GOVERNANCE ON ALL DATA ELEMENTS

Description

All information elements must be subjected to information architecture governance

Benefits

- Sustain data quality.
- Improve operational efficiency.

Implication

- Design the business process application of the data element.
- Assign Applications sourcing the information.
- Align with corporate data model, rules, validations, naming standard.
- Define data management policies *e.g.* security, back-up, archiving/retrieval.
- Assign data ownership.

Counter Argument

- Lack training to adhere to information governance.
- Information governance is not adequately communicated.

DATA PRIVACY AND LEGALITY

Description

Client privacy must be respected and legal requirements must be complied with, in any event of data exchange or commerce.

Benefit

- Maintain good relationships with clients and protect premium income
- Avoid legal costs due to mismanagement of information resulting in lawsuits.

Implication

- The enterprise must be up to date with laws relating to information
- Communicating The enterprise's data policy to clients

- Legal department needs to be up to date with laws governing information usage, commerce and distribution

Counter Argument

- Uncertainty of what constitutes data privacy might make it difficult to implement this principle.

Bottom line: Design principles for enterprise architecture must provide a decision framework based on a clear rationale defined in terms of the benefits, implications and counter argument relating to the design principle

UNIFIED MODELING LANGUAGE (UML)

The Unified Modeling Language or UML is is a mostly graphical modelling language that is used to express designs. It is a standardized language in which to specify the artefacts and components of a software system. It is important to understand that the UML describes a notation and not a process. It does not put forth a single method or process of design, but rather is a standardized tool that can be used in a design process.

STATE DIAGRAM

The state diagram shows the change of an object through time. Based upon events that occur, the state diagram shows how the object changes from start to finish.

States are represented as a rounded rectangle with the name of the state shown. Optionally you can include an activity that represents a longer running task during that state. Connecting states together are transitions. These represent the events that cause the object to change from one state to another. The guard clause of the label is again mutually exclusive and must resolve itself to be either true or false. Actions represent tasks that run causing the transitions.

Actions are different from activities in that actions cannot be interrupted, while an activity can be interrupted by an incoming event. Both ultimately represent an operation on the object being studied. For example, an operation that sets an attribute would be considered an action, while a long calculation might be an activity. The specific separation between the two depends on the object and the system being studied.

ARCHITECTURAL PATTERNS

Patterns for system architecting are very much in their infancy. They have been introduced into TOGAF essentially to draw them to the attention of the systems architecture community as an emerging important resource, and as a placeholder for hopefully more rigorous descriptions and references to more plentiful resources in future versions of TOGAF. They have not (as yet) been integrated into TOGAF. However, in the following, we attempt to indicate the potential value to TOGAF, and to which parts of the TOGAF Architecture Development Method (ADM) they might be relevant.

Background

A "pattern" has been defined as: "an idea that has been useful in one practical context and will probably be useful in others" [*Analysis Patterns - Reusable Object Models*]. In TOGAF, patterns are considered to be a way of putting building blocks into context; for example, to describe a re-usable solution to a problem. Building blocks are what you use: patterns can tell you how you use them, when, why, and what trade-offs you have to make in doing so. Patterns offer the promise of helping the architect to identify combinations of Architecture and/or Solution Building Blocks (ABBs/SBBs) that have been proven to deliver effective solutions in the past, and may provide the basis for effective solutions in the future.

Content of a Pattern

Several different formats are used in the literature for

describing patterns, and no single format has achieved widespread acceptance. However, there is broad agreement on the types of things that a pattern should contain. The headings which follow are taken from *Pattern-Oriented Software Architecture: A System of Patterns.* The elements described below will be found in most patterns, even if different headings are used to describe them.

Name

A meaningful and memorable way to refer to the pattern, typically a single word or short phrase.

Problem

A description of the problem indicating the intent in applying the pattern - the intended goals and objectives to be reached within the context and forces described below (perhaps with some indication of their priorities).

Context

The preconditions under which the pattern is applicable - a description of the initial state before the pattern is applied.

Forces

A description of the relevant forces and constraints, and how they interact/conflict with each other and with the intended goals and objectives. The description should clarify the intricacies of the problem and make explicit the kinds of trade-offs that must be considered. (The need for such trade-offs is typically what makes the problem difficult, and generates the need for the pattern in the first place.) The notion of "forces" equates in many ways to the "qualities" that architects seek to optimize, and the concerns they seek to address, in designing architectures.

For example:

- Security, robustness, reliability, fault-tolerance
- Manageability
- Efficiency, performance, throughput, bandwidth requirements, space utilization

- Scalability (incremental growth on-demand)
- Extensibility, evolvability, maintainability
- Modularity, independence, re-usability, openness, composability (plug-and-play), portability
- Completeness and correctness
- Ease-of-construction
- Ease-of-use
- etc....

A description, using text and/or graphics, of how to achieve the intended goals and objectives. The description should identify both the solution's static structure and its dynamic behaviour - the people and computing actors, and their collaborations. The description may include guidelines for implementing the solution. Variants or specializations of the solution may also be described.

Resulting Context

The post-conditions after the pattern has been applied. Implementing the solution normally requires trade-offs among competing forces. This element describes which forces have been resolved and how, and which remain unresolved. It may also indicate other patterns that may be applicable in the new context. (A pattern may be one step in accomplishing some larger goal.) Any such other patterns will be described in detail under Related Patterns.

Examples

One or more sample applications of the pattern which illustrate each of the other elements: a specific problem, context, and set of forces; how the pattern is applied; and the resulting context.

Rationale

An explanation/justification of the pattern as a whole, or of individual components within it, indicating how the pattern actually works, and why - how it resolves the forces to achieve the desired goals and objectives, and why this is "good". The Solution element of a pattern describes the external structure and behaviour of the solution: the Rationale provides insight into its internal workings.

Related Patterns

The relationships between this pattern and others. These may be predecessor patterns, whose resulting contexts correspond to the initial context of this one; or successor patterns, whose initial contexts correspond to the resulting context of this one; or alternative patterns, which describe a different solution to the same problem, but under different forces; or co-dependent patterns, which may/must be applied along with this pattern.

Known Uses

Known applications of the pattern within existing systems, verifying that the pattern does indeed describe a proven solution to a recurring problem. Known Uses can also serve as Examples.

Patterns may also begin with an Abstract providing an overview of the pattern and indicating the types of problems it addresses. The Abstract may also identify the target audience and what assumptions are made of the reader.

LOW LEVEL DESIGN

The low level design document should contain a listing of the declarations of all the classes, non-member-functions, and class member functions that will be defined during the implementation stage, along with the associations between those classes and any other details of those classes (such as member variables) that are firmly determined by the low level design stage. The low level design document should also describe the classes, function signatures, associations, and any other appropriate details, which will be involved in testing and evaluating the project according to the evaluation plan defined in the project's requirements document.

More importantly, each project's low level design document should provide a narrative describing (and comments in your declaration and definition files should point out) how the high level design is mapped into its detailed low-level design, which is just a step away from the implementation itself. This should be an English description of how you converted the technical diagrams (and text descriptions) found in your high level design into appropriate class and function declarations in your low level design. You should be especially careful to explain how the class roles and their methods were combined in your low level design, and any changes that you decided to make in combining and refining them.

DESCRIPTION

Control systems elements like Advanced Metering Infrastructure (AMI) networks fully field wireless sensors and controls outside a utility's physical security perimeter, placing them at a high risk of compromise. System attackers have every opportunity to damage, sniff, spoof, or tamper communications hardware platforms for malicious, hobbyist, or incidental reasons.

This paper demonstrates the relevance of common control systems communications hardware vulnerabilities that lead to direct control systems compromise. The paper describes several enabling vulnerabilities exploitable by an attacker, the design principles that causing them to arise, the economic and electronic design constraints that restrict their defence, and ideas for vulnerability avoidance.

Topics include design induced vulnerabilities such as the extraction and modification of communications device firmware, man-in-the-middle attacks between chips of a communications devices, circumvention of protection measures, bus snooping, and other attacks. Specific examples are identified in this report, ranked by attack feasibility. Each attack was investigated against actual IEEE 802.15.4 radio architectures.

Embedded System Architecture

Standard wireless embedded implementation technologies such as IEEE 802.15.4 are generally designed to serve specific market needs. Therefore, the market offers components that translate such standards to mass producible designs. Embedded wireless technologies typically, but not always, have relatively low power consumption, component cost, computational power requirements, design cost, and implementation cost.

Commodity variants of components that implement wireless technology generally have higher individual reliability than custom designs, and a ready and willing engineer talent pool to integrate them. Almost all such components are designed to leverage or integrate with existing mass production components and subcomponents such as microcontrollers, RAM chips, ROM chips, and others.

All of the above is highly desirable. As with all such technologies that have the potential to achieve economy of scale in design and implementation, vulnerability generally follows or surpasses all cost optimizations and design trade-offs unless specifically mitigated. Such optimizations and economies of scale can serve to broaden the impact of overlooked security flaws, turning their advantage into a weakness.

This paper does not attempt to cover all potential aspects for such wireless technology implementations, much less the entire range of implementation issues for a single technology. We present security vulnerabilities for typical components found in specific IEEE 802.15.4 implementations; and abstract them to help translate real-world tactical security vulnerabilities as recognizable design classes requiring consideration for mitigation. This paper does not educate the reader in the many nuances of RF design. For RF design and implementation issues, see individual standards such as and engineering references including, but not limited to. We present an abstraction of monolithic vulnerable aspects of a typical commodity IEEE 802.15.4 platform, the Telos-B development kit.

While the Telos-B is a basic user-programmable development kit, its architecture is close enough to most typical applications to be considered general. This abstraction is intended to give the reader a repeatable context as a starting point when looking at other platform architectures.

The RF physical, media access, link layer, and sometimes network layers will be offloaded onto an RF component such as the pictured CC2420. Breaking up the design lets designers implement the RF portion of the application with the best possible RF module for the lowest time to market while targeting host applications to the optimal host processor. Most standalone communications modules will be linked to their host processor by a trivial board-level serial bus such as SPI or I2C. In some designs the host processor also contains the RF stack implementation, eliminating the board-level serial bus. Components such as microcontrollers or host processors rarely fully implement the analog portion of an RF module.

Antennae, inbound and outbound amplifiers, RF switches, and various filters are generally integrated separately as their requirements vary widely across potential applications. Due to their application orientation, host processors will have external timing means.

In general external oscillators reduce processor chip cost and allow the designer to scale the system to the cheapest clock source meeting application requirements. Though typically not used, many 802.15.4 RF modules have a means to slave a host's clock to the RF module to further reduce design cost. Power is supplied to the devices as required by the module, though often platform power requirements are aligned to reduce component count and subsequent cost.

Confidentiality

- Snooping Bus Traffic
- Extracting Firmware for Vulnerability Analysis
- Extracting Stored Information
- Snooping Side Channels

Integrity

- Tampering Bus Traffic
- Replacing Hardware Components
- Modifying Existing Components

- Bypassing Hardware Components
- Disrupting or Distorting Normal Hardware Operation
- Bypassing Software Components

Availability

- Jamming or Shrouding
- Alert/Condition Flooding
- Run Battery Down

PHY, Link Transceiver

The subcomponent that deals with PHY, MAC, and LINK layer issues. Potentially executes link layer cryptography algorithms.

Key Subcomponents: Registers, RAM, other storage, boot loader, internal programme storage, internal timing source, and architecture specific functionality

Key External Dependencies: RF Front End, NET & App Controller, data bus to NET & App Controller, external timing source, power supply, RF/EM environment, temperature environment

Potentially Vulnerable to: DoS, Disruption, Distortion, Spoofing, Snooping, live code injection, serial Bus tampering, reconfiguration, firmware analysis, firmware tampering, snooping side channels, environmental tampering, etc.

NET & APP Controller

The subcomponent that primarily focuses on executing any higher layer network functionality. This is generally an independent microprocessor or microcontroller that may also run the application.

Key Subcomponents: Registers, RAM, other storage, boot loader, internal programme storage, internal timing source, and architecture specific functionality

Key External Dependencies: PHY, Link Transceiver, external buses, data bus to the PHY, Link Transceiver, external timing source, power supply, RF/EM environment, temperature environment, external storage

Potentially Vulnerable to: DoS, Disruption, Distortion, Spoofing, Snooping, live code injection, serial Bus Tampering, reconfiguration, flash/RAM snooping, flash/RAM tampering, firmware analysis, firmware tampering, snooping side channels, environmental tampering, tampering of external flash, etc.

LOW-LEVEL DOCUMENT

On PC-class hardware, there are two basic mechanisms for sending rendering commands to the graphics device: PIO/ MMIO (see glossary for specific definitions) and DMA. The architecture described in this document is designed around DMA-style hardware, but can easily be extended to accommodate PIO/MMIO-style hardware.

- *Client* is a user-space X11 client which has been linked with various modules to support hardware-dependent direct rendering. Typical modules may include:
  - libGL.so, the standard OpenGL (or Mesa) library with our device and operating system independent acceleration and GLX modifications.
  - libDRI.so, our device-independent, operating-system dependent driver.
  - libHW3D.so, our *device-dependent* driver.
- X *server* is a user-space X server which has been modified with *device and operating-system independent* code to support DRI. It may be linked with other modules to support hardware-dependent direct rendering.

  Typical modules may include:
  - libDRI.so, our *device-independent, operating-system dependent* driver.
  - libH2D.so, our *device-dependent* driver. This library may provide hardware-specific 2D rendering, and 3D initialization and finalization routines that are not required by the client.
- *Kernel Driver* is a kernel-level device driver that performs the bulk of the DMA operations and

provides interfaces for synchronization. [Note: Although the driver functionality is hardware-dependent, the actual implementation of the driver may be done in a generic fashion, allowing all of the hardware-specific details to be abstracted into libH3D.so for loading into the Kernel Driver at DRI initialization time. An implementation of this type is desirable since the Kernel Driver will not then have to be updated for each new graphics device. The details of this implementation are discussed in an accompanying document, but are mentioned here to avoid later confusion.]

- PROTO is the standard X protocol transport layer (*e.g.*, a named pipe for a local client).
- SAREA is a special shared-memory area that we will implement as part of the DRI. This area will be used to communicate information from the X server to the client, and may also be used to share state information with the kernel. This area should not be confused with DMA buffers. This abstraction may be implemented as several different physical areas.
- DMA BUFFERS are memory areas used to buffer graphics device commands which will be sent to the hardware via DMA. These areas are not needed if memory-mapped IO (MMIO) is used exclusively to access the hardware.
- IOCTL is a special interface to the kernel device driver. Requests can be initiated by the user-space programme, and information can be transfered to and from the kernel. This interface incurs the overhead of a system call and memory copy for the information transfered. This abstract interface also includes the ability of the kernel to signal a listening user-space application (*e.g.*, the X server) via I/O on a device (which may, for example, signal the user-space application with the SIGIO signal).
- MMIO is direct memory-mapped access to the graphics device.

Initialization Analysis

The X server is the first application to run that is involved with direct rendering. After initializing its own resources, it starts the kernel device driver and waits for clients to connect. Then, when a direct rendering client connects, SAREA is created, the XFree86-GLX protocol is established, and other direct rendering resources are allocated. This section describes the operations necessary to bring the system to a steady state.

X Server Initialization

When the X server is started, several resources in both the X server and the kernel must be initialized if the GLX module is loaded. Obviously, before the X server can do anything with the 3D graphics device, it will load the GLX module if it is specified in the XFree86 configuration file. When the GLX module (which contains the GLX protocol decoding and event handling routines) is loaded, the device-independent DRI module will also be loaded. The DRI module will then call the graphics device-dependent module (containing both the 2D code and the 3D initialization code) to handle the resource allocation outlined below.

X *Resource Allocation Initialization*

Several global X resources need to be allocated to handle the client's 3D rendering requests. These resources include the frame buffer, texture memory, other ancillary buffers, display list space, and the SAREA.

Frame 3Buffer

There are several approaches to allocating buffers in the frame buffer: static, static with dynamic reallocation of the unused space, and fully dynamic. Static buffer allocation is the approach we are adopting in the sample implementation for several reasons that will be outlined below.

Static allocation. During initialization, the resources supported by the graphics device are statically allocated. For example, if the device supports front, back and depth buffers in the frame buffer, then the frame buffer is divided into four areas. The first three are equal in size to the visible display area and are used for the three buffers (front, back and depth). The remaining frame buffer space remains unallocated and can be used for hardware cursor, font and pixmap caches, textures, pbuffers, etc.

Texture memory

Texture memory is shared among all 3D rendering clients. On some types of graphics devices, it can be shared with other buffers, provided that these other buffers can be "kicked out" of the memory. On other devices, there is dedicated texture memory, which might or might not be sharable with other resources. Since memory is a limited resource, it would be best if we could provide a mechanism to limit the memory reserved for textures. However, the format of texture memory on certain graphics devices is organized differently (banked, tiled, etc.) than the simple linear addressing used for most frame buffers. Therefore, the "size" of texture memory is device-dependent. This complicates the issue of using a single number for the size of texture memory.

Another complication is that once the X server reports that a texture will fit in the graphics device memory, it must continue to fit for the life of the client (*i.e.*, the total texture memory for a client can never get smaller). Therefore, at initialization time, the maximum texture size and total texture memory available will need to be determined by the device-dependent driver. This driver will also provide a mechanism to determine if a set of textures will fit into texture memory.

Other Ancillary Buffers

All buffers associated with a window (*e.g.*, back, depth, and GID) are preallocated by the static frame-buffer allocation. Pixmap, pbuffers and other ancillary buffers are allocated out of the memory left after this static allocation.

During X server initialization, the size off-screen memory available for these buffers will be calculated by the device-dependent driver. Note that pbuffers can be "kicked out" (at least the old style could), and so they don't require virtualization like pixmaps and potentially the new style pbuffers.

Display Lists

For graphics devices that support display lists, the display list memory can be managed in the same way as texture memory. Otherwise, display lists will be held in the client virtual-address space.

SAREA

The SAREA is shared between the clients, the X server, and the kernel. It contains four segments that need to be shared: a per-device global hardware lock, per-context information, per-drawable information, and saved device state information.

- *Hardware lock segment.* Only one process can access the graphics device at a time. For atomic operations that require multiple accesses, a global hardware lock for each graphics device is required. Since the number of cards is known at server initialization time, the size of this segment is fixed.
- *Per-context segment.* Each GLXContext is associated with a particular drawable in the per-drawable segment and a particular graphics device state in the saved device state segment. Two pointers, one to the drawable that the GLXContext is currently bound and one to the saved device state is stored in the per-context segment. Since the number of GLXContexts is not known at server start up time, the size of this segment will need to grow. It is a reasonable assumption to limit the number of direct rendering contexts so the size of this segment can be fixed to a maximum. The X server is the only process that writes to this segment and it must maintain a list of available context slots that needs to be allocated and initialized.
- *Per-drawable segment.* Each drawable has certain information that needs to be shared between the X server and the direct rendering client:

- Buffer identification (*e.g.*, front/back buffer) (int32)
- Window information changed ID
- Flags (int32)

The window information changed ID signifies that the user has either moved, unmapped or resized the window, or the clipping information has changed and needs to be communicated to the client via the XFree86-GLX protocol.

Since OpenGL clients can create an arbitrary number of GLXDrawables, the size of this segment will need to grow. As with the per-context segment, the size of this segment can be limited to a fixed maximum. Again, the X server is the only process that writes to this segment, and it must maintain a list of available drawable slots that needs to be allocated and initialized.

- *Saved device state segment*. Each GLXContext needs to save the graphics hardware context when another GLXContext has ownership of the graphics device. This information is fixed in size for each graphics device, but will be allocated as needed because it can be quite large. In addition, if the graphics device can read/write its state information via DMA, this segment will need to be locked down during the request.

Kernel Initialization

When the X server opens the kernel device driver, the kernel loads and initializes the driver. See the next section for more details of the kernel device driver.

Double Buffer Optimizations

There are typically three approaches to hardware double buffering:

1. *Video Page Flipping*: The video logic is updated to refresh from a different page. This can happen very quickly with no per pixel copying required. This forces the entire screen region to be swapped.
2. *Bitblt Double Buffering*: The back buffer is stored in

offscreen memory and specific regions of the screen can be swapped by coping data from the offscreen to onscreen. This has a performance penality because of the overhead of copying the swapped data, but allows for fine grain independent control for multiple windows.

2. *Auxillary Per Pixel Control*: An additional layer contains information on a per pixel basis that is used to determine which buffer should be displayed. Swapping entire regions is much quicker than Bitblt Double Buffering and fine grain independed control for multiple windows is achieved. However, not all hardware or modes support this method.

If the hardware support Auxillary Per Pixel Control for the given mode, then that is the preferred method for double buffer support. However, if the hardware doesn't support Auxillary Per Pixel Control, then the following combined opproach to Video Page Flipping and Bitblt Double Buffering is a potential optimization.

- Initialize in a *Bitblt Double Buffering* mode. This allows for X Server performance to be optimized while not double buffering is required.
- Transition to a *Video Page Flipping* mode for the first window requiring double buffer support. This allows for the fastest possible double buffer swapping at the expense of requiring the X Server to render to both buffers. Note, for the transition, the contents of the front buffer will need to be copied to the back buffer and all further rendering will need to be duplicated in both buffers for all non-double buffered regions while in this mode.
- Transition back to *Bitblt Double Buffering* mode when additional double buffering windows are created. This will sacrifice performance for the sake of visual accuracy. Now all windows can be independently swapped.

In the initial SI, only the Bitblt Double Buffering mode will be implemented.

Kernel Driver Initialization

When the kernel device driver is opened by the X server, the device driver might not be loaded. If not, the module is loaded by kerneld and the initialization routine is called. In either case, the open routine is then called and finishes initializing the driver.

Kernel DMA Initialization

Since the 3D graphics device drivers use DMA to communicate with the graphics device, we need to initialize the kernel device driver that will handle these requests. The kernel, in response to this request from the X server, allocates the DMA buffers that will be made available to direct rendering clients.

Kernel Interrupt Handling Initialization

Interrupts are generated in a number of situations including when a DMA buffer has been processed by the graphics device. To acknowledge the interrupt, the driver must know which register to set and to what value to set it. This information could be hard coded into the driver, or possibly a generic interface might be able to be written. If this is possible, the X server must provide information to the kernel as to how to respond to interrupts from the graphics device.

Hardware Context Switching

Since the kernel device driver must be able to handle multiple 3D clients each with a different GLXContext, there must be a way to save and restore the hardware graphics context for each GLXContext when switching between them. Space for these contexts will need to be allocated when they are created byglXCreateContext(). If the client can use this hardware context (*e.g.*, for software fallbacks or window moves), this information might be stored in the SAREA.

Client DMA wait Queues

Each direct rendering context will require a DMA wait

queue from which its DMA buffers can be dispatched. These wait queues are allocated by the X server when a new GLXContext is created (glXCreateContext()).

Client Initialization

This section examines what happens before the client enters steady state behaviour. The basic sequence for direct-rendering client initialization is that the GL/GLX library is loaded, queries to the X server are made (*e.g.*, to determine the visuals/FBConfigs available and if direct rendering can be used), drawables and GLXContexts are created, and finally a GLXContext is associated with a drawable. This sequence assumes that the X server has already initialized the kernel device driver and has pre-allocated any static buffers requested by the user at server startup (as described above).

Library Loading

When a client is loaded, the GL/GLX library will automatically be loaded by the operating system, but the graphics device-specific module cannot be loaded until after the X server has informed the DRI module which driver to load (see below). The DRI module might not be loaded until after a direct rendering GLXContext has been requested.

Client Configuration Queries

During client initialization code, several configuration queries are commonly made. GLX has queries for its version number and a list of supported extensions. These requests are made through the standard GLX protocol stream. Since the set of supported extensions is device-dependent, similar queries in the device-dependent driver interface (in the X server) are provided that can be called by device-independent code in GLX.

One of the required GLX queries from the client is for the list of supported extended visuals (and FBConfigs in GLX 1.3). The visuals define the types of colour and ancillary buffers that are available and are device-dependent. The X server must provide the list of supported visuals (and

FBConfigs) via the standard protocol transport layer (*e.g.*, Unix domain or TCP/IP sockets). Again, similar interfaces in the device-dependent driver are provided that can be called by the device-independent code in GLX. All of this information is known at server initialization time (above).

Drawable creation

The client chooses the visual (or FBConfig) it needs and creates a drawable using the selected visual. If the drawable is a window, then, since we use a static resource allocation approach, the buffers are already allocated, and no additional frame buffer allocations are necessary at this time. However, if a dynamic resource allocation approach is added in the future, the buffers requested will need to be allocated.

Not all buffers need to be pre-allocated. For example, accumulation buffers can be emulated in software and might not be pre-allocated. If they are not, then, when the extended visual or FBConfig is associated with the drawable, the client library will need to allocate the accumulation buffer. In GLX 1.3, this can happen withglXCreateWindow(). For earlier versions of GLX, this will happen when a context is made current (below).

Pixmaps and Buffers

GLXPixmaps are created from an ordinary X11 pixmap, which is then passed to glXCreatePixmap(). GLXPbuffers are created directly by a GLX command. Since we are using a static allocation scheme, we know what ancillary buffers need to be created for these drawables. In the initial SI, these will be handled by indirect rendering or software fallbacks.

GLXContext creation

The client must also create at least one GLXContext. The last flag to glXCreateContext() is a flag to request direct rendering. The first GLXContext created can trigger the library to initialize the direct rendering interface for this client. Several steps are required to setup the DRI. First, the DRI library is loaded and initialized in the client and X server.

The DRI library establishes the private communication mechanism between the client and X server (the XFree86-GLX protocol). The X server sends the SAREA shared memory segment ID to the client via this protocol and the client attaches to it. Next, the X server sends the device-dependent client side 3D graphics device driver module name to client via the XFree86-GLX protocol, which is loaded and initialized in the client.

The X server calls the kernel module to create a new WaitQueue and hardware graphics context corresponding to the new GLXContext. Finally, the client opens and initializes the kernel driver (including a request for DMA buffers).

Making a GLXContext current

The last stage before entering the steady state behaviour occurs when a GLXContext is associated with a GLXDrawable by making the context "current". This must occur before any 3D rendering can begin. The first time a GLXDrawable is bound to a direct rendering GLXContext it is registered with the X server and any buffers not already allocated are now allocated. If the GLXDrawable is a window that has not been mapped yet, then the buffers associated with the window are initialized to size zero. When a window is mapped, space in the pre-allocated static buffers are initialized, or in the case of dynamic allocation, buffers are allocated from the available offscreen area (if possible).

For GLX 1.2 (and older versions), some ancillary buffers (*e.g.*, stencil or accumulation), that are not supported by the graphics device, or unavailable due to either resource constraints or their being turned off through X server config options (see above), might need to be allocated.

At this point, the client can enter the steady-state by making OpenGL calls.

Steady-state Analysis

The initial steady-state analysis presented here assumes that the client(s) and X server have been started and have established all necessary communication channels (*e.g.*, the

X, GLX and XFree86-GLX protocol streams and the SAREA segment). In the following analysis, we will impose simplifying assumptions to help direct the analysis towards the main line rendering case. We will then relax our initial assumptions and describe increasingly general cases.

Single 3D Client (1 GLXContext, 1 GLXWindow), X Server Inactive

Assume: No X server activity (including hardware cursor movement). This is the optimized main line rendering case. The primary goal is to generate graphics device specific commands and stuff them in a DMA buffer as fast as possible. Since the X server is completely inactive, any overhead due to locking should be minimized.

Processing rendering requests

In the simplest case, rendering commands can be sent to the graphics device by putting them in a DMA buffer. Once a DMA buffer is full and needs to be dispatched to the graphics device, the buffer can be handed immediately to the kernel via an ioctl.

The kernel then schedules the DMA command buffer to be sent to the graphics device. If the graphics device is not busy (or the DMA input queue is not full), it can be immediately sent to the graphics device. Otherwise, it is put on the WaitQueue for the current context.

In hardware that can only process a single DMA buffer at a time, when the DMA buffer has finished processing, an IRQ is generated by the graphics device and handled by the kernel driver.

In hardware that has a DMA input FIFO, IRQs can be generated after each buffer, after the input FIFO is empty or (in certain hardware) when a low-water mark has been reached. For both types of hardware, the kernel device driver resets the IRQ and schedules the next DMA buffer(s).

A further optimization for graphics devices that have input FIFOs for DMA requests is that if the FIFO is not full, the DMA request could be initiated directly from client space.

Synchronization

GLX has commands to synchronize direct rendering with indirect rendering or with ordinary X11 operations. These include glFlush(), glFinish(), glXWaitGL() and glXWaitX() synchronization primitives. The kernel driver provides several ioctls to handle each of the synchronization cases. In the simplest case (glFlush()), any partially filled DMA buffer will be sent to the kernel.

Since these will eventually be processed by the hardware, the function call can return. WithglFinish(), in addition to sending any partially filled DMA buffer to the kernel, the kernel will block the client process until all outstanding DMA requests have been completely processed by the graphics device. glXWaitGL() can be implemented using glFlush(), glXWaitX() can be implemented with XSync().

Buffer Swaps

Buffers swaps can be initiated by glXSwapBuffers(). When a client issues this request, any partially filled DMA buffers are sent to the kernel and all outstanding DMA buffers are processed before the buffer swap can take place. All subsequent rendering commands are blocked until the buffer has been swapped, but the client is not blocked and can continue to fill DMA buffers and send them to the kernel.

If multiple threads are rendering to a GLXDrawable, it is the client's responsibility to synchronize the threads. In addition, the idea of the *current* buffer (*e.g.*, front or back) must be shared by all GLXContexts bound to a given drawable. The X double buffer extension must also agree.

Kernel-driver Buffer Swap Ioctl

When the buffer swap ioctl is called, a special DMA buffer with the swap command is placed into the current GLXContext's WaitQueue. Because of sequentiality of the DMA buffers in the WaitQueue, all DMA buffers behind this are blocked until all DMA buffers in front of this one have been processed. The header information associated with this buffer lets the scheduler know how to handle the request.

There are three ways to handle the buffer swap:

1. *No vert sync*: Immediately schedule the buffer swap and allow subsequent DMA buffers in the WaitQueue to be scheduled. With this policy there will be tearing. In the initial SI, we will implement this policy.
2. *Wait for vert sync*: Wait for the vertical retrace IRQ to schedule the buffer swap command and allow subsequent DMA buffers in the WaitQueue to be scheduled. With this policy, the tearing should be reduced, but there might still be some tearing if a DMA input FIFO is present and relatively full.
3. *No tearing*: Wait for vertical retrace IRQ and all DMA buffers in the input FIFO to be processed before scheduling the buffer swap command. Since the buffer swap is a very fast bitblt operation, no tearing should be present with this policy.

Software Fallbacks

Not all OpenGL graphics primitives are accelerated in all hardware. For those not supported directly by the graphics device, software fallbacks will be required. Mesa and SGI's OpenGL SI provide a mechanism to implement these fallbacks; however, the hardware graphics context state needs to be translated into the format required by these libraries. The hardware graphics context state can be read from the saved device state segment of SAREA. An implicit glFinish() is issued before the software fallback can be initiated to ensure that the graphics state is up to date before beginning the software fallback. The hardware lock is required to alter any device state.

Image Transfer Operations

Many image transfer operations are required in the client-side direct rendering library. Initially these will be software routines that read directly from the memory mapped graphics device buffers (*e.g.*, frame buffer and texture buffer). These are device-dependent operations since the format of the transfer might be different, though certain abstractions should be possible (*e.g.*, linear buffers). An optimization is to allow the client to perform DMA directly to/from the client's address space. Some hardware has support for page table translation and paging. Other hardware will require the ability to lock down pages and have them placed contiguously in physical memory.

The X server will need to manage how the frame and other buffers are allocated at the highest level. The layout of these buffers is determined at X server initialization time.

Texture Management

Each GLXContext appears to own the texture memory. In the present case, there is no contention. In subsequent cases, hardware context switching will take care of texture swapping as well (see below).

For a single context, the image transfer operations described above provides the necessary interfaces to transfer textures and subtextures to/from texture memory.

Display List Management

Display lists initially will be handled from within the client's virtual address space. For graphics devices that supports display lists, they can be stored and managed the same as texture memory

Selection and Feedback

If there is hardware support for selection and feedback, the rendering commands are sent to the graphics pipeline, which returns the requested data to the client. The amount of data can be quite large and are usually delivered to a collection of locked-down pages via DMA. The kernel should provide a mechanism for locking down pages in the client address space to hold the DMA buffer.

Queries

Queries are handled similarly to selection and feedback, but the data returned are usually much smaller. When a query is made, the hardware graphics context state has to be read.

If the GLXContext does not currently own the graphics device, the state can be read from the saved device state segment in SAREA. Otherwise, the graphics pipeline is temporarily stalled, so that the state can be read from the graphics device.

Events

GLX has a "pbuffer clobbered" event. This can only be generated as a result of reconfiguring a drawable or creating a new one. Since pbuffers will initially be handled by the software, no clobbered events will be generated. However, when they are accelerated, the X server will have to wrap the appropriate routine to determine when the event needs to be generated.

Single 3D Client (1 GLXContext, 1 GLXWindow), X Server can Draw

Assume: X server can draw (*e.g.*, 2D rendering) into other windows, but does not move the 3D window. This is a common case and should be optimized if possible. The only significant different between this case and the previous case, is that we must now lock the hardware before accessing the graphics device directly directly from the client, X server or kernel space.

The goal is to minimize state transitions and potentially avoid a full hardware graphics context switch by allowing the X server to save and restore 3D state around its access for GUI acceleration.

Hardware Lock

Access to graphics device must be locked, either implicitly or explicitly. Each component of the system requires the hardware lock at some point. For the X server, the hardware lock is required when drawing or modifying any state. It is requested around blocks of 2D rendering, minimizing the potential graphics hardware context switches.

In the 3D client, the hardware lock is required during the software fallbacks (all other graphics device accesses are handled through DMA buffers). The kernel also must request the lock when it needs to send DMA requests to the graphics device. The hardware lock is contained in the *Hardware lock segment* of the SAREA which can be accessed by all system components. A two-tiered locking scheme is used to minimize the process and kernel context switches necessary to grant the lock. The most common case, where a lock is requested by the last process to hold the lock, does not require any context switches. See the accompanying locks.txt file for more information on two-tiered locking (available late February 1999).

Graphics Hardware Context Switching

In addition to locking the graphics device, a graphics hardware context switch between the client and the X server is required. One possible solution is to perform a full context switch by the kernel (see the "multiple contexts" section below for a full explanation of how a full graphics hardware context switch is handled). However, the X server is a special case since it knows exactly when a context switch is required and what state needs to be saved and restored.

For the X server, the graphics hardware context switch is required only (a) when directly accessing the graphics device and (b) when the access changes the state of the graphics device. When this occurs, the X server can save the graphics device state (either via a DMA request or by reading the registers directly) before it performs its rendering commands and restore the graphics device state after it finishes.

Three examples will help clarify the situations where this type of optimization can be useful. First, using a cfb/mi routine to draw a line only accesses the frame buffer and does not alter any graphics device state. Second, on many vendor's cards changing the position of the hardware cursor does not affect the graphics device state. Third, certain graphics devices have two completely separate pipelines for 2D and 3D commands. If no 2D and 3D state is shared, then they can proceed independently (but usually not simultaneously, so the hardware lock is still required).

Single 3D Client (1 GLXContext, 1 GLXWindow), X Server Active

Assume: X server can move or resize the single 3D window. When the X server moves or resizes the 3D window, the client needs to stop drawing long enough for the X server to change the window, and it also needs to request the new window location, size and clipping information. Current 3D graphics devices can draw using window relative coordinates, though the window offset might not be able to be updated asynchronously (*i.e.*, it might only be possible to update this information between DMA buffers). Since this is an infrequent operation, it should be designed to have minimal impact on the other, higher priority cases.

X Server Operations

On the X server side, when a window move is performed, several operations must occur. First, the DMA buffers currently being processed by the graphics device must be completely processed before proceeding since they might associated with the old window position (unless the graphics device allows asynchronous window updates). Next, the X server grabs the hardware lock and waits for the graphics device to become quiescent.

It then issues a bitblt to move the window and all of its associated buffers. It updates the window location in all of the contexts associated with the window, and increments the "Window information changed" ID in the SAREA to notify all clients rendering to the window of the change. It can then release the hardware lock.

Since the graphics hardware context has been updated with the new window offset, any outstanding DMA buffers for the context associated with the moved window will have the new window offset and thus will render at the correct screen location. The situation is slightly more complicated with window resizes or changes to the clipping information.

When a window is resized or when the clipping information changes due to another window popping up on top of the 3D window, outstanding DMA buffers might draw outside of the new window (if the window was made smaller). If the graphics device supports clipping planes, then this information can be updated in the graphics hardware context between DMA buffers.

However, for devices that only support clipping rectangles, the outstanding DMA requests cannot be altered with the new clipping rects.

To minimize this effect, the X server can:

- Flush the DMA buffers in all contexts' WaitQueues associated with the window,
- Wait for these DMA buffers to be processed by the graphics device. However, this does not completely solve the problem as there could be a partially filled DMA buffer in the client(s) rendering to the window (see below).

3D Client Operations

On the client side, during each rendering operation, the client checks to see if it has the most current window information. If it does, then it can proceed as normal. However, if the X server has changed the window location, size or clipping information, the client issues a XFree86-DRI protocol request to get the new information.

See the accompanying XFree86-DRI.txt file for more information on the XFree86-DRI protocol implementation. This information will be mainly used for software fallbacks. Since there could be several outstanding requests in the partially filled "current" DMA buffer, the rendering commands already in this buffer might draw outside of the window. The simplest solution to this problem is to send an expose event to the windows that are affected.

This could be accomplished as follows:

- Send the partially filled DMA buffer to the kernel,
- Wait for it to be processed,
- Generate a list of screen-relative rectangles for the affected region,
- Send a request to the X server to generate an expose event in the windows that overlap with that region.

On graphics devices that do not allow the window offset to be updated between DMA buffers, the situation described above will also occur for window moves. The "generate expose events" solution also will be used to solve the problem. It is not known at this time if any graphics devices of this type exist.

Multiple 3D Clients

Assume: There are now multiple 3D clients, each of which has their own GLXContext(s). As with the previous case, multiple GLXContexts are actively used in rendering, and this case can be handled the same as the previous one.

Finalization Analysis

This section examines what happens after exiting steady state behaviour via destroying a rendering surface or context, or via process termination. Process suspension and switching virtual consoles are special cases and are dealt with in this section.

Destroying a Drawing Surface

If the drawing surface is a window, it can be destroyed by the window manager. When this occurs, the X server must notify the direct rendering client that the window was destroyed. However, before the window can be removed, the X server must wait until all outstanding DMA buffer requests associated with the window have been completely processed in order to avoid rendering to the destroyed window after it has been removed. When the client tries to draw to the window again, it recognizes that the window is no longer valid and cleans up its internal state associated with the window (*e.g.*, any local ancillary buffer), and returns an error. GLX 1.3 uses glXDestroyWindow() to explicitly notify the system that the window is no longer associated with GLX, and that its resources should be freed.

Destroying a GLXContext

Since there are limited context slots available in the per-context segment of SAREA, a GLXContext's resources can be freed by calling glXDestroyContext()when it is no longer needed. If the GLXContext is current to any thread, the context cannot be destroyed until it is no longer current. When this happens, the X server marks the GLXContext's per-context slot as free, frees the saved device state, and notifies the kernel that the WaitQueue can be freed.

Destroying Shared Resources

Texture objects and display lists can be shared by multiple GLXContexts. When a context is destroyed in the share list, the reference count should be decremented. If the reference count of the texture objects and/or display lists is zero, they can be freed as well.

Process Finalization

When a process exits, its direct rendering resources should be freed and returned to the X server.

Graceful Termination

If the termination is expected, the resources associated with the process are freed. The kernel reclaims its DMA buffers from the client. The X server frees the GLXDrawables and GLXContexts associated with the client. In the process of freeing the GLXContexts, the X server notifies the kernel that it should free any WaitQueues associated with the GLXContexts it is freeing. The saved device state is freed. The reference count to the SAREA is decremented. Finally, any additional resources used by the GLX and XFree86-GLX protocol streams are freed.

Unexpected Termination

Detecting the client death is the hardest part of unexpected process termination. Once detected, the resources are freed as in the graceful termination case outlined above. The kernel detects when a direct rendering client process dies since it has registered itself with the kernel exit procedure. If the client does not hold the hardware lock, then it can proceed as in the graceful termination case. If the hardware lock is held, the lock is broken. The graphics device might be in an unusable state (*e.g.*, waiting for data during a texture upload), and might need to be reset. After reset, the graceful termination case can proceed.

Process Suspension

Processes can suspend themselves via a signal that cannot be blocked, SIGSTOP. If the process holds the hardware lock during this time, the SIGSTOP signal must be delayed until the lock is freed. This can be handled in the kernel. As an initial approximation, the kernel can turn off SIGSTOP for all direct rendering clients.

Switching Virtual Consoles

XFree86 has the ability to switch to a different virtual console when the X server is running. This action causes the X server to draw to a copy of the frame buffer in the X server virtual address space. For direct rendering clients, this solution is not possible. A simple solution to use in the initial SI is to halt all direct access to the graphics device by grabbing the hardware lock.

In addition to switching virtual consoles, XFree86 can be started on multiple consoles (with different displays). Initially, only the first display will support direct rendering.

Future Enhancements

MMIO

This architecture has been designed with MMIO based 3D solution in mind, but the initial SI will be optimized for DMA based solutions. A more complete MMIO driven implementation can be added later. Base support in the initial SI that will be useful for an MMIO-only solution is unprivileged mapping of MMIO regions and a fast two-tier lock. Additional optimizations that will be useful are virtualizing the hardware via a page fault mechanism and a mechanism for updating shared library pointers directly.

Device-specific Kernel Driver

Several optimizations (mentioned above) can be added by allowing a device-specific kernel driver to hook out certain functions in the generic kernel driver.

Other Enhancements

We should consider additional enhancements including:

- Multiple displays and multiple screens
- More complex buffer swapping (cushion buffering, swap every N retraces, synchronous window swapping)

Glossary

MMIO

Memory-Mapped Input-Output. In this document, we use the term MMIO to refer to operations that access a region of graphics card memory that has been memory-mapped into the virtual address space, or to operations that access graphics hardware registers via a memory-mapping of the registers into the virtual address space (in contrast to PIO).

Note that graphics hardware "registers" may actually be pseudo-registers that provide access to the hardware FIFO command queue.

PIO

Programmed Input-Output. In this document, we use the term PIO to refer specifically to operations that *must* use the Intel in and out instructions (or equivalent non-Intel instructions) to access the graphics hardware (in contrast to using memory-mapped graphics hardware registers, which allow for the use ofmov instructions).

MODULARIZATION

MODULAR SOFTWARE DESIGN

In order to produce programmes that are readable, reliable, and can be easily maintained or modified, one must use modular software design. This means that, instead of having a large collection of statements strung together in one partition of in-line code, we segment or divide the statements into logical groups called modules. Each module performs one or two tasks, then passes control to another module. By breaking up the code into "bite-sized chunks", so to speak, we are able to better control the flow of data and control. This is especially true in large software systems.

OVERVIEW OF MODULAR SOFTWARE DESIGN

We begin with several definitions (*Hint:* These may be useful to learn for a future exam) in support of a brief discussion of software design goals. We then progress to examples of code segmentation.

Observation

In the early days of computer programming, when people coded programmes in *machine code* (ones and zeroes), it was quite difficult to determine programme function and structure from looking at the code. Humans tend to look at problems solved on a computer in a linguistic sort of way, *i.e.*, expect some flow of control or data to be expressed in the programming language. Ones and zeros don't tell us much, and they certainly give little indication of programme structure or data/control flow.

Definition

Spaghetti code is the term used for a computer programme that is not well structured and tends to have highly tangled flows of data and control.

Example

Most *assembly language code* and *machine code* are good examples of spaghetti code. The following sample of machine code is illustrative:

```
110101010010001000111001001
010101001000100001011101001
000111001101110001101101010
```

001111010010010101011001010
001010101111110100101010001

Clearly, there is very little discernable structure in this type of code. Definition In programming languages, the *semantic gap* is the difference between the language you use to programme the hardware (machine code) and the language you would like to use to programme the computer as a system. We call the latter, more abstract language a *high-level language* or HLL.

Observation

Throughout the history of computing, there have been at least hundreds of attempts to make computer programming languages something like English — easy to read and implicitly easy to understand. PASCAL is the result of one such effort. The co-creator of PASCAL, Nicholas Wirth, wanted to have an HLL that was easy to learn, read, and write.

So, he designed PASCAL around the following concepts:

- PASCAL should close or significantly narrow the semantic gap.
- Every PASCAL statement should be like a *clause* in an English-language sentence.
- The PASCAL programme can be thought of as a *sentence* in English (namely, a concatenation of clauses).
- Names of procedures, data structures, and variables in PASCAL should be easily recognizable.

Remark. PASCAL facilitates modular coding via:

- Encapsulating code in PROCEDUREs and FUNCTIONs that constitute a PROGRAMME;
- The use of BEGIN and END statements to define a functional block of code;
- Strict *variable typing* (*i.e.*, assigning datatypes such as *integer*, *real*, or *string* to variables) in support of parameter passing between procedures; and
- User-friendly syntax that narrows (but does not close) the semantic gap.

In the 1960s and 1970s, software designers were faced with large accumulations of spaghetti code from preceding years. Programmes were becoming more complex, and it was more difficult to keep software running correctly. After trying various strategies for organizing this morass of code, the following guidelines for software development emerged:

- *Clarity*: Code must be easily understandable by humans, and variable/function names should have obvious meaning.
- *Modularity*: Programmes must be divided into small modules.
- *Concision*: Modules must perform a few tasks only, using compact (but not cryptic) notation.
- *Reliability*: Programmes must run correctly, in a repeatable manner.
- *Ease of Maintenance*: Software must be easy to maintain and modify, and must be accompanied by comprehensive documentation.

Clearly written software is often an elusive goal, because technical programmers tend to prefer cryptic variable names (*e.g.*, PR2CD$ instead of clear notation such as PRICE). Furthermore, there are many programmers who do not have good writing skills, and definitely don't enjoy writing documentation. Thus, to be a good programmer, must concentrate on improving the quality of your software not only through careful design and programming, but also through careful documentation.

Modular code is easy to produce from a design, but often hard to produce from spaghetti code. We discuss this process below, where we show general examples of code modularization. Modern software development tools facilitate the generation of modular code, and often check syntax of programming statements, with some variable type checking possible. Thus, there exists a variety of evolving techniques for software design in modular form.

Concisely written code is important to ensuring proper programme function. For example, if your code is so tangled that you can't determine what it does, how easy will it be for others to understand your work? It is also important not to create excessively complicated procedures, which are difficult to debug and maintain, and thus tend to be unreliable.

Software reliability follows from rigorous software design, checking one's work, and carefully debugging and testing the software you write in an incremental fashion. By *incremental development,* we mean the construction of a software system and testing of that software on a piece-by-piece basis. For example, after you write the lowest-level routines, you should test them all thoroughly before you write the functions or procedures that call those routines.

PASCAL PROCEDURAL ORGANIZATION

PASCAL supports *hierarchical programme structure,* in which there is a high-level procedure, often called the *main programme* or *root procedure.* Other procedures are subordinate to the root procedure, and may call each other, but usually do not call the root procedure. Each procedure is comprised of*statements,* which are lines of code that perform a given function.

The PASCAL language provides three methods for encapsulating code in procedures. First, the FUNCTION statement specifies a function that accepts values from its argument list and returns a value or result through the function name. Second, the PROCEDURE statement specifies a procedure that accepts values from its argument list and returns one or more values through its argument list.

Third, the PROGRAMME statement allows the programmer to specify high-level source code that calls predefined procedures to implement a structured software system. We define these statements as follows:

Programme Specification Statement

Purpose: The Programme statement specifies the name of a main programme (*i.e.,* the top-level procedure).

Syntax:

```
PROGRAM program-name ( input-file , output-
file ) ; where
```

```
program-name denotes the name of the program
input-file denotes the name of the file from which the program reads input
output-file denotes the filename to which the program writes output.
```

Example:

```
PROGRAM Progl (myfile.dat, myfile.rpt);
PROGRAM Progl;
```

Function Specification Statement

Purpose: The Function statement specifies the name of a procedure that inputs values through its argument list and can be thought of as returning a result through its name.

Syntax:

```
FUNCTION function-name ( argument- 1 ..., argument-N ); where
function-name denotes the name of the function
argument-i denotes the name of the i-th argument of the function.
```

Example:

```
FUNCTION sine(x);
FUNCTION Distance(x,y);
```

Notes: Do not try to pass output values through the argument list of a function. This can cause problems in some PASCAL implementations.

Procedure Specification Statement

Purpose: The Procedure statement specifies the name of a procedure that can input and output values through its argument list.

Syntax:

```
PROCEDURE proc-name ( argument- 1 ..., argument-N ); where
proc-name denotes the name of the procedure
argument-i denotes the name of the i-th argument of the procedure.
```

Example:

```
PROCEDURE  sine(x,output);
PROCEDURE  Distance(x,y,output);
PROCEDURE  Smile;
```

BEGIN...END Block Specification Statement

Purpose: The BEGIN...END statement delimits a block of *compound statements*.

Syntax: `BEGIN andltstatements> END` where statements denotes more than one Pascal statement.

Example:

```
BEGIN
  WRITELN('Hello,  world');
  WRITELN('Second  statement');
  WRITELN('Last  statement');
END;
```

General Comments

Indentation is used to highlight and clarify programme structure. For example, each new level of statements should be indented two or three spaces to the right. When a block of statements is closed (*e.g.*, with an END statement), then the indent shifts two or three spaces to the left. Each statement begins on a new line, except for multiple short assignment statements that initialize values in a programme.

PASCAL VARIABLES AND DATATYPES

Programming languages use abstractions called *variables* to store values. Because there are many different types of values (*e.g.*, integer, real, string, etc.), there exists a method called *datatyping* by which one such type can be assigned to each variable. PASCAL supports *strict typing*, that is, the datatype is assigned to the variable at compile time and does not change thereafter.

In PASCAL, valid datatypes that we will consider in this class are:

- *Integer*: a whole number, such as 1, 2, etc.;
- *Real*: a decimal number, such as -22.7, 231.8942, etc.;

- *Char*: a single character, such as 'H' or 'i';
- *String* : A list of characters, such as 'Hello'; and
- *Array* : A list of variables, such as (1.1, 2.4..., 3.7) or a two-dimensional array. Higher-dimensional structures are possible.

Most (but not all) compiled languages adopt the strict typing convention, to simplify compiler design and maintenance. However, there are some interpreted languages (*e.g.*, SNOBOL) that allow flexible datatyping. This can produce great difficulty when debugging a programme in which a given variable's value is type-dependent.

In PASCAL, a variable name is any string of valid PASCAL characters. We recommend that you use the characters {A-Z,a-z,0-9,_} for your variable names.

The following example is illustrative:

```
VALID NAMES          INVALID NAMES
Cost, Price          $amount, @price
score                score+exam-grade
```

In each case of invalid names, reserved symbols or characters that have multiple meanings are used in the name string. This is bad practice that can lead to compiler errors (*i.e.*, your programme won't compile), or can lead to confusion when debugging or modifying programmes that contain such names.

VAR Specification Statement

Purpose: The VARiable statement specifies the name and datatype of procedure or programme variables.

Syntax:

```
VAR varname-1...,varname N : datatype )
; where
    varname-i denotes the name of the i-th
    variable in the list
    datatype denotes a valid PASCAL datatype
```

Example:

```
VAR x,y,z: integer;
VAR sum,prod: real;
VAR name,ssn: string;
```

Notes: It is good programming style to specify only one datatype in each VAR statement. It is also good style not to continue VAR statements on multiple lines. This makes the programme easier to read. We next consider the issue of *scope of variables*. This issue is discussed in detail in Chapter 6 of Koffman, the textbook for t12his class, from which we condense the following discussion.

In above, we illustrate the following procedure nesting hierarchy:

`(Nest > (Outer > Inner, Too))`

The statements in each procedure operate only on *local variables*. This is good programming practice, and facilitates modularity. If we were to use*global variables*, which are declared once at the beginning of the main programme and then hold through all procedures, this would be bad software engineering practice, because:

- Global variables lead to confusion in debugging, when trying to trace variable types through many pages of code.
- Global variables are convenient to programmers, but they do not make procedures re-usable, since there is no variable declaration at the top of the procedure. In the absence of proper documentation, one cannot know for sure what datatype is assigned to a given variable. This adversely impacts the clarity, reliability, and maintainability of software.

MODULAR DESIGN

The basic idea underlying modular design is to organize a complex system (such as a large programme, an electronic circuit, or a mechanical device) as a set of distinct components that can be developed independently and then plugged together. Although this may appear a simple idea, experience shows that the effectiveness of the technique depends critically on the manner in which systems are divided into components and the mechanisms used to plug components together.

Provide Simple Interfaces

Simple interfaces reduce the number of interactions that

must be considered when verifying that a system performs its intended function. Simple interfaces also make it easier to reuse components in different circumstances. Reuse is a major cost saver. Not only does it reduce time spent in coding, design, and testing, but it also allows development costs to be amortized over many projects. Numerous studies have shown that reusing software is by far the most effective technique for reducing software development costs. As an example, a modular implementation of a climate modeling system may define distinct modules concerned with atmosphere modeling, ocean modeling, etc. The interfaces to each module can comprise a small set of procedures that access boundary data, advance the simulation, and so on.

Ensure that Modules Hide Information

The benefits of modularity do not follow automatically from the act of subdividing a programme. The way in which a programme is decomposed can make an enormous difference to how easily the programme can be implemented and modified. Experience shows that each module should encapsulate information that is not available to the rest of a programme. This*information hiding* reduces the cost of subsequent design changes.

For example, a module may encapsulate:

- Related functions that can benefit from a common implementation or that are used in many parts of a system,
- Functionality that is likely to change during later design or deployment,
- Aspects of a problem that are particularly complex, and/or
- Code that is expected to be reused in other programmes.

Use Appropriate Tools

While modular designs can in principle be implemented in any programming language, implementation is easier if the language supports information hiding by permitting the encapsulation of code and data structures. Fundamental mechanisms in this regard include the procedure (or subroutine or function) with its locally scoped variables and argument list, used to encapsulate code; the user-defined datatype, used to encapsulate data; and dynamic memory allocation, which allows subprograms to acquire storage without the involvement of the calling programme. These features are supported by most modern languages (*e.g.*, C++, Fortran 90, and Ada) but are lacking or rudimentary in some older languages (*e.g.*, Fortran 77).

Design Checklist

The following design checklist can be used to evaluate the success of a modular design. As usual, each question should be answered in the affirmative.

- Does the design identify clearly defined modules?
- Does each module have a clearly defined purpose? (Can you summarize it in one sentence?)
- Is each module's interface sufficiently abstract that you do not need to think about its implementation in order to understand it? Does it hide its implementation details from other modules?
- Have you subdivided modules as far as usefully possible?
- Have you verified that different modules do not replicate functionality?
- Have you isolated those aspects of the design that are most hardware specific, complex, or otherwise likely to change?

Example Database Search

We use a simple example to illustrate how information hiding considerations can influence design. To search a database for records matching a specified search pattern, we must read the database, search the database, and write any matching records found. One possible decomposition of this problem defines input, search, and output modules with the following interfaces.

```
input(in_file, database)
search(database, search_pattern,
matches)
output(out_file, database, matches)
```

An examination of what must be done to read a database, perform a search, and so on could then lead us to define the procedures that comprise the input, search, and output modules. This design provides simple interfaces. However, all three modules depend on the internal representation used for the database, and hence must be modified if this representation is changed. In addition, each module probably duplicates database access functions.

STRUCTURAL CHARTS

A Structure Chart (SC) in software engineering and organizational theory is achart, which shows the breakdown of the configuration system to the lowest manageable levels. It is used to show the hierarchical arrangement of the modules in a structured programme. Each rectangular box represents a module. The names of the modules are written inside the box. An arrow joins two modules that have an invocation relationship.

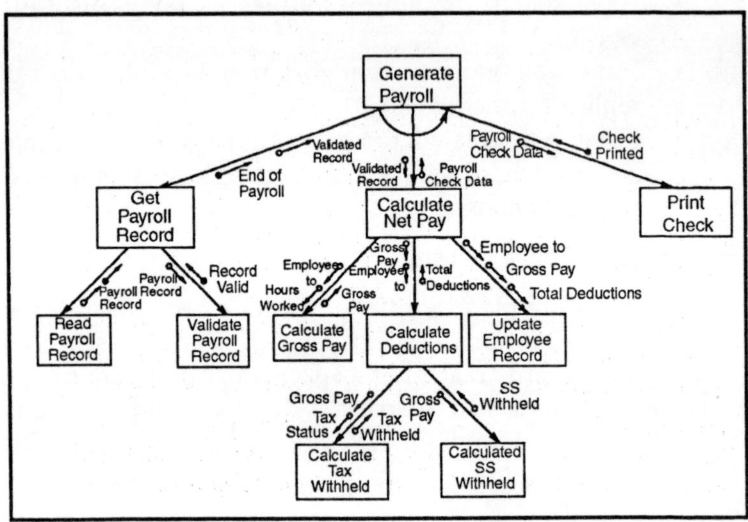

A structure chart is a top-down modular design tool, constructed of squares representing the different modules in the system, and lines that connect them. The lines represent the connection and or ownership between activities and subactivities as they are used inorganization charts. In structured analysis structure charts, according to Wolber (2009), "are used to specify the high-level design, or architecture, of a computer programme.

As a design tool, they aid the programmer in dividing and conquering a large software problem, that is, recursively breaking a problem down into parts that are small enough to be understood by a human brain. The process is called top-down design, or functional decomposition.

Programmers use a structure chart to build a programme in a manner similar to how an architect uses a blueprint to build a house.

In the design stage, the chart is drawn and used as a way for the client and the various software designers to communicate. During the actual building of the programme (implementation), the chart is continually referred to as the master-plan".

A structure chart depicts:

- The size and complexity of the system, and
- Number of readily identifiable functions and modules within each function.

A structure chart is also used to diagram associated elements that comprise a run stream or thread. It is often developed as a hierarchical diagram, but other representations are allowable. The representation must describe the breakdown of the configuration system into subsystems and the lowest manageable level.

An accurate and complete structure chart is the key to the determination of the configuration items, and avisual representation of the configuration system and the internal interfaces among its CIs.

During the configuration control process, the structure chart is used to identify CIs and their associated artifacts that a proposed change may impact.

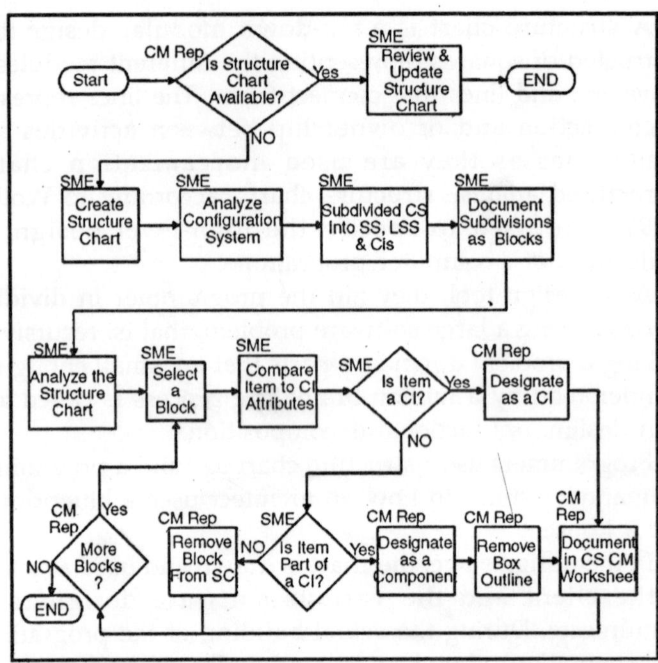

According to Wolber, "a structure chart can be developed starting with the creating of a structure, which places the root of an upside-down tree which forms the structure chart. The next step is to conceptualize the main sub-tasks that must be performed by the programme to solve the problem. Next, the programmer focuses on each sub-task individually, and conceptualizes how each can be broken down into even smaller tasks. Eventually, the programme is broken down to a point where the leaves of the tree represent simple methods that can be coded with just a few programme statements". In practice, see figure, first is checked is a Structure Chart has been developed already. If so an expert need to review to ensure it represents the current structure and update the chart where needed.

DESIGN STRUCTURE CHART

Once the flow of data and control in the system is decided using tools like DFDs and CFDs, the system is given shape through programming. Prior to this, the basic infrastructure of the programme layout is prepared based on the concepts of modular programming. In modular programming, the complete system is coded as small independent interacting modules. Each module is aimed at doing one specific task. The design for these modules is prepared in the form of structure charts. A structure chart is a design tool that pictorially shows the relation between processing modules in computer software. Describes the hierarchy of components modules and the data are transmitted between them. Includes analysis of input-to-output transformations and analysis of transaction.

Structure charts show the relation of processing modules in computer software. It is a design tool that visually displays the relationships between programme modules. It shows which module within a system interacts and graphically depicts the data that are communicated between various modules. Structure charts are developed prior to the writing of programme code. They identify the data passes existing between individual modules that interact with one another.

They are not intended to express procedural logic. This task is left to flowcharts and pseudocode. They don't describe the actual physical interface between processing functions.

Data Passing

When one module calls another, the calling module can send data to the called module so that it can perform the function described in its name. The called module can produce data that are passed back to the calling module. Two types of data are transmitted. The first, parameter data, are items of data needed in the called module to perform the necessary work.

A small arrow with an open circle at the end is used to note the passing of data parameters. In addition, control information (flag data) is also passed. Its purpose is to assist in the control of processing by indicating the occurrence of, say, errors or end-of-conditions. A small arrow with a closed circle indicates the control information. A brief annotation describes the type of information passed. Structure chart is a tool to assist the analyst in developing software that meets the objectives of good software design.

PSEUDO CODES

Pseudo-code is a non-formal language, a way to create a logical structure, describing the actions, which will be executed by the application. Using pseudo-code, the developer describes the application logic using his native language, without applying the structural rules of a specific programming language.

The big plus of the pseudo-code is that the application logic can be easily understood by any developer in the development team (in this case, it doesn't depend, which programming language knows each team member). Also, when the application algorithm is described in pseudo-code, it is very easy to transform the pseudo-code into real code (using any programming language).

For a better understanding of what is pseudo-code, let's take a look at an example. Suppose that you have to develop an application, that gets the number of students in a high school and then it gets each student's final grade (100, 90, 80, 60 and 50) and processes the average grade for the whole school. Instead of creating the programme at a computer, let's describe the application logic using pseudo-code. First, I will describe the general purpose of the application:

Pseudo-Code is simply a numbered list of instructions to perform some task. In this course we will enforce three standards for good pseudo code

1. *Number each instruction*: This is to enforce the notion of an *ordered sequence of... operations*. Furthermore we introduce a *dot* notation (*e.g.* 3.1 come*after* 3 but *before* 4) to number subordinate operations for conditional and iterative operations
2. Each instruction should be *unambiguous* (that is the computing agent, in this case the reader, is capable of carrying out the instruction) and *effectively computable* (do-able).
3. *Completeness*: Nothing is left out.

Pseudo-code is best understood by looking at examples. Each example below demonstrates one of the control structures used in algorithms: sequential operations, conditional operations, and iterative operations. We also list all variables used at the end of the pseudo-code.

FLOW CHARTS

DEFINITION

The flowchart is a means of visually presenting the flow of data through an information processing systems, the operations performed within the system and the sequence in which they are performed. In this lesson, we shall concern ourselves with the programme flowchart, which describes what operations (and in what sequence) are required to solve a given problem. The programme flowchart can be likened to the blueprint of a building. As we know a designer draws a blueprint before starting construction on a building. Similarly, a programmer prefers to draw a flowchart prior to writing a computer programme. As in the case of the drawing of a blueprint, the flowchart is drawn according to defined rules and using standard flowchart symbols.

A flowchart is a diagrammatic representation that illustrates the sequence of operations to be performed to get the solution of a problem. Flowcharts are generally drawn in the early stages of formulating computer solutions. Flowcharts facilitate communication between programmers and business people. These flowcharts play a vital role in the programming of a problem and are quite helpful in understanding the logic of complicated and lengthy problems. Once the flowchart is drawn, it becomes easy to write the programme in any high level language. Often we see how flowcharts are helpful in explaining the programme to others. Hence, it is correct to say that a flowchart is a must for the better documentation of a complex programme.

GUIDELINES

Flowcharts are usually drawn using some standard

symbols; however, some special symbols can also be developed when required. Some standard flowchart symbols, which are frequently required for flowcharting many computer programmes are shown in Figure.

Start or end of the Programme

Computational Steps or Processing Function of a Programme

Input or Output Operation

Decision Making and Branching

Connector or Joining of Two Parts of Programmme

Magnetic Tape

Mangnetic Disk

Off-Page Connector

Flow Line

← → ↑ ↓

Annotation

Display

A SET OF USEFUL STANDARD FLOWCHART SYMBOLS

It is not strictly necessary to use boxes, circles, diamonds or other such symbols to construct a flowchart, but these do help to describe the types of events in the chart more clearly. Described below are a set of standard symbols which are applicable to most situations without being overly complex.

- *Rounded box*: Use it to represent an event which occurs automatically. Such an event will trigger a subsequent action, for example 'receive telephone call or describe a new state of affairs.
- *Rectangle or box*: Use it to represent an event which is controlled within the process. Typically this will be a step or action which is taken. In most flowcharts this will be the most frequently used symbol.
- *Diamond*: Use it to represent a decision point in the

process. Typically, the statement in the symbol will require a 'yes' or 'no' response and branch to different parts of the flowchart accordingly.

- *Circle*: Use it to represent a point at which the flowchart connects with another process. The name or reference for the other process should appear within the symbol.

7

Function Oriented Software Design

INTRODUCTION

The design of a piece of software is usually captured in some kind of document—all but the most trivial software projects benefit from good design documentation, particularly when there is more than one participant involved in the creation of the software. Two major classes of design documentation have been placed into widespread practice:

- *Requirements*: The requirements define the intended functionality of the software for users and external systems. For example, one requirement of an automated teller machine is that the users that meet certain criteria must be able to withdraw cash.
- *Specifications*: The specifications state the constraints that must be met by users and external systems before the software will function properly (as defined by the requirements). For example, part of the specification of some automated teller machines is that the user must bring a bank card and swipe it in the machine. Users that do not comply with this part of the specification will be unable to use it.

The initial practice of designing software often focuses on creating work products that capture the desired requirements and specifications of the proposed software. There are many different approaches to software design, but most software will never reach a point where all of the desired requirements are met because the requirements will change and grow as soon as the software goes into use. So, software design is principally concerned with designing software that is expected to continuously evolve to meet an ever-changing list of requirements.

It is far easier to make sense of software design and development processes when this crucially important but subtle notion is grasped: good design is about creating software that can evolve and adapt over a long period of time and an indefinite number of versions, it is *not* chiefly concerned with creating a pristine finished product that is intended to remain untouched upon completion.

The first software was designed with a procedural paradigm in mind. The procedural paradigm envisions software simply as a list of instructions, usually contained across many files, to be executed. As computers became more powerful, programmes grew to a size that made this approach unmanageable without adopting designs specifying complex organizational procedures for keeping track of all of the files containing these instructions.

Since then, many programming paradigms have been envisioned, the most popular of which is the object oriented paradigm. Supporting the object oriented paradigm is the process of object oriented design, or OOD. OOD aims to design software such that it is broken up into manageable chunks called classes.

A class is a unit of code that contains information and defines behaviours that manage that information. In this way, the information managed by the class can only be changed by the outside world in the ways defined by the class.

The world outside that class need not understand the details of how such information must be manipulated; ensuring that the information is complete and consistent is managed within the class itself, greatly simplifying the task of working with that information for the outside world.

DESCRIPTION

- The fundamental unit of an object oriented system is the

class. A *class* is a set of data and the behaviours that operate upon that data. Each behaviour is captured in a method, which is a function associated with a class. A class defines a type of object that can exist within the system.

It is instructive to consider an example. An object is related to its class much in the same way a specific dog (let's call him Rover) is related to the class of all dogs. In the object oriented approach we say that Rover is an instance of a dog.

Similarly, we would refer to an object as an instance of a particular class. Just as Rover and Fido are two distinct instances of dogs, at any given time there may be many instances of a particular class existing in an object oriented system. If we are designing an object oriented system designed to represent dogs, then, we would use this analogy to create a class called Dog. On this class we can define variables like hairColor, hairLength, eyeColor, weight, height, etc. We can also define behaviours that all dogs share such aseat(), sleep(), bark(), and run().

The behaviours we define may use the state stored in the variables to determine how to correctly carry out the behaviour (for instance, a large dog will eat more and bark louder than a small dog). When we instantiate, or create, a new dog we would initialize it with all the properties of the specific dog we wish to represent.

So, even though we'd have two instances of the Dog class in our system, fido and rover, they would exhibit the same behaviours in different ways based on their individual state. There are three principles fundamental to the definition of all object oriented software: encapsulation, inheritance, and polymorphism.

We will discuss each in turn, but it's important to realise that all three principles work in combination to define a particular class. The principle of *encapsulation* refers to the scope and visibility of state within a class. It is important for each class to define behaviours usable by the outside world in such a way that the internal state is not known outside the object, nor would it be necessary for that state to be known for objects of the class to serve a purpose within the system.

Encapsulation goes hand-in-hand with the principle of information hiding, which says that any information that need not be known by outside agents should be hidden from view. In this way, the outside world sees only what it needs to see in order to use the object, simplifying its usage.

To use the example above, the eat() method of our Dog class might use a very complex algorithm based on the weight, height, and any other characteristics of that particular dog to calculate how much food it should eat when invoked. The outside world ought to regard the particular process used by the class with disinterest—it simply calls the eat() method and, from that outside perspective, the dog eats.

Inheritance refers to a particular relationship that two or more classes can share. After we define our Dog class, we may wish to design some classes that represent particular breeds: German Shepherd, Pointer, and Retriever, for example. All of these are different kinds of dogs. As such, any behaviour or characteristic our more generic Dog class contains ought to also be contained by each of these classes. It would be a terrible waste of effort, however, to duplicate all of the work we've done defining those characteristics and behaviours on the Dog class.

Furthermore, whenever we update such code shared by all dogs (such as when fixing a bug), we would have to apply the same update to all classes with copies of that same code. Fortunately, because object oriented systems allow inheritance, we need not define the same functionality multiple times.

We can simply say that the different breeds of dog extend or inherit from the Dog class, and instances of those classes automatically get all of the characteristics and behaviours defined on Dog. *Polymorphism* refers to a particular feature of classes that define an inheritance relationship. Above, we said that a Pointer is a specific kind of Dog, and therefore the Pointer class can extend the Dog class. Once this inheritance-type relationship is defined between these two classes, the outside world can treat any pointer specifically as a pointer, or it may also treat it more generally as simply a dog. When dealing with a particular instance, in fact, the outside world need not even know its dealing with a pointer. For example, if the Pointer class defines an additional behaviour unique to pointers, such as point(), when dealing with an instance of the Pointer class—let's call this particular dogpointy—we may invoke the point() method and observe Pointy point. However, if we are only interested in requesting that Pointy do things that all dogs can do, such as eat() and sleep(), we may forget altogether that Pointy is in fact a Pointer and simply treat him just as though he were directly an instance of the Dog class. Polymorphism is the ability of objects to behave as though they are instances of a superclass.

OBJECT ORIENTED DESIGN

INTRODUCTION

The object-oriented approach to software development extends and improves on traditional methods of system development. Object-oriented models effectively capture and communicate system requirements in a way that closely resembles the real world and which is extensible in response to change. This chapter presents some common approaches to designing and implementing object-oriented software which satisfies system requirements. This design occurs after relevant requirements have been specified, and detailed analysis has begun within the problem domain.

As part of learning such design techniques, students use elements of UML to describe how collections of collaborating objects, each with a well-defined and carefully-chosen set of responsibilities, can together realise the required behaviour of a software system under development. Students also learn how to express their software class discoveries using UML's class diagram and related notation.

Objectives:

- Analyse use cases and identify the important messages between external users and the internal software system;

- Design a collaboration of objects which implement these messages;
- Discover relevant software classes, including their attributes and methods which are part of an object of some class;
- Evaluate existing software class designs, identifying potential problems and possible solutions;
- Employ design heuristics, which give useful guidance in inventing good designs, as well as improving existing designs.

Includes:

- Review of domain class modeling and UML class diagrams.
- Introduction to Course Exercise (CE).
- Transforming use cases and domain models into working software: an overview.
- Discovering the important messages within a use case.
- Describing messages using a UML Sequence Diagram.
- Bridging the gap between analysis and design: responsibility-centered design of software classes.
- Some design guidance: the GRASP heuristics (General Responsibility Assignment Software Patterns) of C. Larman
- Core GRASP heuristics.
- Designing and diagramming a collaboration of objects.
- Designing with CRC Cards.
- Diagramming collaboration using UML Communication (Collaboration) Diagrams.
- Turning object collaborations into OO code.
- Other GRASP heuristics.
- Evaluating software designs.
- OO design heuristics
- Iterative development, software design, and design heuristics.
- Refactoring software designs

- Course review, summaries, and conclusions

TO DOWN AND BOTTOM UP DESIGN

OVERVIEW

Top-down and bottom-up are strategies of information processing and knowledge ordering, mostly involving software, but also other humanistic and scientific theories (see systemics). In practice, they can be seen as a style of thinking and teaching. In many cases *top-down*is used as a synonym of *analysis* or *decomposition,* and *bottom-up* of *synthesis.*

A top-down approach is essentially breaking down a system to gain insight into its compositional sub-systems. In a top-down approach an overview of the system is first formulated, specifying but not detailing any first-level subsystems. Each subsystem is then refined in yet greater detail, sometimes in many additional subsystem levels, until the entire specification is reduced to base elements.

A top-down model is often specified with the assistance of "black boxes", these make it easier to manipulate. However, black boxes may fail to elucidate elementary mechanisms or be detailed enough to realistically validate the model. A bottom-up approach is piecing together systems to give rise to grander systems, thus making the original systems sub-systems of the emergent system.

In a bottom-up approach the individual base elements of the system are first specified in great detail. These elements are then linked together to form larger subsystems, which then in turn are linked, sometimes in many levels, until a complete top-level system is formed. This strategy often resembles a "seed" model, whereby the beginnings are small but eventually grow in complexity and completeness. However, "organic strategies" may result in a tangle of elements and subsystems, developed in isolation and subject to local optimization as opposed to meeting a global purpose.

Good engineering has a balance between top-down and bottom-up design, but there should generally be a bias towards top-down because your ultimate goal is to meet the system requirements which flow in at the top level. Bottom-up engineering is important to answer questions of technical feasibility or organisational capability, and ensure that the high level design decisions don't impose burdensome constraints on lower level components.

But too much bottom-up engineering can lead to missed requirements and the classic "integration problems" that occur when engineers realise too late in the process that the subcomponents aren't going to work together efficiently at the system level. While requirements flow down the system hierarchy, the balancing force is feasibility which flows back up to ensure that higher level design decisions don't result in downstream requirements which are excessively difficult or impossible to meet.

Including an experienced engineer on the design review team is often a more cost-effective way of answering questions of feasibility than bottom-up activities such as building a prototype or building an experimental ASIC. Engineers generally enjoy building things along the way during a large project, but bear in mind that the ultimate project goal is the final deliverables; all the throw-away prototypes and design revisions constructed along the way are simply steps towards that goal.

What counts is what the end customer gets. Multiple ASIC tape-outs, PCB revisions and software releases can simply point to an inefficient development process. Each of these has a cost associated with it, and only the final ASIC, PCB or software release actually gets delivered to the customer. Including design reviews in the process helps reduce the number of design iterations, prototypes and rework required to meet the end goal.

By contrast in bottom-up design individual parts of the system are specified in detail, and may even be coded. The parts are then linked together to form larger components, which are in turn linked until a complete system is arrived at. Top down approaches emphasise planning, and a complete understanding of the system.

It is inherent that no coding can begin until a sufficient level of detail has been reached on at least some part of the system. Bottom up emphasises coding, which can begin as soon as the first module has been specified. However bottom-up coding runs the risk that modules may be coded without having a clear idea of how they link to other parts of the system, and that such linking may not be as easy as first thought.

Top-down design was promoted in the 1970s by IBM researcher Harlan Mills and by Nicklaus Wirth. Mills developed structured programming concepts for practical use and tested them in a 1969 project to automate the *New York Times* morgue index. The engineering and management success of this project led to the spread of the top-down approach through IBM and the rest of the computer industry.

Nicklaus Wirth, among other achievements the developer of Pascal programming language, wrote the influential paper 'Programme Development by Stepwise Refinement'. Top-down methods were favored in software engineeringuntil the rise of object-oriented programming in the late 1980s. Modern software design approaches usually combine both of these approaches. Although an understanding of the complete system is usually considered necessary for good design, leading theoretically to a top-down approach, most software projects attempt to make use of existing code to some degree. Pre-existing modules give designs a 'bottom-up' flavour. Some design approaches also use an approach where a partially-functional system is designed and coded to completion, and this system is then expanded to fulfill all the requirements for the project.

TECHNIQUES IN SOFTWARE DEVELOPMENT

Top-down approaches emphasize planning and a complete understanding of the system. It is inherent that no coding can begin until a sufficient level of detail has been reached in the design of at least some part of the system. The Top-Down Approach is done by attaching the stubs in place of the module.

This, however, delays testing of the ultimate functional units of a system until significant design is complete. Bottom-up emphasizes coding and early testing, which can begin as soon as the first module has been specified. This approach, however, runs the risk that modules may be coded without having a clear idea of how they link to other parts of the system, and that such linking may not be as easy as first thought.

The engineering and management success of this project led to the spread of the top-down approach through IBM and the rest of the computer industry. Among other achievements, Niklaus Wirth, the developer of Pascal programming language, wrote the influential paper *Programme Development by Stepwise Refinement*.

ince Niklaus Wirth went on to develop languages such as Modula and Oberon (where one could define a module before knowing about the entire programme specification), one can infer that top down programming was not strictly what he promoted. Top-down methods were favored in software engineering until the late 1980s, and object-oriented programming assisted in demonstrating the idea that both aspects of top-down and bottom-up programming could be utilized.

Modern software design approaches usually combine both top-down and bottom-up approaches. Although an understanding of the complete system is usually considered necessary for good design, leading theoretically to a top-down approach, most software projects attempt to make use of existing code to some degree.

Pre-existing modules give designs a bottom-up flavour. Some design approaches also use an approach where a partially-functional system is designed and coded to completion, and this system is then expanded to fulfill all the requirements for the project

Programming

Top-down is a programming style, the mainstay of traditional procedural languages, in which design begins by specifying complex pieces and then dividing them into successively smaller pieces. Eventually, the components are specific enough to be coded and the programme is written. This is the exact opposite of the bottom-up programming approach which is common in object-oriented languages such as C++ or Java.

The technique for writing a programme using top-down methods is to write a main procedure that names all the major functions it will need. Later, the programming team looks at the requirements of each of those functions and the process is repeated. These compartmentalized sub-routines eventually will perform actions so simple they can be easily and concisely coded. When all the various sub-routines have been coded the programme is done.

By defining how the application comes together at a high level, lower level work can be self-contained. By defining how the lower level abstractions are expected to integrate into higher level ones, interfaces become clearly defined.

Top-down Approach

Practicing top-down programming has several advantages:

- Separating the low level work from the higher level abstractions leads to a modular design.
- Modular design means development can be self contained.
- Having "skeleton" code illustrates clearly how low level modules integrate.
- Fewer operations errors (to reduce errors, because each module has to be processed separately, so programmers get large amount of time for processing).
- Much less time consuming (each programmer is only involved in a part of the big project).
- Very optimized way of processing (each programmer has to apply their own knowledge and experience to their parts (modules), so the project will become an optimized one).
- Easy to maintain (if an error occurs in the output, it

is easy to identify the errors generated from which module of the entire programme).

BOTTOM UP DESIGN

In accordance with this principle, a large programme must be divided into pieces, and the larger the programme, the more it must be divided. How do you divide a programme? The traditional approach is called *top-down design:* you say "the purpose of the programme is to do these seven things, so I divide it into seven major subroutines.

The first subroutine has to do these four things, so it in turn will have four of its own subroutines," and so on. This process continues until the whole programme has the right level of granularity— each part large enough to do something substantial, but small enough to be understood as a single unit. Experienced Lisp programmers divide up their programmes differently. As well as top-down design, they follow a principle which could be called *bottom-up design*— changing the language to suit the problem.

In Lisp, you don't just write your programme down towards the language, you also build the language up towards your programme. As you're writing a programme you may think "I wish Lisp had such-and-such an operator." So you go and write it. Afterward you realise that using the new operator would simplify the design of another part of the programme, and so on.

Language and programme evolve together. Like the border between two warring states, the boundary between language and programme is drawn and redrawn, until eventually it comes to rest along the mountains and rivers, the natural frontiers of your problem. In the end your programme will look as if the language had been designed for it. And when language and programme fit one another well, you end up with code which is clear, small, and efficient.

It's worth emphasizing that bottom-up design doesn't mean just writing the same programme in a different order. When you work bottom-up, you usually end up with a different programme. Instead of a single, monolithic programme, you will get a larger language with more abstract operators, and a smaller programme written in it. Instead of a lintel, you'll get an arch. In typical code, once you abstract out the parts which are merely bookkeeping, what's left is much shorter; the higher you build up the language, the less distance you will have to travel from the top down to it.

This brings several advantages:

- By making the language do more of the work, bottom-up design yields programmes which are smaller and more agile. A shorter programme doesn't have to be divided into so many components, and fewer components means programmes which are easier to read or modify. Fewer components also means fewer connections between components, and thus less chance for errors there. As industrial designers strive to reduce the number of moving parts in a machine, experienced Lisp programmers use bottom-up design to reduce the size and complexity of their programmes.
- Bottom-up design promotes code re-use. When you write two or more programmes, many of the utilities you wrote for the first programme will also be useful in the succeeding ones. Once you've acquired a large substrate of utilities, writing a new programme can take only a fraction of the effort it would require if you had to start with raw Lisp.
- Bottom-up design makes programmes easier to read. An instance of this type of abstraction asks the reader to understand a general-purpose operator; an instance of functional abstraction asks the reader to understand a special-purpose subroutine.
- Because it causes you always to be on the lookout for patterns in your code, working bottom-up helps to clarify your ideas about the design of your programme. If two distant components of a programme are similar in form, you'll be led to notice the similarity and perhaps to redesign the programme in a simpler way.

Bottom-up design is possible to a certain degree in languages other than Lisp. Whenever you see library functions, bottom-up design is happening. However, Lisp gives you much broader powers in this department, and augmenting the language plays a proportionately larger role in Lisp style— so much so that Lisp is not just a different language, but a whole different way of programming.

It's true that this style of development is better suited to programmes which can be written by small groups. However, at the same time, it extends the limits of what can be done by a small group. In *The Mythical Man-Month,* Frederick Brooks proposed that the productivity of a group of programmers does not grow linearly with its size. As the size of the group increases, the productivity of individual programmers goes down.

FEATURES

In bottom-up organized organizations, *e.g.* ministries and their subordinate entities, decisions are prepared by experts in their fields, which define, out of their expertise, the policy they deem necessary. If they cannot agree, even on a compromise, they *escalate* the problem to the next higher hierarchy level, where a decision would be sought.

Finally, the highest common principal might have to take the decision. Information is in the debt of the inferior to the superior, which means that the inferior owes information to the superior. In the effect, as soon as inferiors agree, the head of the organization only provides his or her "face3 for the decision which their inferiors have agreed upon.

Among several countries, the German political system provides one of the purest forms of a bottom-up approach. The German Federal Act on the Public Service provides that any inferior has to consult and support any superiors, that he or she – only – has to follow "general guidelines" of the superiors, and that he or she would have to be fully responsible for any own act in office, and would have to follow a specific, formal complaint procedure if in doubt of the legality of an order.

The historical foundation of this approach lies with the fact that, in the 19th century, many politicians used to be noblemen without appropriate education, who more and more became forced to rely on consultation of educated experts, which (in particular after the Prussian reforms of Stein and Hardenberg) enjoyed the status of financially and personally independent, indismissable, and neutral experts as *Beamte* (public servants under public law).

A similar approach can be found in British police laws, where entitlements of police constables are vested in the constable in person and not in the police as an administrative agency, this leading to the single constable being fully responsible for his or her own acts in office, in particular their legality.

The experience of two dictatorships in the country and, after the end of such regimes, emerging calls for the legal responsibility of the "aidees of the aidees" (*Helfershelfer*) of such regimes also furnished calls for the principle of personal responsibility of any expert for any decision made, this leading to a strengthening of the bottom-up approach, which requires maximum responsibility of the superiors.

In the opposite, the French administration is based on a top-down approach, where regular public servants enjoy no other task than simply to execute decisions made by their superiors. As those superiors also require consultation, this consultation is provided by members of a *cabinet*, which is distinctive from the regular ministry staff in terms of staff and organization.

Those members who are not members of the *cabinet* are not entitled to make any suggestions or to take any decisions of political dimension. The advantage of the bottom-up approach is the great level of expertise provided, combined with the motivating experience of any member of the administration to be responsible and finally the independent "engine" of progress in that field of personal responsibility. A disadvantage is the lack of democratic control and transparency, this leading, from a democratic viewpoint, to the deferment of actual power of policy-making to faceless, if even unknown, public servants. Even the fact that certain politicians might "provide their face" to the actual decisions of their inferiors might not mitigate this effect, but rather strong parliamentary rights of control and influence in legislative procedures (as they do exist in the example of Germany). The advantage of the top-bottom principle is that political and administrative responsibilities are clearly distinguished from each other, and that responsibility for political failures can be clearly identified with the relevant office holder.

Disadvantages are that the system triggers demotivation of inferiors, who know that their ideas to innovative approaches might not be welcome just because of their position, and that the decision-makers cannot make use of the full range of expertise which their inferiors will have collected. Administrations in *dictatorships* traditionally work according to a strict top-down approach.

As civil servants below the level of the political leadership are discouraged from making suggestions, they use to suffer from the lack of expertise which could be provided by the inferiors, which regularly leads to a breakdown of the system after an few decades.

Modern communist states, which the People's Republic of Chinaforms an example of, therefore prefer to define a framework of permissible, or even encouraged, criticism and self-determination by inferiors, which would not affect the major state doctrine, but allows the use of professional and expertise-driven knowledge and the use of it for the decision-making persons in office.

SOFTWARE MEASUREMENTS

The measurement information model is a structure linking information needs to the relevant entities and attributes of concern. Entities include processes, products, projects, and resources. The measurement information model describes how the relevant attributes are quantified and converted to indicators that provide a basis for decision-making. The selection or definition of appropriate measures to address an information need begins with a measurable concept: an idea of which measurable attributes are related to an information need and how they are related. The measurement planner defines measurement constructs that link these attributes to a specifiedinformation need. Each construct may involve several types or levels of measures.

This measurement information model (see Figure) identifies the basic terms and concepts with which the measurement analyst must deal. The measurement modelhelps to determine what the measurement planner needs to specify during measurement planning, performance, and evaluation.

ENTITY

An entity is an object (for example, a process, product, project, or resource) that is to be characterized by measuring its attributes. Typical software engineering objects can be classified as products (*e.g.*, design document, source code, and test case), processes (*e.g.*, design process, testing process, requirements analysis process), projects, and resources (*e.g.*, the programmers and the testers).

An entity may have one or more properties that are of interest to meet the information needs. In practice, an entity can be classified into more than one of the above categories.

MEASURABLE ATTRIBUTE

An attribute is a property or characteristic of an entity that can be distinguished quantitatively or qualitatively by human or automated means. An entity may have many attributes, only some of which may be of interest for measurement.

The first step in defining a specific instantiation of the measurement information model is to select the attributes that are most relevant to the measurement user's information needs. A given attribute may be incorporated in multiple measurement constructs supporting different information needs.

BASE MEASURE

A base measure is an attribute and the method for quantifying it. A base measure is functionally independent of other measures. A base measure captures information about a single attribute. Data collection involves assigning values to base measures. Specifying the expected range and/or type of values of a base measure helps to verify the quality of the data collected.

Measurement Method

A measurement method is a logical sequence of operations, described generically, used in quantifying an attribute with respect to a specified scale. The operations may involve activities such as counting occurrences or observing the passage of time. The same measurement method may be applied to multiple attributes.

However, each unique combination of an attribute and a method produces a different base measure. Some measurement methods may be implemented in multiple ways. A measurement procedure describes the specific implementation of a measurement method within a given organizational context.

Type of Measurement Method

The type of measurement method depends on the nature of the operations used to quantify an attribute.

Two types of method may be distinguished:

1. *Subjective*: Quantification involving human judgment
2. *Objective*: Quantification based on numerical rules such as counting. These rules may be implemented via human or automated means.

Scale

A scale is an ordered set of values, continuous or discrete, or a set of categories to which the attribute is mapped. The measurement method maps the magnitude of the measured attribute to a value on a scale. A unit of measurement often is associated with a scale.

Type of Scale

The type of scale depends on the nature of the relationship between values on the scale.

Four types of scales are commonly defined:

1. *Nominal*: The measurement values are categorical. For example, the classification of defects by their type.
2. *Ordinal*: The measurement values are rankings. For example, the assignment of defects to a severity level.
3. *Interval*: The measurement values have equal distances corresponding to equal quantities of the *attribute*. For example, cyclomatic complexity has the minimum value of one, but each increment represents an additional path.
4. *Ratio:* The measurement values have equal distances corresponding to equal quantities of the *attribute* where the value of zero corresponds to none of the *attribute*. For example, the size of a software component in terms of LOC.

The method of measurement usually affects the type of *scale* that can be used reliably with a given *attribute*. For example, subjective methods of measurement usually only support ordinal or nominal scales.

Unit of Measurement

A *unit of measurement* is a particular quantity, defined and adopted by convention, with which other quantities of the same kind are compared in order to express their magnitude relative to that quantity. Only quantities expressed in the same units of measurement are directly comparable. Example of units include the hour and the metre.

DERIVED MEASURE

A derived measure is a measure that is defined as a function of two or more base measures. Derived measures capture information about more than oneattribute. Simple transformations of base measures (for example, taking the square root of a base measure) do not add information, thus do not produce derived measures. Normalization of data often involves converting base measures into derived measures that can be used to compare different entities.

Measurement Function

A measurement function is an algorithm or calculation performed to combine two or more base measures. The scale and unit of the derived measure depend on the scales and units of the base measures from which it is composed as well as how they are combined by the function.

INDICATOR

An indicator is an estimate or evaluation of specified attributes derived from a model with respect to defined information needs. Indicators are the basis for analysis and decision-making. These are what should be presented to measurement users.

Measurement is always based on imperfect information, so quantifying the uncertainty, accuracy, or importance of indicators is an essential component of presenting the actual indicator value. Therefore, an interpretation of indicators is performed to provide the desired information product.

Measurement Model

A measurement model is an algorithm or calculation combining one or more base and/or derived measures with associated decision criteria. It is based on an understanding of, or assumptions about, the expected relationship between the component measures and/or their behaviour over time. Models produce estimates or evaluations relevant to defined information needs. The scale and measurement method affect the choice of analysis techniques or models used to produceindicators.

Decision Criteria

Decision criteria are numerical thresholds or targets used to determine the need for action or further investigation, or to describe the level of confidence in a given result. Decision criteria help to interpret the results of measurement. Decision criteria may be calculated or based on a conceptual understanding of expected behaviour. Decision criteria may be derived from historical data, plans, and heuristics, or computed as statistical control limits or statistical confidence limits.

SOFTWARE METRICS

Effective management of any process requires quantification, measurement, and modeling. Software metrics provide a quantitative basis for the development and validation of models of the software development process. Metrics can be used to improve software productivity and quality. This module introduces the most commonly used software metrics and reviews their use in constructing models of the software development process.

Although current metrics and models are certainly inadequate, a number of organizations are achieving promising results through their use. Results should improve further as we gain additional experience with various metrics and oftware metrics are numerical data related to software development. Metrics strongly support software project management activities.

They relate to the four functions of management as follows:

1. *Planning*: Metrics serve as a basis of cost estimating, training planning, resource planning, scheduling, and budgeting.
2. *Organizing*: Size and schedule metrics influence a project's organization.
3. *Controlling*: Metrics are used to status and track software development activities for compliance to plans.
4. *Improving*: Metrics are used as a tool for process improvement and to identify where improvement efforts should be concentrated and measure the effects of process improvement efforts.

A metric quantifies a characteristic of a process or product. Metrics can be directly observable quantities or can be derived from one or more directly observable quantities. Examples of raw metrics include the number of source lines of code, number of documentation pages, number of staff-hours, number of tests, number of requirements, etc. Examples of derived metrics include source lines of code per staff-hour, defects per thousand lines of code, or a cost performance index.

The term *indicator* is used to denote a representation of metric data that provides insight into an ongoing software development project or process improvement activity. Indicators are metrics in a form suitable for assessing project behaviour or process improvement. For example, an indicator may be the behaviour of a metric over time or the ratio of two metrics.

Indicators may include the comparison of actual values versus the plan, project stability metrics, or quality metrics. Examples of indicators used on a project include actual versus planned task completions, actual versus planned staffing, number of trouble reports written and resolved over time, and number of requirements changes over time.

Indicators are used in conjunction with one another to provide a more complete picture of project or organization behaviour. For example, a progress indicator is related to requirements and size indicators. All three indicators should be used and interpreted together.

METRICS SET

The metrics to be collected provide indicators that track ongoing project progress, software products, and software development processes.

Depending upon the nature of the project, specific contractual requirements, or management preference, a project may choose to collect additional metrics or to tailor the recommended set.

CHART CONSTRUCTION

Charts are prepared for the standard metrics. All charts require titles, legends, and labels for all axes. They should clearly and succinctly show the metrics of interest, with no excessive detail to detract the eye. Do not overuse different line types, patterns, or colour, or added dimensionality unless used specifically to differentiate items. Overlayed data is preferable to multiple charts when the different data are related to each other and can be meaningfully depicted without obscuring other details.

The most common type of chart is the tracking chart. This chart is used extensively for the Progress indicator, and is used in similar forms for many of the other indicators. For task progress, it depicts the cumulative number of planned and actual task completions (or milestones) against time. For other indicators, it may show actual versus planned staffing profiles, actual versus planned software size, actual versus planned resource utilization or other measures compared over time.

There are many ways to modify the tracking chart. A horizontal planned line representing the cumulative goal can be drawn at the top, multiple types of tasks can be overlaid on a single tracking chart (such as design, code, and integration), or the chart can be overlaid with other types of data. It is recommended that tracked quantities be shown as a line chart, and that replanned task progress be shown as a separate planning line. The original planned baseline is kept on the chart, as well as all replanning data if there is more than a single replan.

The following sections provide brief descriptions of the different metrics categories with samples of the required charts. Individual projects may enhance the charts for their situations or have additional charts for the categories.

PROGRESS

Progress indicators provide information on how well the project is performing with respect to planned task completions and keeping schedule commitments. Tasks are scheduled and then progress is tracked to the schedules. Metrics are collected for the activities and milestones identified in the project schedules. Metrics on actual completions are compared to those of planned completions to determine whether there are deviations to the plan. The difference between the actual and planned completions indicates the deviations from the plan. Each project identifies tasks for which progress metrics will be collected. The completion criteria for each task must be well defined and measurable. The project should establish range limits (thresholds) on the planned task progress for the project. The thresholds are used for management of software development risk.

Figure depicts the cumulative number of planned and actual completions (or milestones) over time. Note that this chart is generic, and each project will substitute specific tasks (units, milestones, SLOCs, etc.). Additionally, each project is expected to produce multiple progress charts for different types of tasks, different teams, etc.

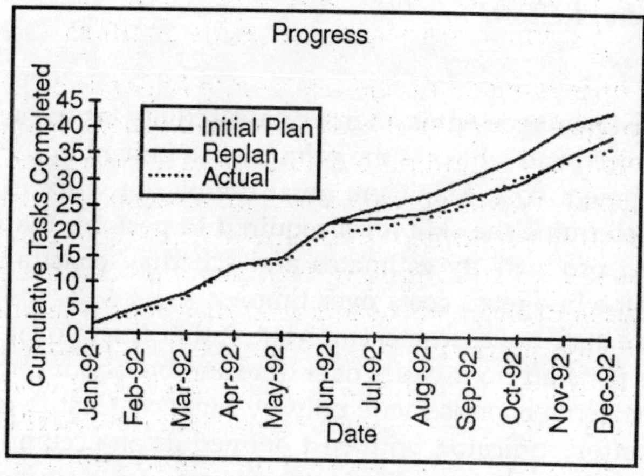

Fig. Progress Indicator.

EFFORT

Effort indicators allow the software manager to track personnel resources. They provide visibility into the contribution of staffing to project costs, schedule adherence, product quality and the amount of effort required for each activity. Effort indicators include trends in actual staffing levels, staffing profile by activity or labour category, or a profile of unplanned staff loses. Effort indicators may be used by all levels of project software management to measure the actual profile against the plan. Each level of management forms a profile for its area of control and monitors the actual profile against the plan. Determining the number of staff needed at any one time is an important function performed by software management. By summing the number of staff during each reporting period, the composite staffing profile for the project can be determined. These indicators are applied during all life-cycles phases, from project inception to project end. Effort metrics are to be collected and reported at least on a monthly basis.

The effort and cost metrics are related. By convention, effort metrics are non-cumulative expenditures of human resources, and cost metrics are cumulative levels of effort as tracked by earned value. Thus, cost metrics are a cumulative depiction of effort.

COST

Cost management is an important activity for the success of a project, and labour is the primary component of software development cost. Managers must define the work in their area, determine the skill level required to perform the work, and use productivity estimates and schedule constraints to determine budgeted costs over time.

Use staff-hours to measure cost, rather than dollars. The dollars per staff-hour varies over time and by labour category, and the conversion is made only by Finance. Cost is related to the effort indicator, with cost defined as an accumulation of effort expenditures. (The total project cost also includes non-labour costs, but they are not tracked here.) Only those projects using earned value can report the earned value quantities.

A Work Breakdown Structure (WBS) is established to define the structures that will be used to collect the costs. The WBS identifies separate elements for requirements, design, documentation, code and unit test, integration, verification, and system testing. Costs can also be segregated by component, function, or configuration item. Work packages are derived from the WBS. Costs are allocated to work packages using an earned value method. This system allows managers to track the actual costs and measure them against the budget for their respective areas of responsibility.

REVIEW RESULTS

Review Results indicators provide insight into the status of action items from life-cycle reviews.

The term Action Item (AI) refers to inspection defects and customer comments. Reviews include the following:

- Formal inspections of software documents or code
- Formal customer milestones, *e.g.*, SSR, PDR, CDR, or TRR
- Informal peer evaluations of products, *e.g.*, walk throughs, technical reviews, or internal PDRs
- Management reviews
- Process reviews, *e.g.*, SQA audits, SEI CMM assessments, or the causal analysis from formal inspections.

There are standards for some reviews, as well as procedures for conducting them. For example, formal inspections result in assertion logs that document the minor and major defects uncovered by the inspection process.

Therefore, standard review result indicators for formal inspections are:

- Counts of minor/major defects
- Rates of defect detection (*e.g.*, assertions per inspection meeting minute, defects per inspected document page, or defects per KSLOC of code inspected)
- Defect status (*e.g.*, age of open defects, number of open/closed defects, and breakdown by defect categories).

A customer-conducted review such as a Preliminary Design Review (PDR) generates AIs that must be closed before approval of the Software Design Document. Therefore, standard review result indicators for a PDR are the number of comments written and their status (open, closed, and age).

Review metrics record the AIs identified in the review findings and track them until they are resolved. These metrics provide status on both products and processes. Review results are not to be used to evaluate the performance of individuals.

TROUBLE REPORTS

TR indicators provide managers with insight into the quality of the product, software reliability, and the effectiveness of testing. They also provide information on the software development process. The terms defect and problem will be used interchangeably herein.

Monthly tracking of TR indicators shows the project's trends in the following areas:

1. The rate at which TRs are being written and resolved.
2. The type and severity of the TRs.
3. Relationship between the number of TRs and the number of test cases passed or the number of test steps passed.
4. The TR density (the number of TRs per unit size).
5. The number of defects in each software application/ unit.

TR indicators are applicable only in the following life cycle stages (and each release of the software within these stages, and during the informal and formal test segments of these stages)

- Application test and integration,
- System test,
- Acceptance test.

Thus the TR indicators are applicable only to defects during the operation or execution of a computer programme. Due to the shortness of testing periods, and the dynamics involved between the test team and the implementation team that analyses the TRs and fixes the defects, the TR indicators are generally evaluated on a weekly basis. The terms open and closed are defined as follows: Open The problem has been reported. Closed The investigation is complete and the action required to resolve the problem has been proposed, implemented, and verified to the satisfaction of all concerned. In some cases, a TR will be found to be invalid as part of the investigative process and closed immediately.

REQUIREMENTS STABILITY

Requirements Stability provides an indication of the completeness, stability, and understanding of the requirements. It indicates the number of changes to the requirements and the amount of information needed to complete the requirements definition. A lack of requirements stability can lead to poor product quality, increased cost, and schedule slippage.

Requirements stability indicators are in the form of trend charts that show the total number of requirements, cumulative changes to the requirements, and the number of TBDs over time. A TBD refers to an undefined requirement. Based on requirements stability trends, corrective action may be necessary.

Requirements stability is applicable during all life-cycles phases, from project inception to the end. The requirements stability indicators are most important during requirements and design phases. Requirements stability metrics are collected and reported on a monthly basis.

SIZE STABILITY

Software size is a critical input to project planning. The size estimate and other factors are used to derive effort and schedule before and during a project. The software manager tracks the actual versus planned software product size. Various indicators show trends in the estimated code size, trends by code type, the variation of actual software size from estimates or the size variation by release.

Size stability is derived from changes in the size estimate as time goes on. It provides an indication of the completeness and stability of the requirements, the understanding of the requirements, design thoroughness and stability, and the capability of the software development staff to meet the current budget and schedule.

Size instability may indicate the need for corrective action. Size metrics are applicable during all life-cycle phases. Size metrics are collected and reported on a monthly basis, or more often as necessary.

COMPUTER RESOURCE UTILIZATION

Computer Resource Utilization indicators show whether the software is using the planned amount of system resources. The computer resources are normally CPU time, I/O, and memory. For some software, the constraints of computer resources significantly affect the design, implementation, and testing of the product. They can also be used to replan, re-estimate, and guide resource acquisition.

Computer resource utilization is planned during the requirements activity and reviewed during the design activity. Resources are monitored from the start of implementation activity to the end of the life cycle.

For memory utilization, the unit of data is the byte, word, or half-word. For CPU time, the unit of data is either MIPS (millions of instructions per second), or the percentage of CPU time used during a peak period. For I/O time, the unit of data is the percentage of I/O time used during a peak period.

Resource Utilization data is collected and reported at least monthly, with the period between collection and reporting becoming shorter as the software system nears completion and a better picture of software performance can be seen. Note that the resource utilization is normally an estimate until integration occurs, at which time the actual data is available.

TRAINING

Training indicators provide managers with information on the training programme and whether the staff has necessary skills. A trained staff is a commitment. The manager must ensure that the staff has the skills needed to perform their assigned tasks. The objective of the training indicator is to provide visibility into the training process, to ensure effective utilization of training, and to provide project software managers with an indication of their staff's skill mixture. The manager should investigate the deviations in the number of classes taught from the number of classes planned, and the deviation of the number of staff taught to the planned number. The quality of the training programme should also be determined from completed course evaluation sheets. The number of waivers requested and approved for training should also be tracked.

HALSTEAD'S SOFTWARE SCIENCE

Maurice Halstead's approach relied on his fundamental assumption that a programme should be viewed as an expression of language. His work was based on studying the complexities of languages — both programming and written languages.

Halstead found what he believed were mathematically sound relationships among the number of variables, the type of programming language statements and the complexity of the code. He attacked part of the first and second reasons a programmer might find code complex. Halstead derived more than a dozen formulas relating properties of code. Although not all of them can be covered here, the following is a representative sample of his work.

Halstead found these quantities significant:

- The number of distinct operators in the code (h1)
- The number of distinct operands in the code (h2)
- The number of all operators in the code (N1)
- The number of all operands in the code (N2).

From them, he defined the following entities:

- Vocabulary (h) as h = h1 + h2
- Length (N) as N = N1 + N2
- Volume (V) as V = N log2 h (the program's physical size)
- Potential volume (V*) as V* = (2 + h2*) log2 (2 + h2*) (the smallest possible implementation of an algorithm). H2* is the smallest number of operands required for the minimal implementation, which Halstead stated are the required input and output parameters.
- Programme level (L) as L = V*/V (The closer L is to 1, the tighter the implementation.) Starting with the assumption that code complexity increases as vocabulary and length increase, Halstead observed the following:

- Code complexity increases as volume increases.
- Code complexity increases as programme level decreases.

PROBLEMS

Halstead's groundbreaking work is criticized on several fronts. Some find fault with his methodology for deriving some mathematical relationships. Others find fault with some of his assumptions. For example, Halstead used a number called the Stroud number (ranging from five to 20), which represents how many elementary discriminations the human brain can perform in a "moment."

Another "fact" is that Halstead postulated the human brain can handle up to five chunks of material simultaneously. Many find equations derived on these assumptions represent very wishful thinking.

Another difficulty with the Halstead metrics is that they are difficult to compute. How do you easily count the distinct and total operators and operands in a programme? Imagine counting these quantities every time you made a significant change to a programme. A metric is useless if you can't compute it quickly and easily.

Halstead stated that the lower the programme level, the more complex the programme. Unfortunately, he went no further. Is a programme with level.100 complex? How about one with level.005? All you can do is compare versions of the same programme and compare their programme levels. Recall that the McCabe metric gives an upper limit of 10 for complexity.

The computation of the Halstead metrics for the bubble sort suggest that the bubble sort, as implemented, is very complex. The problem is that the computation for the potential volume mandates the number of input and output parameters.

For the bubble sort, only the array to be sorted is needed. The low number for the potential volume skews the programme and language levels. Most programmers would agree that this algorithm is not complex.

STATE OF SOFTWARE COMPLEXITY MEASUREMENT

Code-level complexity measures have met with mixed success. Although their assumptions have an intuitively sound basis, they are not that good at predicting error rates or cost. Some studies have shown that both McCabe and Halstead do no better at predicting error rates and cost than simple lines-of-code measurements.

Some researchers use McCabe's and Halstead's work as a starting point. For example, Albrecht and Gafffney used some of Halstead's work to derive function points and code size based on operand count. Hansen suggests incorporating both cyclomatic complexity and software science. (Refer to "Measurement of Programme Complexity by the Pair - Cyclomatic Number, Operator Count," ACM SIGPLAN). Some researchers have incorporated several code complexity measurements into design complexity measurement schemes.

There is no silver-bullet formula or methodology that yields exact results for software complexity. Studies that attempt to correlate error rates with computed complexity measures show mixed results. Some studies show that experienced programmers provide the best prediction of error rates and software complexity.

FUNCTION POINT BASED MEASURE

INTRODUCTION

Function Points and the Function Point Model are measurement tools to manage software. Function Points, with other business measures, become Software Metrics. Function Points measure Software size. Function Points measure functionality by objectively measuring functional requirements.

Function Points quantify and document assumptions in Estimating software development. Function Points and Function Point Analysis are objective; Function Points are consistent, and Function Points are auditable. Function Points are independent of technology.

Function Points even apply regardless of design. But Function Points do not measure people directly. Function Points is a macro tool, not a micro tool. Function Points are the foundation of a Software Metrics programme. Software Metrics include Function Points as a normalizing factor for comparison. Function Points in conjunction with time yield Productivity Software Metrics. Function Points in conjunction with defects yield Quality Software Metrics. Function Points with costs provide Unit Cost, Return on Investment, and Efficiency Software Metrics, never before available.

Function Points connect Software Metrics to measure Risk. Function Points can verify Staffing metrics. Function Points can evaluate Build, Buy and/or Outsource decisions. Function Points combine with SEI CMM measures, TQM measures, Baldrige measures, ISO and/or other software and business measures to prove overall status and value.

DOING THE RIGHT THINGS!

Function Points and Usage or Volume measures create Software Metrics that demonstrate an organization's ability to Leverage software's business impact. The Leverage of E Commerce is obvious, but until now unmeasured. Function Points support Customer Satisfaction measures to create Value Software Metrics. Function Points and Skill measures provide Software Metrics for Employee Service Level Agreements to meet current and future company skill needs. Function Points can even measure the Corporate Vision and generate Software Metrics to report progress towards meeting it.

Function Points, Function Point Analysis, the Function Point Model, Supplemental Software Measures, and the Software Metrics they generate, are only the third measure that transcend every part of every organization. (The other two are time and money.) Without them your organization is only two thirds whole.

DEFINITION

A function point is a unit of measurement to express the amount of business functionality an information system provides to a user. Function points are the units of measure used by the IFPUG Functional Size Measurement Method.

The IFPUG FSM Method is an ISO recognized software metric to size an information system based on the functionality that is perceived by the user of the information system, independent of the technology used to implement the information system.

Function points were defined in 1979 in New Way of Looking at Tools by Allan Albrecht at IBM. The functional user requirements of the software are identified and each one is categorized into one of five types: outputs, inquiries, inputs, internal files, and external interfaces.

Once the function is identified and categorized into a type, it is then assessed for complexity and assigned a number of function points. Each of these functional user requirements maps to an end-user business function, such as a data entry for an Input or a user query for an Inquiry.

This distinction is important because it tends to make the functions measured in function points map easily into user-oriented requirements, but it also tends to hide internal functions (*e.g.* algorithms), which also require resources to implement.

Over the years there have been different approaches proposed to deal with this perceived weakness, however there is no ISO recognized FSM Method that includes algorithmic complexity in the sizing result. The variations of the Albrecht based IFPUG method designed to make up for this (and other weaknesses) include:

- *Early and easy function points*: Adjusts for problem and data complexity with two questions that yield a somewhat subjective complexity measurement; simplifies measurement by eliminating the need to count data elements.
- *Engineering function points*: Elements (variable names) and operators (*e.g.*, arithmetic, equality/inequality, Boolean) are counted. This variation highlights computational function.
- *Bang measure*: Defines a function metric based on

twelve primitive (simple) counts that affect or show Bang, defined as "the measure of true function to be delivered as perceived by the user." Bang measure may be helpful in evaluating a software unit's value in terms of how much useful function it provides, although there is little evidence in the literature of such application. The use of Bang measure could apply when re-engineering (either complete or piecewise) is being considered, as discussed in Maintenance of Operational Systems—An Overview.

FIVE COMPONENTS OF FUNCTION POINTS

Data Functions

- Internal Logical Files
- External Interface Files

Transactional Functions

- External Inputs
- External Outputs
- External Inquiries

INTERNAL LOGICAL FILES

The first data function allows users to utilize data they are responsible for maintaining. For example, a pilot may enter navigational data through a display in the cockpit prior to departure.

The data is stored in a file for use and can be modified during the mission. Therefore the pilot is responsible for maintaining the file that contains the navigational information. Logical groupings of data in a system, maintained by an end user, are referred to as Internal Logical Files (ILF).

EXTERNAL INTERFACE FILES

The second Data Function a system provides an end user is also related to logical groupings of data. In this case the user is not responsible for maintaining the data. The data resides in another system and is maintained by another user or system. The user of the system being counted requires this data for reference purposes only.

For example, it may be necessary for a pilot to reference position data from a satellite or ground-based facility during flight. The pilot does not have the responsibility for updating data at these sites but must reference it during the flight. Groupings of data from another system that are used only for reference purposes are defined as External Interface Files (EIF).

The remaining functions address the user's capability to access the data contained in ILFs and EIFs. This capability includes maintaining, inquiring and outputting of data. These are referred to as Transactional Functions.

EXTERNAL INPUT

The first Transactional Function allows a user to maintain Internal Logical Files (ILFs) through the ability to add, change and delete the data. For example, a pilot can add, change and delete navigational information prior to and during the mission.

In this case the pilot is utilizing a transaction referred to as an External Input (EI). An External Input gives the user the capability to maintain the data in ILF's through adding, changing and deleting its contents.

EXTERNAL OUTPUT

The next Transactional Function gives the user the ability to produce outputs. For example a pilot has the ability to separately display ground speed, true air speed and calibrated air speed.

The results displayed are derived using data that is maintained and data that is referenced. In function point terminology the resulting display is called an External Output (EO).

EXTERNAL INQUIRIES

The final capability provided to users through a

computerized system addresses the requirement to select and display specific data from files. To accomplish this a user inputs selection information that is used to retrieve data that meets the specific criteria.

In this situation there is no manipulation of the data. It is a direct retrieval of information contained on the files. For example if a pilot displays terrain clearance data that was previously set, the resulting output is the direct retrieval of stored information. These transactions are referred to as External Inquiries (EQ).

In addition to the five functional components described above there are two adjustment factors that need to be considered in Function Point Analysis.

FUNCTIONAL COMPLEXITY

The first adjustment factor considers the Functional Complexity for each unique function. Functional Complexity is determined based on the combination of data groupings and data elements of a particular function.

The number of data elements and unique groupings are counted and compared to a complexity matrix that will rate the function as low, average or high complexity. Each of the five functional components (ILF, EIF, EI, EO and EQ) has its own unique complexity matrix. The following is the complexity matrix for External Outputs.

	1-5 DETs	6 - 19 DETs	20+ DETs
0 or 1 FTRs	L	L	A
2 or 3 FTRs	L	A	H
4+ FTRs	A	H	H

Complexity	UFP
L (Low)	4
A (Average)	5
H (High)	7

Using the examples given above and their appropriate complexity matrices, the function point count for these functions would be:

Function Name	Function Type	Record Element Type	Data Element Type	File Types Referenced	Unadjusted FPs
Navigational data	ILF	3	36	n/a	10
Positional data	EIF	1	3	n/a	5
Navigational data - add	EI	n/a	36	1	4
Navigational data - change	EI	n/a	36	1	4
Navigational data - delete	EI	n/a	3	1	3
Ground speed display	EO	n/a	20	3	7
Air speed display	EO	n/a	20	3	7
Calibrated air speed display	EO	n/a	20	3	7
Terrain clearance display	EQ	n/a	1	1	3
Total unadjusted count					50 UFPs

All of the functional components are analysed in this way and added together to derive an Unadjusted Function Point count.

VALUE ADJUSTMENT FACTOR

The Unadjusted Function Point count is multiplied by the second adjustment factor called the Value Adjustment Factor. This factor considers the system's technical and operational characteristics and is calculated by answering 14 questions. The factors are:

Data Communications

The data and control information used in the application are sent or received over communication facilities.

Distributed Data Processing

Distributed data or processing functions are a characteristic of the application within the application boundary.

Performance

Application performance objectives, stated or approved by the user, in either response or throughput, influence (or will influence) the design, development, installation and support of the application.

Heavily Used Configuration

A heavily used operational configuration, requiring special design considerations, is a characteristic of the application.

Transaction Rate

The transaction rate is high and influences the design, development, installation and support.

On-line Data Entry

On-line data entry and control information functions are provided in the application.

End -User Efficiency

The on-line functions provided emphasize a design for end-user efficiency.

On-line Update

The application provides on-line update for the internal logical files.

Complex Processing

Complex processing is a characteristic of the application.

Reusability

The application and the code in the application have been specifically designed, developed and supported to be usable in other applications.

Installation Ease

Conversion and installation ease are characteristics of the application. A conversion and installation plan and/or conversion tools were provided and tested during the system test phase.

Operational Ease

Operational ease is a characteristic of the application. Effective start-up, backup and recovery procedures were provided and tested during the system test phase.

Multiple Sites

The application has been specifically designed, developed and supported to be installed at multiple sites for multiple organizations.

Facilitate Change

The application has been specifically designed, developed and supported to facilitate change. Each of these factors is scored based on their influence on the system being counted. The resulting score will increase or decrease the Unadjusted Function Point count by 35%. This calculation provides us with the Adjusted Function Point count.

APPROACH TO COUNTING FUNCTION POINTS

There are several approaches used to count function points. Q/P Management Group, Inc. has found that a structured workshop conducted with people who are knowledgeable of the functionality provided through the application is an efficient, accurate way of collecting the necessary data. The workshop approach allows the counter to develop a representation of the application from a functional perspective and educate the participants about function points. Function point counting can be accomplished with minimal documentation. However, the accuracy and efficiency of the counting improves with appropriate documentation. Examples of appropriate documentation are:

- Design specifications
- Display designs
- Data requirements (Internal and External)
- Description of user interfaces

Function point counts are calculated during the workshop and documented with both a diagram that depicts the application and worksheets that contain the details of each function discussed.

Benefits of Function Point Analysis

Organizations that adopt Function Point Analysis as a software metric realise many benefits including: improved project estimating; understanding project and maintenance productivity; managing changing project requirements; and gathering user requirements. Each of these is discussed below. Estimating software projects is as much an art as a science. While there are several environmental factors that need to be considered in estimating projects, two key data points are essential. The first is the size of the deliverable. The second addresses how much of the deliverable can be produced within a defined period of time.

Size can be derived from Function Points, as described above. The second requirement for estimating is determining how long it takes to produce a function point. This delivery rate can be calculated based on past project performance or by using industry benchmarks.

The delivery rate is expressed in function points per hour (FP/Hr) and can be applied to similar proposed projects to estimate effort (*i.e.* Project Hours = estimated project function points FP/Hr). Productivity measurement is a natural output of Function Points Analysis.

Since function points are technology independent they can be used as a vehicle to compare productivity across dissimilar tools and platforms. More importantly, they can be used to establish a productivity rate (*i.e.* FP/Hr) for a specific tool set and platform. Once productivity rates are established they can be used for project estimating as described above and tracked over time to determine the impact continuous process improvement initiatives have on productivity.

In addition to delivery productivity, function points can be used to evaluate the support requirements for maintaining systems. In this analysis, productivity is determined by calculating the number of function points one individual can support for a given system in a year (*i.e.* FP/FTE year). When compared with other systems, these rates help to identify which systems require the most support. The resulting analysis helps an organization develop a maintenance and replacement strategy for those systems that have high maintenance requirements.

Managing Change of Scope for an in-process project is another key benefit of Function Point Analysis. Once a project has been approved and the function point count has been established, it becomes a relatively easy task to identify, track and communicate new and changing requirements.

As requests come in from users for new displays or capabilities, function point counts are developed and applied against the rate. This result is then used to determine the impact on budget and effort. The user and the project team can then determine the importance of the request against its impact on budget and schedule.

At the conclusion of the project the final function point count can be evaluated against the initial estimate to determine the effectiveness of requirements gathering techniques. This analysis helps to identify opportunities to improve the requirements definition process.

Communicating Functional Requirements was the original objective behind the development of function points. Since it avoids technical terminology and focuses on user requirements it is an excellent vehicle to communicate with users. The techniques can be used to direct customer interviews and document the results of Joint Application Design (JAD) sessions. The resulting documentation provides a framework that describes user and technical requirements. In conclusion, Function Point Analysis has proven to be an accurate technique for sizing, documenting and communicating a system's capabilities. It has been successfully used to evaluate the functionality of real-time and embedded code systems, such as robot based warehouses and avionics, as well as traditional data processing.

CYCLOMATIC COMPLEXITY MEASURES

OVERVIEW

One of the more popular complexity measures is McCabe's Cyclomatic Complexity (CC). The theory behind CC is simple: CC is a measure of the number of control flows within a module. A module is defined as a set of executable code that has an entrance and an exit.

Control flow helps determine the number of paths through the module. The greater the number of paths through the module, the greater is the module's complexity. The cyclomatic number for a module is equivalent to the number of linearly independent paths through the module and can be used to determine the minimum number of distinct tests that must be executed to test every executable statement at least once.

CC measurements may be performed:

1. By counting the nodes (correspond to the corners) and edges (correspond to the bodies of the arrows) of the module graph
   `CC = # of edges - # of nodes + 2`
2. By counting the number of binary decision points.
   `CC = # of binary decisions + 1`

After we calculate the CC number for a module, what do we do with it and what does the CC number mean ? Stated simply, a higher CC signifies greater complexity of the module and corresponds to greater difficulty to test and maintain the module. Rules have been put forth on interpreting CC numbers.

One such rule indicates that a CC > 20 signifies a high degree of complexity and risk of code being prone to defects. There are also rules that try to predict the probability of introducing regressions or inserting defects while trying to fix another defect, using the CC number.

Here too, the higher CC corresponds to a greater probability of introducing new/ additional defects while trying to make fixes to other defects. CC is helpful in trying to gain an insight into the difficulty to maintain and test code.

DESCRIPTION

Cyclomatic complexity measures the amount of decision logic in a single software module. It gives the number of recommended test for software. Cyclomatic complexity is based entirely on the structure of software's control flow graph.

Control flow graph: Control flow graphs describe the logic structure of software module.

Each flow consists of nodes and edges:

- *Nodes*: computation statements or expresions.
- *Edges*: represent transfer of control between nodes.

Each possible execution path of a software module has a corresponding path from the entry to the exit node of the module's control flow graph.

Example

Consider the C function, which implements Euclid's algorithm for finding greatest common divisors.

```
A0 euclid(int m, intn) {
int r;
A1 if (n>m) {
A2 r = m;
A3 m = n;
A4 n = r;
A5 }
A6 r = m%n;
A7 while (r != 0) {
A8 m = n;
A9 n = r;
A10 r = m% n;
A11 }
A12 return n;
A13 }
```

The nodes are numbered A0 through A13.

CYCLOMATIC COMPLEXITY

- C.C. is defined for each module to be:e-n+2
  e,n: the number of edges and nodes in the control flow graph,respectively.

- C.C is also know as: v(G)
- v: Cyclomatic number.
- G: Indicates that the complexity is a function of the graph.

The cyclomatic number gives the number of independent paths through the control flow graph of the module. This means that cyclomatic number is precisely the minimal number of paths that can, in linear combination, generate all possible paths through the module.

Let us consider the following mathematical model: Each path has an associated row vector, with the elements corresponding to the edges in the flow graph. The value of each element is the number of times the edges is traversed by the path.

Example

Consider the path through the graph of euclid module:
0 1 2 3 4 5 6 7 8 9 10 7 8 9 10 7 11 12 13
(the numbers represent the nodes which are traversed by the path)

This path has an associated vector:
0 1 2 3 4 5 6 7 8 9 10 11 12 13 14
1 1 0 1 1 1 1 1 2 1 2 2 2 1 1

FROM LINEAR ALGEBRA

Rank of a matrix: number of linear independent rows. Each matrix has an unique rank that is less than or equal to the number of columns.

The minimal set of vectors with maximum rank is known as a basis,and a basis can also be described as a linear independent set of vectors that generate all the vectors in the space by linear combination.

Considering any set of paths gives a matrix in which the columns correspond to edges and the rows correspond to paths. The maximum value of rank of this matrix is exactly the c.c. of the graph. This means that the c.c. is the number of paths in any independent set of paths that generate all possible paths by linear combination.

There are a few important points to note about the linear algebra of control flow graphs:

- Each basis set has the same number of paths in it (c.c.), but there is no restriction on the number of different sets of basis paths,it means it is possible to have considerable freedom in selecting a basis set of paths to testing.
- Although every path has corresponding vector, not every vector has a correcponding path.
- Linear combination vectors of vectors that correspond to actual paths may be vectors that do not correspond to actual paths.

SIMPLIFIED COMPLEXITY COMPUTATION Y

Counting Predicates From the Flow Graph

- *Binary decisions*: If all decisions are binary and there are p binary decisions predicates,then v(G)=p+1. This formula is a simple consequence of the complex definition.A straight-line control flow graph,which has exactly one edge emanating from each node except the module exit node has complexity equal to one. Each node with two edges out of it adds one to complexity, since the "e" in the e-n+2 formula is increased by one while the "n" is unchanged.
- *Multiway decisions*: As in the p+1 formula for binary predicates:
  - Start with a complexity value 1 and add x to it for each decision node in the control flow graph.
  - x=one less the number of edges out of the decision node.

Counting Predicates Directly From Source Code

For most programming language constructs, the construct has direct mapping to the control flow graph, thus, contributes a fixed amount to complexity.

However, constructs that appear similar in different languages may not have identical control flow semantics:

- "If", "while" statements and so on are binary decisions and therefore add 1 to complexity.
- Boolean operators add either one or nothing, depending on whether they have short-circuit evaluation semantics.
- An implicit default or fall-through branch, if specified by the language, must be taken into account when calculating complexity. For example, in C there is an implicit default if no default outcome is specified. In that case, the complexity contribution of the "swith" statement is exactly the number of case-labeled statements., which is one less than the total number of edges out of the multiway decision node in the control flow graph. The distinction between "case-labeled statements" and "case labels" has great impact on complexity. When several case labels apply to the same programme statement, this is modeled as a single decision outcome edge in the control flow graph, adding one to complexity.

8

Formal Technical Reviews

REVIEW

In our deliberations over that standard in the early 1980's, only the most generic parts of a review process were retained, from the many successful variations with which the standards committee was familiar. The process defined basically elaborates on: *"You plan, prepare, review, and follow-up"*. Little guidance is provided on exactly *how* to do those activities. The real action of a review process, however, is in those details.

Regardless of an organization's maturity level, however, there is a review process appropriate for it. In an organization with absolutely no formally defined development process, people can sit down together, look over one another's work, and productively find flaws in their acts of software design and construction. In such an organization, that is probably the single most important thing to do to improve the quality of a delivered system.

As an organization matures (by whatever scale chosen), however, so should its technical review process. As an organization documents its processes, defining roles and responsibilities for people and entry and exit criteria for activities, so too should this be done for the review process. As measurement and baselines are established, the review process should be updated to track data.

As root cause analysis becomes understood, it should be integrated with reviews. And as the overall development process becomes better understood and more finely tuned, the standard review process has been seen to evolve into several processes, each appropriate to the very different types of workproducts within the development cycle. Another dimension of variation among review processes is influenced by an organization's management style.

Just as the varying cognitive styles of people influence how best they learn and mature, the management style of organizations influence the maturing of their review process. In an autocratic organization, a process, once somehow defined or selected, is imposed and changed by executive fiat. Management with a participative or consensual focus will have processes designed (at least in part) by the technical staff, thus opening the door to nearly unlimited process variations.

In the body of this paper, review processes for differing maturity levels are delineated. The basic outline of the CMM's process plateaus is used here, providing a common framework with the SEI's work.

The influence of management style is then highlighted. My particular expertise in technical review processes comes from a long consulting relationship across a diversity of development organizations. My intuition tells me that a multi-level model of a review process, as discussed herein, has analogues in other software development practices. I hope others with a breadth of experience across these other practices can profit from this model and apply it within their realms.

REVIEW PROCESSES

The basic outline of the CMM is preserved, as a common framework. For any one development organization, the details may vary, but the general outline of the levels remains.

INITIAL PLATEAU

In an ad hoc development, peer reviews can prove particularly important. Any professional realises that mistakes are likely in developing complex systems, and the independent perspective of another person is key in discovering oversights and blind spots. Babbage and von

Neuman, long before "software development" was a phrase, reviewed with their peers the logic they attempted to implement on the earliest of computers.

An early model of software peer reviews was that familiar from referred journals: circulate a draft and consolidate returned commentary. To be effective for software, this model relies on the software artefact to be reasonably stand-alone and self explanatory. Another model, the buddy-check or desk-check, has roots in the multi-person office, where one could turn to a peer and ask them to, *"look this over, could you?"*

In this case, as questions arose, the author was close at hand to fill in missing context and detail. Too close, some would argue. Often these practices were "recommended" to be followed during software systems development, but the general lack of fine-grained project scheduling and tracking typical of organizations at this level precluded strict following of what actually occurred.

Some of the problems noted in the ad hoc practices of this stage were that of inconsistent practice both within and across teams, and a feeling among some that the time spent reviewing was wasted since it took away from time which could be otherwise be spent coding (which is the only real productive activity at this level, of course). Generally, the code's author runs the review, since the product *is* their responsibility.

UP TO THE REPEATABLE PLATEAU

At the repeatable level, the techniques with which people experimented at the *"initial"* level were improved based on experience, and generally documented. The processes were written down in their basic form to establish a common set of expectations across the team.

The advocates of reviews then began to make headway in achieving an initial degree of acceptance by looking at the success stories and qualitative feedback from the *"initial"* process efforts. With this process now a generally "recommended practice", their may be some degree of planning to help integrate review activities into the rest of the work to be done. The review process, at this level, generally has this structure: first, material for review is distributed somewhat in advance of when the comments are needed; then, depending on the process used by the development team, the comments are consolidated by the author or by the group of reviewers as a team; the author then adjourns to independently correct the identified items. Typical processes at this level are the basic group peer reviews and walkthroughs.

New problems appear. Along with the structure added to the review process, other processes in the development lifecycle are being similarly examined and recommended, and software people are now asked to write down requirements, document designs, and develop test plans, in addition to the "real work" of cutting code.

Reviews, along with these other activities, are put into detailed project plans, which developers are held to follow. Under severe resource constraints, reviews begin to buckle: reviewers are given little advance review notice (since everything's running late); they often don't prepare adequately; they are given massive work products to review in a single sitting; and some identified items never get addressed because the author's deadlinés are yesterday. *"Quality"*, an attribute far less visible than cost, schedule, and functionality, is left behind as a good intention.

DEFINED PLATEAU

By now, in the overall development process itself, there is enough data on development effort to show that maintenance is a nightmare sucking up project resources. Because of their ability to catch problems early and avoid potentially large downstream costs, reviewers *must get serious* about this review process, the thinking goes.

This is usually where the term "formal" is introduced, as in *"Formal Peer Reviews"*. Guidelines are established, such as lines-of-code/hour or pages/hour to help size a review to a realistic task. This also helps managers quantify the overall effort involved in reviews, which turns out to be large, but not as large as the maintenance numbers. A common review process is once again improved to address the problems of the past. The process at this level looks much like that defined by the IEEE [IEE] or by Fagan [FAG]. Entry criteria are established (with specifics for different review types, such as design, code, test) defining amount of material to be covered in a review, materials to be distributed to reviewers, etc.

Roles and responsibilities (such as reader, scribe, moderator) are assigned to review team members to improve the meeting effectiveness. Since the author has emotion and schedule vested in the work product, the running of the review is often given to a more independent person to act as leader.

Since historically people have never prepared well, the meeting is run as a group walkthrough, with issues identified and delineated by the group as a reader summarizes the material sequentially. Follow-up activities are established to assure that identified items are resolved. Data are collected to support the cost-benefit of the reviews.

Since reviews have proven effective in avoiding problems, all the work-products of the lifecycle are expected to be reviewed. The cost of reviewing *everything* becomes enormous. Teams try to follow the proscribed process activities, but its overall effectiveness is lacking.

In monitoring code reviews at this level, I have seen meetings where the most serious item discussed was basic syntax or structure a compiler or quick test would have identified, but the process said: *"No compiling or testing before the review"*. A well-intended process has been over-generalized, and now its details stand in need of evaluation.

MANAGING AND OPTIMIZE - QUANTITATIVELY

The large scale tradeoff of reduced maintenance efforts

used to finance solid review methodologies has been made at this point. The question now becomes how to manage and optimize *within* a process, the review process in this case. An organization having been through all this now has a base of experience and data which can drive either further changes or the status quo, depending on how it is used. Some high-level data, along with probable process inferences, lead to refocusing review efforts at different levels. Across the software profession, there is less experience of reviews at this level, though some studies are being published.

As an example of process managing, Christenson [CHR] uses a baseline of data and a classical statistical paradigm to establish control limits for reviews. Using test and field data as driving quality measures, he relates these back to the data from individual reviews to characterize why some were better than others, and then establishes control limits and monitors ongoing reviews to these limits.

There are several problems in this approach, however. First and foremost is that development processes are human-based, not machine based, and the humans are conscious of the expectations on them; numbers can then be easily manipulated to fall within the desired norms.

Another is the long-term nature of the feedback from a review, when one ultimately finds out how many of the total defects in a work-product the review found or which got through; long term feedback admits many intervening events, which may contaminate any results.

Machines have a rather short-term feedback from control to output, permitting quicker loops for isolating and understanding events, and for controlling them. As an example of process optimizing, Votta [VOT] takes a somewhat different course, using more immediate effectiveness measures to tune the process itself.

In the environment studied, reviewers came to code review meetings having thoroughly prepared, with issues identified in advance, and the meetings were used to discuss, evaluate, and consolidate their findings.

Over a series of many reviews, he studied the union of all reviewers' issues before the meeting, and compared it to the list of issues documented during the meeting. The effect of synergy in finding new errors as a group (an advertised selling point of the process) was shown to counterbalance the effect of items which were on someone's list at the start, but were never discussed, and thus lost in the final reporting. The bottom line in this work was that for code reviews, group meetings added little to review effectiveness.

One possible conclusion is that the staff cost of the meeting time outweighed its marginal benefit, and thus should be abandoned under the circumstances studied. Another option may be to change the meeting's discussion protocol so that all issues get due consideration. What seems to be happening as we gain more insight into review processes is that the one-process-for-all workproducts becomes less applicable as we tune the process.

TO MANAGE AND OPTIMIZE - QUALITATIVELY

We are enamored of metrics because they give an air of objectivity to our work. Measurements of software development are human-based, however, and will always have a subjective element. Much can be gained and learned from qualitative information, as well.

The developers themselves, those doing the work, can often give insights which data could never illuminate. This is one of the articles of faith of the current-day quality thrust, as propounded by Juran. Work with current clients has focused not on the steps of the review process, which are rather straightforward and generic, but on the details of how best to implement each.

For example, all review processes have a box labeled *"Preparation"*, where a reviewer studies a workproduct before the group meeting. But how is that best accomplished? Rifkin [RIF] argues that software people can well benefit from the current work and insights developed in the field of programme comprehension.

INFLUENCE OF MANAGEMENT STYLE ON ROCESS

Autocratic organizations are often thought to be easiest when technology transfer is addressed: import or create a process, train people, and demand it. Drawbacks though are compliance and subterfuge.

Will everyone follow the process, and if policed, will people report compliance accurately? Looking at process variations in this light is not productive, since once established, there is little room for conscious change.

For quantitatively driven managers, a process must be well-instrumented to demonstrate its value, or it will not survive.

One reason for Fagan's success [FAG] in implementing a software inspection process at IBM is the integration of data collection into the process. Reviews are expensive in staff effort, and to justify their ongoing existence, data-driven managers need to see review costs displayed against the alternatively postulated maintenance savings to keep reviews in place.

Process designers under data-driven managers must be sure to integrate ongoing data capture, collection, analysis, and reporting into any process to justify its continuance. Of course this information is useful to know, but once established, the physical and intellectual expenses will be better directed towards understanding the next generation of process changes necessary.

For example, dollars-per-defect is certainly important in balancing review effort with maintenance effort, but defects-per-page is a more valuable statistic in exploring process variations which result in better defect removal. Managers with a participative focus will rely on people more than numbers to deliver an effective review process to the overall development environment.

One way to view this perspective is that a somewhat sub optimal process without compliance problems (since the developers who created it are vested in making it work) is preferable to a theoretically better process which no one is seriously motivated to follow. Given that varying sets of people are now responsible for the ultimate shape of a process, there are many process variations which may be implemented.

The implications for process evolution are:

- Less need to instrument a process for data collection,
- More need for periodic re-evaluation of process by developers themselves.

IMPACT ON PROCESS ENGINEERING

As an overall software development process matures, and so do its individual key component processes. This paper has pulled out one well-understood key process threaded among the many of software development, and separately examined its story.

Each Process An Unending Task

The maturing of an overall software development organization is depicted by the CMM incrementally: a few basic key processes are established, and then on that foundation others are introduced. Much as in human development, where a child masters a task like reading and then moves on to other things.

Process engineers therefore focus on the introduction and integration of rather statically-defined processes, each at its appropriate place in the maturity timeline. But the review process story, revealed here, is not that of a static process. It is the story of a process that begins in the infancy of software development, and matures on a parallel track with development processes as a whole.

Process Experimentation

Key to ongoing process improvement is experimentation, to understand and verify improvement opportunities. In a manufacturing environment, a line can often be run under varying conditions to isolate improvements. Software development processes rarely give us that opportunity. Software development projects are large and costly, and rarely is there an opportunity to develop something more than once under controlled conditions.

Here are some rather basic issues which must be addressed for adequate software process experimentation:

- If end-product quality is the measure of success correlated to process changes, there is a long wait for results. Test data may be confounded by testing strategies, and the ultimate customer usage data is yet many more months out. More immediate measures need to be explored; Votta [VOT], for example, structured his study to measure the gross number of issues a review identified.
- Software development projects generally have many processes running simultaneously. There are thus many opportunities for confounding factors to come into play, especially in long-term studies. Weller [WEL] looks at review process data over three years, but makes no mention of other events in the development process over that time frame.
- Since software development processes are human-based, data submitted by people, can have a high degree of subjectivity. This adds significantly to noise at the data source.
- Traditional statistical advice dictates large sample sizes to average out the effects of noise and confounding effects. Thus the data collection task becomes yet more ambitious.
- Software engineering has been continuously plagued by the failure of results to scale up. Small projects and research on undergraduates has not helped large, industrial efforts. For results applicable to a large industrial environment, one must study its large industrial projects.

Within the CMM optimization is at the highest of maturity plateaus. Unfortunately, this can lead process engineers working in organizations below level 5 to forgo experimentation. While experimentation with instrumented processes is certainly a long-term goal, there are experiments appropriate to all maturity levels, also.

At the earliest of maturities, small-scale, controlled

studies can be useful to justify initial process design and establish basic ranges for process parameters. As an example, Buck [BUC] documented initial parameters for IBM's inspection process, using data from early process training classes.

Operating ranges for material coverage rates and team size were indicated in the early work. These early parameters must be viewed cautiously, though, as they become used in the very different environment of day-to-day practice. Process studies are ultimately needed to confirm and tune initial estimates. As an example of middle-maturity process structuring,Weller [WEL] consolidated three years of experience with review processes.

He pulls out several large scale themes from the data, which are likely to be relevant in his environment. There are many other possible explanation s that fit the data, however, which remain undiscussed; there is little basis to judge how portable the results are to other organizations.

Speciation

The evolution of species teaches that from variation and succession, the more fit can come to dominate. Thus in developing processes, designers should value variation and learn from it. A less obvious lesson parallels the evolutionary creation of several species from one, when there are varying environmental niches to fill.

I posit that this is what we are seeing in higher maturity projects, as review processes for requirements, design, and maintenance differentiate themselves to better meet their tasks. Hawks and sparrows are both recognized as birds, though feeding by hunting vs. gathering have given them very different styles and appearances.

The lesson for process engineering is to allow this to happen. Many organizations are pushing for a "common process", and the underlying standardization that implies. Consider an extreme case: should the review process for a newly developed subsystem be the same as that for a 5-line patch immediately required by a customer? It is certainly important to review both. But developing one process for both will likely lead to a process ill-suited to either.

Technology Training

In attempting to improve a review process, one must be cognizant of how mature the reviews themselves are, and focus efforts from that baseline. Rudimentary, industry-wide cost-benefit studies are not what's needed in working to improve an organization already at a CMM level three baseline. Similarly, thorough root-cause analysis will be lost on a project just starting to collect defect data. Training is needed on an ongoing, and updated, basis as processes evolve, to establish a common framework.

But training must focus on the delta: many organizations have at least some exposure to reviews; few are starting from scratch. This is an ideal opportunity for trainers to capitalize on the existing experience base. Developers are often cognizant of needed improvements, and more experientially-based instruction can lead them constructively onward.

FORMAL TECHNICAL REVIEWS (FTR)

The FTR (Formal Technical Review) is a software quality assurance activity with the objectives to uncover errors in function, logic or implementation for any representation of the software; to verify that the software under review meets its requirements; to ensure that the software has been represented according to predefined standards; to achieve software that is developed in a uniform manner and to make projects more manageable.

FTR (Formal Technical Review) is also a learning ground for junior developers to know more about different approaches to software analysis, design and implementation. It also serves as a backup and continuity for the people who are not exposed to the software development so far. FTR (Formal Technical Review) activities include walkthroughs, inspection and round robin reviews and other technical assessments. The above-mentioned methods are different FTR (Formal Technical Review) formats.

REVIEW MEETINGS

Review meeting is important form of FTR (Formal Technical Review) and there are some essential parameters for the meeting such as there should be reasonable number of persons conducting the meeting and that too after each one of them has done his/her homework *i.e.* some preparation and the meeting should not be carried out very long which may lead to wastage of time but rather for duration just enough to churn out some constructive results.

FTR (Formal Technical Review) is effective when a small and specific part of the overall software is under scrutiny. It is easier and more productive to review in small parts like each module one by one rather than to review the whole thing in one go. The target of the FTR (Formal Technical Review) is on a component of the project, a single module.

The individual or the team that has developed that specific module or product intimates the product is complete and a review may take place. Then the project leader forwards the request to the review leader who further informs the reviewers who undertake the task.

The members of the review meeting are reviewers who undertake the task. The members of the review meeting are reviewers, review-leader, product developers (or the module leader alone) and there one of the reviewers takes up the job of the recorder and notes down all the important issues raised in the meeting.

At the end of each review meeting the decision has to be taken by the attendees of the FTR (Formal Technical Review) on whether to accept the product without further modification or to reject the product due to severe errors or to accept the product provisionally. All FTR (Formal Technical Review) attendees sign off whatever decision taken. At the end of the review a review issues list and a review summary is report is generated.

WALK THROUGH

Introduction

A static analysis technique in which a designer or programmer leads members of the development team and other interested parties through a segment of documentation or code, and the participants ask questions and make comments about possible errors, violation of development standards, and other problems. Software testing is all about caring for software quality.

It helps in deploying error free software, in time. Software testing helps to find out the deviations of software developed from the result expected. The quality analyst engineers assure that the software testing reveals appropriate results with respect to what the software was intended for ?

A software testing company works to deliver quality assured software applications – be it big or small project. Software testing company analysis the difficulties keeping in view that each project developed is unique. A project may have undergone several alterations, while its way to deployment.

Bugs get incorporated due to many factors. Starting form miscommunication, defecting software coding, use of software development tools, timely delivery pressures, and the ever changing requirements, all can contribute for flawed software. No matter what the case may be, what counts is the defects should be fixed before the customer makes use of it.

Software testing company has a wide area to work on. The IT industry may be flooded with a variety of software testing services, not to mention the wide diversity found in their baptism scheme. There is compatibility testing, functional testing, performance testing, load testing, regression testing, stress testing, and unit testing among a few to mention.

A reliable software testing company realises the need for validating the software product not just once, but also repeated validation for each new release of the software product or website. A reputed software testing company follows specific guidelines in accordance to the client's requirements. They ensure to comply with the quality system with regards to software validation.

Software testing company follows the bug testing processes, to the max. The head quality analyst (project manager) of software testing company is responsible for project planning and scheduling it.

Monitoring and reporting the project of software testing is handled with utmost diligence. For each project, the software testing is different. This depends on the size, scope and usability of the project. Each factor looked on with minute details prove worth in delivering a quality software output after software testing services. Software testing is all about caring for software quality.

It helps in deploying error free software, in time. Software testing helps to find out the deviations of software developed from the result expected. The quality analyst engineers assure that the software testing reveals appropriate results with respect to what the software was intended for?

A software testing company works to deliver quality assured software applications - be it big or small project. Software testing company analysis the difficulties keeping in view that each project developed is unique. A project may have undergone several alterations, while its way to deployment.

Bugs get incorporated due to many factors. Starting form miscommunication, defecting software coding, use of software development tools, timely delivery pressures, and the ever changing requirements, all can contribute for flawed software. No matter what the case may be, what counts is the defects should be fixed before the customer makes use of it. Software testing company has a wide area to work on. The IT industry may be flooded with a variety of software testing services, not to mention the wide diversity found in their baptism scheme. There is compatibility testing, functional testing, performance testing, load testing, regression testing, stress testing, and unit testing among a few to mention.

A reliable software testing company realises the need for validating the software product not just once, but also repeated validation for each new release of the software product or website. A reputed software testing company follows specific guidelines in accordance to the client's requirements.

They ensure to comply with the quality system with regards to software validation. Software testing company follows the bug testing processes, to the max. The head quality analyst (project manager) of software testing company is responsible for project planning and scheduling it. Monitoring and reporting the project of software testing is handled with utmost diligence.

For each project, the software testing is different. This depends on the size, scope and usability of the project. Each factor looked on with minute details prove worth in delivering a quality software output after software testing services.

Software testing has positive impacts on quality software. It helps clients business and makes the software developed more usable and more user-friendly.

The objectives of Walkthrough can be summarized as follows:

- Detect errors early.
- Ensure (re)established standards are followed:
- Train and exchange technical information among project teams which participate in the walkthrough.
- Increase the quality of the project, thereby improving morale of the team members.

The participants in Walkthroughs assume one or more of the following roles:

- Walk-through leader
- Recorder
- Author
- Team member

To consider a review as a systematic walk-through, a team of at least two members shall be assembled. Roles may be shared among the team members. The walk-through leader or the author may serve as the recorder. The walk-through leader may be the author.

Individuals holding management positions over any member of the walk-through team shall not participate in the walk-through.

Input to the walk-through shall include the following:

- A statement of objectives for the walk-through
- The software product being examined
- Standards that are in effect for the acquisition, supply, development, operation, and/or maintenance of the software product

Input to the walk-through may also include the following:

- Any regulations, standards, guidelines, plans, and procedures against which the software product is to be inspected
- Anomaly categories

The walk-through shall be considered complete when:

- The entire software product has been examined
- Recommendations and required actions have been recorded
- The walk-through output has been completed

SAMPLE REQUIREMENT SPECIFICATION

Users of this checklist should keep in mind that this is a good starting point of questions that shold be asked to ensure that all requirements are gathered from any phase in a project from specification through to production delivery.

Clarity

- Are the requirements written in non-technical understandable language?
- Are there any requirements that could have more than one interpretation?
- Is each characteristic of the final product described with a unique terminology?
- Is there a glossary in which the specific meaning(s) of each term is(are) defined?

- Could the requirements be understood and implemented by an independent group?

Consistency

- Are there any requirements describing the same object that conflict with other requirements with respect to terminology?
- Are there any requirements describing the same object that conflict with respect to characteristics?
- Are there any requirements that describe two or more actions that conflict logically?
- Are there any requirements that describe two or more actions that conflict temporally?

Traceability

- Are all requirements traceable back to a specific user need?
- Are all requirements traceable back to a specific source document or person?
- Are all requirements traceable forward to a specific design document?
- Are all requirements traceable forward to a specific software module?

Verifiability

- Are any Requirements included which are impossible to implement?
- For each requirement is there a process that can be executed by either a human or a machine to verify the requirement?
- Are there any requirements that will be expressed in verifiable terms at a later time?

Modifiability

- Is the requirements document clearly and logically organized?
- Does the organization adhere to an accepted standard?

- Is there any redundancy in the requirements?

COGNITIVE WALKTHROUGH

Usability Inspection is referred as a systematic procedural review of a system, based on a number of stipulated guidelines where the user interface is inspected by a number of evaluators.

Therefore usability inspection is focused in finding out the usability problems in design, which has always been problematic for users, some areas that get evaluated are the language used in the system, the amount of recall required by the user at each step in a process, the amount of feedback provided by the system to the user. Specific issues such as clarity, consistency, navigation, and error minimisation are analysed thoroughly. Once the problems are identified, the experts give their reviews and recommendations for resolving these issues.

There are also some methods in which, issues like the severity of the usability problems and the overall usability of the entire system is identified. There are many inspection methods, which contribute themselves to the inspection of the user interface specifications that hasn't necessarily been implemented but then it is clearly feasible that inspection can be performed at an early stage in the usability-engineering life cycle.

Usability Inspection is preferred to any of the traditional laboratory evaluation methods, as usability inspection tools are economical, much cheaper, faster and very reliable as it deals with real time users. Moving ahead we shall delve about the types usability inspection methods. The first one would be Heuristic Evaluation.

Heuristic Evaluation is the most popular and an informal method of the usability inspection, which involves having usability experts who examine the interface and judge its compliance with a set of principles, also known as the ("Heuristics"). A heuristic evaluation can be carried out at different phases of the development lifecycle; though it's better to carry out some type of context analysis to help out the experts focus on the actual product usage. Cognitive Walkthrough is another usability inspection method, which is used to identify usability issues through a particular software or a website, focusing on how easy and user friendly it is for the new users to accomplish tasks with the system.

Cognitive walkthrough uses a more explicitly detailed and a simple procedure to simulate a user's problem-solving process at each step through the dialogue, checking if the simulated user's goals and memory content can be assumed to lead the users to the next best correct action. Expert Review - a group of experts inspect a website to identify the potential usability problems faced by the users. Usability Testing is a priceless usability inspection method, which is used to evaluate a product by testing it on real time users. This method is a very valuable one due to its irreplaceable usability practice, as it gives direct input on how real users use the system.

This is in contrast with the usability inspection method where experts use different methods to evaluate a user interface without involving users. Usability testing aims in determining a product's capacity to meet its exact purpose. The products that exercise usability testing are websites or web applications, documents, devices and computer interfaces. Usability testing determines the usability of a specific object.

CODE INSPECTION

DEFINITION

A formal testing technique where the programmer reviews source code with a group who ask questions analyzing the programme logic, analyzing the code with respect to a checklist of historically common programming errors, and analyzing its compliance with coding standards.

You can control tasks related to your code directly from your changeset view. This will help you to keep you code clean and up-to-date. From here you can jump to the task list and back in one click to see the whole picture. Status bullets show you the status of the tasks. You may also create, edit and delete tasks by clicking on the left of any code line.

CODE INSPECTION ON COMMERCIAL WEB SERVERS

The prevalent open-source version of the Apache Web server stacks up well with commercial Web servers in terms of the number of code defects, according to a study by Mountain View, Calif.-based automated software inspection service provider Reasoning.

Reasoning recently inspected Apache V2.1 and compared it with other commercial Web servers that were at a similar stage of their development and found 31 code defects in 58,944 lines of code for a defect density of 0.53 per thousand lines of code. Commercial Web servers have a defect density of 0.51 per thousand lines.

Using its homegrown proprietary automated inspection software and processes for Java and C and C++ applications, Reasoning inspected the Apache code looking for memory leaks, NULL point dereference defects, bad deallocation, out-of-bounds array access and uninitialized variables.

Reasoning found 29 instances of NULL point dereferences where expressions dereference a NULL pointer; the company also found two instances of uninitialized variables where a variable was not initialized prior to use.

"Some consider any defect a security defect," said Thomas Fry, Reasoning's director of marketing. "Some resource leaks in Java, for example, lead to denial-of-service attacks. It depends on how you define a security vulnerability [as opposed to a coding problem]."

Earlier this year, Reasoning did a code review of the Linux TCP/IP stack against commercial TCP/IP stacks, and Linux won in a big way. Eight defects were found in 81,852 lines of code of the Linux 2.4.19 networking sample.

Reasoning shares its findings with the open-source community. The findings from the Linux TCP/IP inspection were sent to Linux kernel developers, and some were addressed and fixed immediately, Fry said. Reasoning is waiting to hear from the Apache Group regarding the most recent survey. "We report all of the defects to the community and to our customers," Fry said. "With our customers, 80% to 85% of the [Apache] defects were fixed immediately. They agreed they were serious." Currently, Reasoning is inspecting code in Tomcat, a module in Apache that enables the Web server software to run Java applications.

Fry expects those results within two weeks. "We're only doing reviews right now of open-source projects with large peer reviews [like Linux and Apache]," Fry said. "There are plenty of open-source projects that have smaller followings and less peer reviews. We'll be looking at those eventually to determine how the peer review process improves quality."

CODE INSPECTION TO SPREADSHEET TESTING

In programming, reliability requires an extensive testing phase. Spreadsheet development, which has about the error rate as programme development, also needs to be followed by an extensive testing phase if spreadsheets are to be reliable. In this study, sixty undergraduate MIS students code-inspected a spreadsheet seeded with eight errors.

They first inspected the spreadsheet working alone. They then met in twenty groups of three to reinspect the spreadsheet together. Effort was made to prevent hasty inspection.

Individual code inspection, consistent with past studies of both spreadsheet and programme code inspection, caught only 63 per cent of the errors. Group inspection raised this to 83 per cent. However, the group phase never found new errors; it merely pooled the errors found during the individual phase by the three members.

One group even lost an error found during the individual phase. This raises the question of whether a group code inspection phase is really necessary. Other findings were that subjects were overconfident when inspecting alone, that certain types of errors are especially difficult to detect, and that the benefits of the group phase is greatest for these difficult-to-detect types of errors.

COMPLIANCE WITH DESIGN AND CODING STANDARDS

INTRODUCTION

Compliance is either a state of being in accordance with established guidelines, specifications, or legislation or the process of becoming so. Software, for example, may be developed in compliance with specifications created by some standards body, such as the Institute of Electrical and Electronics Engineers (IEEE), and may be distributed in compliance with the vendor's licensing agreement.

In the legal system, compliance usually refers to behaviour in accordance with legislation, such as the United States Can Spam Act of 2003, theSarbanes-Oxley Act (SOX) of 2002, or HIPAA (United States Health Insurance Portability and Accountability Act of 1996).

Compliance in a regulatory context is a prevalent business concern, perhaps because of an ever-increasing number of regulations and a fairly widespread lack of understanding about what is required for a company to be in compliance with new legislation.

OVERVIEW

New environmental regulations are forcing companies in the electrical and electronic equipment industry to change the way products are designed. With the risks of non-compliance ranging from potential fines to being completely shut out of key markets, manufacturers will need to effectively address these regulations in order to minimize the impact on profit margins and prevent loss of revenue.

Currently, attention is focused on the European Union's Restrictions on the use of certain Hazardous Substances directive and Waste of Electrical and Electronic Equipment recycling mandate.

Similar regulations and voluntary programmes are also being established across the globe in countries such as the U.S., China, Japan and South Korea. July 2006, the time the RoHS directive takes effect, should, therefore, not be perceived as the compliance "finish line," rather the beginning of a new era when environmental impact considerations will be integral to product design decisions.

The optimal time to ensure compliance occurs during the initial product design stages. When non-compliant components and assemblies are identified, changes can be made quickly and easily in computer aided design or product lifecycle management applications where the cost to change designs is relatively inexpensive.

On the other hand, the costs of compliance increase exponentially once the product advances beyond the prototype phase and moves into full production; where changes may require an engineering change order, field replacement or product recall. The phrase, "design for compliance" has been used to describe the proactive approach to managing compliance in the design phase.

While most companies agree that managing product compliance without a robust information system is not feasible; many companies lack the necessary IT infrastructure to manage the complexity introduced by environmental compliance. Compliance cannot be addressed by merely requiring a compliance certification from suppliers, which is then stored in a database for retrieval.

Experience has shown that supplier compliance certificates are often inaccurate due to many factors, including a lack of understanding concerning interpretation of the regulations and the proper reporting of substances at the homogenous material level. These unintentional errors can lead to significant risk for original equipment manufacturers that are ultimately responsible for the compliance of their products.

In order to effectively determine if a product is compliant, various factors must be analysed and tracked such as material content, substance concentrations and product exemptions. Manufacturers can significantly reduce their risk by requiring suppliers to provide material content information in addition to certificates of compliance.

With material data, the substance concentrations can be compared directly with the regulatory requirements to eliminate errors and determine compliance.

Although it may seem counter-intuitive, the analytical approach is much more cost effective than a simple certificate of compliance due to a number of factors. For example, when existing regulations change or new regulations are introduced, the manufacturer can analyse existing data rather than surveying suppliers again. Most importantly, OEMs can eliminate errors, thereby avoiding fines and rework costs.

There are a number of factors to consider when implementing an IT system to manage compliance. In addition to material compliance analysis capabilities, the system should also be able to account for rapidly changing environmental regulations across multiple markets and geographies. Similarly vital is the system's ability to integrate sourcing and product development information.

Material and part suppliers are key partners in a company's drive for compliance, since a single non-compliant supplier could cause the product to be non-compliant. The IT infrastructure should expedite the flow of material content information and supplier compliance certificates across the supply chain and provide design engineers the necessary visibility to use this information during all stages of the product development lifecycle.

In addition, the application should support links to multiple IT systems within a company since many manufacturers often have product management and supply chain systems that vary by product groups and divisions. Synapsis Technology has developed a solution that can easily integrate into a company's existing PLM, CAD and ERP systems while providing a centralized platform to manage compliance.

The Environmental Material Aggregation and Reporting System is a sophisticated solution that addresses the analysis, tracking, data collection and reporting needs of an entire organization and provides the visibility that design engineers require to design for compliance. EMARS helps product development teams assure product compliance starting day one. With EMARS, a design engineer has the ability to confidently select a compliant part or subassembly based on EMARS' extensive evaluation of its compliance, accounting for multi-sourced components and product exemptions.

A design engineer will have similar information available when selecting parts in EMARS. The engineer will know that Part A can be used to design a compliant Server type product for ROHS, but not a consumer product.

Additionally, the Pass with Exemptions status denotes that Part A meets the regulatory requirements by means of a regulatory product exemption such as "lead in solder for server and infrastructure equipment." This is an important capability that helps companies deplete inventory during transition to compliant parts over time as they become commercially available.

The enhanced level of compliance visibility at the part or subassembly level will help the design engineer assure that the product meets all the regulatory requirements of the market or geography where the product will be sold.

Companies that are concerned about minimizing the risk and cost of compliance cannot deal with compliance as a tactical problem or a short-term initiative to assure that the product meets ROHS and WEEE.

Current and future regulations require long-term investments and the implementation of robust processes and flexible systems that embed regulatory compliance into the fabric of the organization.

ANALYTICAL TESTING

Compliance Designs offers comprehensive bottled water analyses to meet Federal, State and/or Industry standards at competitive prices. We also provide flexibility with regards to early notification of results, soft-copy transmittal of analytical data, and a comprehensive summary designed as a marketing tool that consolidates all laboratory results in a concise easy-to-read format.

What CDI accomplishes with their analytical testing programme is ease of sampling and analysis, and increased communication and flexibility.

Administrative Permit Management

We were the first to do it. We are the best at what we do.* Compliance Designs has been providing permit management services to members of the bottled water and beverage industries for over 15 years. We use our wealth of experience and knowledge to keep abreast of state licensing requirements for the manufacture and distribution of bottled waters and beverages.

Our established relationships with many state regulatory agencies allows us to apply for and maintain state licenses, with as little effort on the part of the manufacturing personnel as possible.

PRODUCTS

Label Requirements Report

Summary of the major FDA and State bottled water and beverage labeling requirements

Regulations Binder Set

Comprehensive compilation of all state and federal bottled water rules and regulations (set of 5 binders)

Certificate of Potability

Professionally designed certificate stating that the water tested meets EPA's primary drinking water standards and FDA's quality standards for bottled water based upon a review of analytical data

SERVICES

- Annual Analysis to meet State, Industry, and Federal bottled water monitoring requirements. We obtain volume discounts for bottled water manufacturers from qualified laboratories holding the necessary state certificates and having the capability to analyse for parameters required by regulatory authorities in every state. We act as the liaison between the bottler and each laboratory so that each bottler always has personal and individual attention.

- Weekly Microbiological analysis to meet State and Federal Requirements. Our programme is very competitively priced, and includes sampling supplies and an analysis by certified laboratories to satisfy State and Federal monitoring requirements for Total Coliform and Standard Plate Count. We summarize results in an easy-to-read report that is provided to the bottler each week.
- State Reporting of Weekly Microbiological Analyses Several States require that a bottled water manufacturer submit monthly, quarterly or semi-annual results from the weekly analysis of their sources and products for Total Coliform and Standard Plate Count. For a standard monthly fee, Compliance Designs will submit these reports to the states as required, and provide the bottler with copies of the reports and cover letters.
- Permit/License Management Services. Several States require that Bottled water and beverage manufacturers obtain and maintain licenses to distribute their products. Compliance Designs provides license management services that include a checklist of items/information required to apply for individual state licenses, preparation and submittal of license applications, and liaison services between the bottler and the licensing entity for all regulatory issues.
- Permit Renewal Notification. Compliance Designs will maintain a calendar of license expiration dates for manufacturers and provide early notification of pending renewals so that the facility's permits and licenses remain current.
- Special Projects. Our consultants are qualified by

years of experience regarding bottled water and beverage manufacturing and regulation. Our staff also includes a former laboratory director, and two former bottled water plant managers. The knowledge and expertise of our consultants can be a valuable resource for questions regarding all aspects of bottled water operations.

Bibliography

Alan, C.: *Software Quality: Theory and Management*, London: Free Press, 1992.

Barry, W.: *Software Engineering Economics*, London: Prentice Hall, 2003.

Bertrand, M.: *IEEE Computer*, New York: O'Reilly Media, 2003.

Carlo, G.: *Fundamentals of Software Engineering*, London: Academic Press, 2005.

Daniel, T.: *Object Technology in Application Development*, London: Prentice Hall, 2003.

David, R.: *C++ Programming with the Standard Template Library*, New York: Addison-Wesley Press, 2003.

Donald, C.: *Exploring Requirements: Quality before Design*, London: Manning Publications, 2003.

Edward, Y.: *Decline and Fall of the American Programmer*, US: Yourdon Press, 2005.

Efcall, Y.: *Rise and Resurrection of the American Programmer*, US: Yourdon Press, 1996.

Grady, B.: *Object-Oriented Analysis and Design with Applications*, New York: Yourdon Press, 2001.

Ian, S.: *Software Engineering*, UK : Addison-Wesley Press, 1995.

Ilialy, J.: *The Unified Software Development Process*, New York: Addison Wesley Press, 2003.

Ivar, J.: *Object Oriented Software Engineering: A Use Case Driven Approach*, UK: Addison-Wesley Prees, 1992.

Lawrence, J.: *Software Design: Methods and Techniques,* New York: Yourdon Press, 1998.

Marc R.: *Software Teams: Communications of the ACM,* New York: Addison-Wesley Press, 2003.

Mary, S.: *Software Architecture: Perspective on an Emerging Discipline,* London: Prentice Hall, 1996.

Mohamed, F.: *Communications of the ACM,* New York: Addison-Wesley Press, 2003.

Plauger, J.: *Programming on Purpose: Computer Language,* London: Prentice Hall, 2003.

Tom, D.: *Structured Analysis and System Specification,* US: Yourdon Press, 2000.

William, A.: *Compilers and Computer Architecture: IEEE Computer,* New York: John Wiley & Sons Publication, 2001.

Index